Kafka's Law

Kafka's Law

The Trial *and American Criminal Justice*

ROBERT P. BURNS

THE UNIVERSITY OF CHICAGO PRESS   CHICAGO AND LONDON

ROBERT P. BURNS is professor at Northwestern University School of Law. He is the author of *The Death of the American Trial*, also published by the University of Chicago Press.

The University of Chicago Press, Chicago 60637
The University of Chicago Press, Ltd., London
© 2014 by The University of Chicago
All rights reserved. Published 2014.
Printed in the United States of America

23 22 21 20 19 18 17 16 15 14   1 2 3 4 5

ISBN 13: 978-0-226-16747-3 (cloth)
ISBN-13: 978-0-226-16750-3 (e-book)
DOI: 10.7208/chicago/9780226167503.001.0001

Library of Congress Cataloging-in-Publication Data

Burns, Robert P., 1947– author.
    Kafka's law : The Trial and American criminal justice / Robert P. Burns.
        p. ; cm
    Includes bibliographical references and index.
    ISBN 978-0-226-16747-3 (cloth : alkaline paper) — ISBN 978-0-226-16750-3 (e-book)
    1. Criminal procedure—United States.   2. Criminal justice, Administration of—United States.   3. Kafka, Franz, 1883–1924. Prozess.   4. Law in literature.   I. Title.
    KF9619.B875 2014
    345.73′05—dc23

                                                                    2013048752

♾ This paper meets the requirements of ANSI/NISO Z39.48–1992 (Permanence of Paper).

Contents

Preface

In this book, I look at a system with which we seem to be very familiar through a lens that is, to most of us, quite unfamiliar. We are all exposed to the workings of our criminal justice system. One wag commented that a future civilization attempting to reconstruct contemporary society from its television programs would conclude that half or more of our citizens were either detectives or lawyers. (The rest were emergency room doctors.) Crime programs are ubiquitous, including all the iterations of *Law and Order* and *CSI*. Some prosecutors have even complained that those programs were changing jury behavior, making convictions harder to obtain. Cable news is filled with reports and punditry surrounding crimes and criminal cases. Some shows, former prosecutor Nancy Grace's, for example, are devoted exclusively to crimes and the prosecutions of crimes. Then there are the almost daily crime stories in our newspapers. And the gavel-to-gavel televising of some very high profile criminal trials, the George Zimmerman case, for example, followed by extensive commentary.

It seems that we know this system very well. Alas, this is not so. The actual workings of our machinery of criminal justice are only dimly perceived. To understand it concretely, I argue, it helps to see it through the eyes of one particular artist. Indeed, I believe that many of its gears, nuts, and bolts become clearest when viewed through the eyes of Franz Kafka, author, most relevantly, of *The Trial*. The perspective of a foreign "visitor" often allows us to see what we can see least well, that which is closest to us.

Kafka was born in 1883 in Prague, then a predominantly Czech city with a large German population, in the Austro-Hungarian Empire.[1] His father had worked himself up from the Jewish peasantry to the ownership of a successful dry-goods story in the city. Kafka celebrated his bar mitzvah when he was thirteen, but received a classical German education and entered the German Charles Ferdinand University in Prague, earning a doctorate in law. He moved in literary circles in the city and began limited publication of some short works. He practiced law for private entities for a couple years and then began his major professional work at the Workers' Accident Insurance Company, which lasted from 1908 until just two years before his death from tuberculosis in 1924. He traveled through Europe during the second decade of the twentieth century, attending lectures and readings by some of the era's most important writers and thinkers. His employers insisted that he was too valuable to release into the army for the Great War, which had begun in 1914. He wrote *The Trial* in 1914–15. He struggled about the decision to marry but remained a bachelor, though he had a number of intimate relationships. He was instrumental in establishing a hospital for injured war veterans and continued to publish short stories, but never published any one of his three novels. All were published, after aggressive editing by his friend Max Brod, after his death and despite what may have been a halfhearted instruction that they be destroyed.

Kafka was a genius. W. H. Auden said that Kafka is to our era what Dante and Shakespeare are to theirs, the writer who most comprehensively shows us what we are becoming. His genius was to address institutions and practices as problems specifically for modern people with modern political, psychological, and religious sensibilities. He was also a lawyer who worked for years for a semigovernmental organization that struggled to regulate the new and newly dangerous industries and factories that had grown up in Central Europe and also paid out disability benefits to workers maimed in their machines. (One of his most famous stories, "In the Penal Colony," describes a horrendous execution machine patterned on the machines he knew all too well.) Kafka understood bureaucracy and law from the inside. He was a very good lawyer. He was one of the originators of a perspective that one commentator called "organizational gothic," an understanding that the locus of evil in modern societies often lies within the gears of its bureaucracies. His anticipation of some of the law-ways of the Third Reich, for example, was uncanny.

This book examines aspects of the American criminal justice system through the lens that Kafka provided us in *The Trial*. It assumes no familiarity with Kafka or with *The Trial*. I provide in the first two chapters all that is necessary to the later argument. Although the novel ends grimly, it is often very funny. It *satirizes* dominance. One of Kafka's contemporaries observed that humor can add immeasurably to the clarity of thought. I hope that greater clarity about what we are doing in our criminal justice system will emerge from my efforts here.

I am grateful to Mary Burns and Locke Bowman, both of whom carefully read the manuscript and whose suggestions greatly improved it. I am grateful as well to the Press's anonymous readers who offered both appreciation of the work and positive, forward-looking criticism. And John Tryneski, the Press's executive editor for legal studies, was again a joy to work with. Our discussions often helped me clarify and improve my thinking. Short sections of this book have appeared in earlier forms in the *William and Mary Law Review* and the *Georgia Law Review*.

Introduction

The Trial is actually closer to reality than fantasy as far as the client's perception of the system. It's supposed to be a fantastic allegory, but it's reality. It's very important that lawyers read it and understand this.—Justice Anthony Kennedy

In 1994, David Saraceno[1] was an eighteen-year-old high school student. Saraceno was arrested and brought to the police station where he was interrogated for over ten hours[2] about an apparent arson of fifteen school buses. (The first step in bureaucratic processing of most cases is arrest and interrogation.) He denied any involvement. The detectives[3] refused to accept his denial. "We are not idiots. . . . Don't bother wasting our time" was their response. "As the detectives grew frustrated with Saraceno's denials, they raised their voices, yelled at him and moved in closer." They repeated and repeated (following the scripts of the manuals in which they almost certainly had been trained), "You know you did this. . . . Just admit it." They confronted him with knowingly false evidence: they falsely claimed to have found his fingerprints at the scene and claimed that they had found accelerant on boots taken from his home. When he told them the boots were his father's, they told him they didn't believe him. "I was just thinking this was unreal. They are never going to let me leave here." He asked for an attorney: the detective said that could wait. They told him he could not call his parents, that it was not his right. When his father came to the station to make sure his son had actually waived his right to an attorney, he was falsely told that his son had done that. The detectives told him that they would let him go if he confessed and would support him with the prosecutor and that he would get probation if he confessed. On the other hand, if he continued in his denials, "they would make sure he went to jail, where, they said, he would not survive":

> It would be like "throwing a lamb to the lions," they told him. He would be "raped by a big black nigger." Terrified, and believing that this was a "done deal," Saraceno started to shake uncontrollably. He started to see spots; twice he felt like he was going to pass out. He told the detectives that he felt nauseous and asked them if he could receive medical attention, but they denied his request and responded that his feelings of nausea were really just feelings of guilt and would pass once he confessed. . . . As he had throughout earlier portions of the interrogation, Saraceno cried, this time uncontrollably.
>
> Eventually, Saraceno asked the detectives, "Do you want me to lie? Is that what you are telling me I should do?" One of the detectives responded that Saraceno should do whatever he felt was necessary and right. At this point, Saraceno began fabricating a story, repeating the details the detectives had told him and agreeing to their suggestion of the facts.[4]

Saraceno's oral confession was offered against him in his trial. As is usually the case when the prosecution case is supported by a confession[5] (though the other evidence pointed away from him), Saraceno was convicted and faced a "possible sentence of thirty-five years in prison."

As Kafkaesque as all this was, the denouement was, from the point of view of official conduct, worse:

> While Saraceno's appeal was pending, private investigators learned of the true perpetrators. The state had chosen to protect them rather than disclose their identities to the defense or the court, although one of them had confessed in detail in a privately sealed affidavit and offered to testify against the other three if given immunity. But now it was too late to prosecute them because the district attorney had let the statute of limitations run out. Although the judge set aside Saraceno's conviction, prosecutors threatened further prosecution unless he pled "no contest" to a lesser bus-fire charge. *When Saraceno refused, they, incredibly, offered him a deal requiring that he plead guilty to the misdemeanor of "hindering prosecution by falsely confessing" and receive a suspended sentence. To put an end to this "surreal prosecution," stop draining his family finances, and get his life back on track, Saraceno took the deal.*[6]

A number of things should be noted in this account. *Private* investigators, perhaps working for an insurance company, discovered the true perpetrators. Once the police "clear" a case by a confession, as we will see, their bureaucratic imperatives dictate that they "close their investigation, deem the case solved, and make no effort to pursue any exculpatory evidence or other possible leads—even if the confession is internally inconsistent, contradicted by external evidence, or the result of coercive interrogation."[7] What the detectives did to Saraceno would not occur unless they were reasonably sure that it could be effective: for example, that it actually will extract a confession, that the lies and threats would be held to be permissible, and, to put it bluntly, that any remaining constitutional violations could effectively be lied away. Finally, the prosecutors seemed also to be protecting themselves more than anything else. The two different pleas they offered were, of course, inconsistent. The first was simply false, and the second outrageous, assigning a teenager criminal liability for police misconduct. It looks like they simply wanted *some* expression of guilt from Saraceno, so they could assign him some of the blame and so manage the public relations fallout from the blown statute of limitations.

In *The Trial*, Kafka depicts a recognizably modern man living in a modern society, a man largely defined publicly by his economic role and privately by his fears and desires. He does not seem to have a place to stand outside that system, has no "interiority" except the generalized guilt he feels when the system accuses him. When the system of which he is a mere functionary turns against him, he can hardly complain. A spokesman explains, "The law . . . receives you when you come and dismisses you when you go." (His colleagues and family members in effect shrug and accept that Josef K. has "his process," as if it were a natural condition to be expected.) He becomes the confused target of a system intent on his destruction. The trial process advances like a natural process. "The Court" has relatively little concern for what he had done, but seems very interested in whether he shows sufficient deference, servility really, toward the process itself. And these surmises can only be guesses, because the motivations of his pursuers are hidden, as are the issues to which he could address any counterarguments.

Kafka does portray a nightmare. That nightmare emerged in his imagination from his experience with a modern bureaucratic legal system in a capitalist country during the second decade of the twentieth century. Twenty years later, the nightmare became reality through the awful exaggeration of certain features already implicit in the system he knew.

We shouldn't expect to see in our legal order the dangers Kafka imagined and exaggerated in exactly the form that existed in the public world where he practiced law. Nor are we likely to become the regime that succeeded his, likely the "most terrible regime history has so far produced." Even those most inclined to be pessimistic see only a "*friendly* fascism" or a "*sanitized* version of the brave new world" in our future. This is, of course, some comfort, but not much. Although our public situation is different from the one Kafka experienced, in some troubling ways it is the same. Although our intellectual landscape has changed, the same fundamental issues in political and legal philosophy recur in a somewhat different key. The characteristics of his extreme system may allow us to see features of our system that could become nightmarish and, in Justice Kennedy's view, which may already be showing dangerous signs.

In the first chapter, I will provide a reading of *The Trial* that focuses on the characteristics of the law that Josef K. confronts. In the second chapter, I will argue that the book is centrally concerned with the justice of institutions and practices, such that a "political reading" has its place along with other possible readings of the novel. That chapter describes the "polymorphic" character of modern subjectivity that the novel allows us to experience directly. It then discusses some difficult issues surrounding the interpretation of *The Trial*. It describes explicitly the characteristics of the law that eventually destroys K. I argue that the Kafka's law is unknowable, ubiquitous, bureaucratic and ideological, and dangerously informal. It depends on deception, marginalizes defense counsel, and is relatively unconcerned with the facts of the case. It claims to be "infallible" in its global judgments and merges the political into the religious and psychological. And it claims justification in its inevitability or necessity.

The third chapter turns to our own criminal justice system, "the law in action" as we actually administer it. I first sketch out some of the more salient aspects of the social background against which our criminal justice system operates to imprison about one out of every hundred Americans. I describe the odd centrality of issues of crime and punishment in our politics. I then turn to the characteristics of American criminal process in action. I find that it has many of the same characteristics of the law that Kafka satirized as marks of a system of pure dominance. I describe the unknowability of procedural and substantive criminal law, its expanding breadth, its increasingly bureaucratic character, its elimination of formal proceedings, its reliance on deception in dealing with suspects and jurors, the limited role of defense counsel, the casualness with the facts of the case, claims to infallibility, the merger of the legal into the religious and psychological, and the expansion of the claimed range of inevitability and necessity. It looks like Justice Kennedy was largely correct in his conclusion about our system.

In the last chapter, I identify resources in the tradition of American criminal procedure that offer antidotes to the darkest aspects of Kafka's law. I argue that we still have "spaces of freedom" that Kafka could not have imagined and that can remedy the immobility of that "vast judicial organism" that "remains, so to speak, in a state of eternal equilibrium." I argue that the central resource our tradition offers, the jury trial, must be protected by legislature, appellate courts, and the bureaucracies on which it will remain dependent. Finally, I recognize the power of Kafka's dark view and assess the likelihood that we will be able to avoid its worst aspects.

CHAPTER ONE

A Reading of *The Trial*

The great epiphanic work actually can put us in contact with the sources it taps. It can *realize* the contact. The philosopher or critic tinkers around and shapes images through which he or another *might* one day do so. The artist is like the race-car driver, and we are the mechanics in the pit; except in this case, the mechanics usually have four thumbs, and they have only a hazy grasp of the wiring, much less than the drivers have. . . . [W]e delude ourselves if we think that philosophical or critical language for these matters is somehow more hard-edged and more free from personal index than that of poets or novelists.
—Charles Taylor

Art may not have the power to change the course of history, but it can provide a perspective on historical events that needs to be heard, even if it is seldom heeded. . . . After all the temporary influences that once directed the course of history have vanished, great art survives and continues to speak to each generation.—Dave Brubek

Introduction

Legal themes pervade Kafka's writing. He himself was a lawyer, working for a short time in civil and criminal litigation and for a longer time as a claims adjudicator and what we might call a "risk-manager" in a state-controlled disability insurance company.[1] Kafka's protagonist, Josef K., protests, much as we might, that he "lived in a state governed by law [and] . . . all statutes were in force."[2] Josef K.'s complacent belief does not, of course, prevent him from descending into a legal nightmare. My argument is that *The Trial* represents a critique of and a warning about features, tendencies, and latent dangers of the modern legal world, that those dangers are becoming more threatening for us, and that Kafka's vision illuminates dangers that lurk in any large modern legal system, including ours, as Justice Kennedy intimated. And, as the quote from Charles Taylor recounted above suggests, before we theorize about the legal world, it is wise to spend some time with the artists.

As I will explain at greater length below, modern people experience their world on different levels. As Winton Marsalis put it, explaining a distinctively modern American form of music, "Everything is always going on, all of the time."[3] Kafka represents all of these levels of experience in his novel. This leads him to write a deliberately uninterpretable parable, in the sense that there exists no *single* account, distinct from the story itself, which can adequately capture the conflicting perspectives and experiences embedded in the tale, *and* which most fairly reveals our *actual* concrete experience of the world.[4] The novel is thus impervious to any one "systematic interpretation":

> For what Kafka has done as a writer is to fuse into a unique literary style all the discrete elements of modern experience[,] . . . elements which in our daily life are fragmented and incoherent, although never wholly absent. In *The Trial* Kafka welds into a continuous associative chain the daily bureaucratic routine of Josef K.; the stylizations of a court of law; and the primitive, almost superstitious level of existence at which humanity, fearing the chaotic freedom of its own consciousness, generated the notion of Law in the first place.[5]

Much like the contemporary American trial at its best, *The Trial* seeks to show what cannot otherwise be said[6] and is *designed* to prevent reductionist reinterpretations. We come away from the novel with an understanding that cannot be reformulated in more theoretical language. And so it is imperative to begin with an account of the story itself.[7]

The title of Kafka's masterpiece is *Der Process*. Though I shall follow convention here, "The Trial" is in many ways a misleading translation. As Miriam Damaska explains, continental procedure does not have an institution that directly parallels an American trial. The latter is a relatively compressed and plenary event, with only rare interlocutory interventions by higher courts, at the end of which a judgment is entered. In continental procedure, there are no such sharp discontinuities.[8] The appellate court frequently intervenes in the proceedings in the trial court. There are seldom temporally discrete trials. Rather, the "process," which is tightly controlled by the examining magistrate, continues on as a kind of investigation, punctuated by hearings, until the magistrate thinks he has enough to decide the case. Kafka exaggerates these features of continental procedure for effect. His "process" is relatively "informal" but moves relentlessly, like a very fast-flowing glacier. (It's over in exactly one year, from K.'s arrest to his execution . . . or murder.) In a key scene late in the book, a priest, who turns out to be a prison chaplain and apologist for the law, tells K., "The judgment is simply delivered at some point; the proceedings gradually merge into the judgment" (213). K.'s lawyer tells another anxious client that "in some cases the final judgment comes unexpectedly from some chance person at some random moment" (197). Further, much of the dialogue in the novel makes more sense if the American reader simply substitutes "process" for "trial," since the latter term cannot but carry its local associations.

The Plot of *The Trial*

JOSEF K.'S ARREST AND INITIAL INTERROGATION. *The Trial* opens with a scene that is at the same time ominous and ridiculous. Famously, the first sentence reads, "Someone must have slandered Josef K., for one morning, without having done anything wrong, he was arrested" (1). Upon waking, K. notices that he is being observed through the window by an old lady who lives across the way, who is later joined by others, just staring at him. K. is "on stage" right from the beginning, a central theme of the book. The "officials" throughout the book (K. himself turns out to be an official, a role player, in the bank where he works) are exhausted by the roles they play. "The traditional *topos* of the world as a stage is taken literally by Kafka. . . . The reader is simultaneously in the audience and in the mind of the principal actor."[9] Two "guards" enter Josef K.'s bedroom to "arrest" him. K. realizes too late that by addressing the first guard, "he had, in a sense, acknowledged the stranger's right to oversee his actions" (4).[10] This inability to act, this inclination to "go with the flow," to move things along in the direction set by outside forces is another central theme of the book. It applies both on the psychological and the legal levels. The guards' names are Willem and Franz, echoing the names of the German monarchs (of Prussia and Austria-Hungary) who were, as Kafka wrote *The Trial*, in the process of plunging Europe into the unimaginable nightmare of the First World War, just as the guards begin K.'s personal nightmare. (They soon receive a whipping [in a closet at Josef K.'s bank!] after Josef K. complains about their conduct, just as the most powerful Eastern European czars, emperors, and kaisers were soon to be ignominiously removed from office.) Again, the account is both threatening and ridiculous: when Kafka read the first chapter of his book to his friends, he was laughing so hard that he had to stop.[11]

The guards order him to stay in his room and refuse to tell him why he is being held. They seem a foolish and corrupt duo: they take an interest in K.'s nightshirt and, implying that he will actually be in custody, offer to take care of all his undergarments to prevent them from pilfering by the venal prison bureaucracy. Having eaten K.'s breakfast themselves, they ask for money to buy him a small breakfast at the "filthy all-night café" nearby. K. is at a loss to understand what is happening:

> What sort of men were they? What were they talking about? What office did they represent? After all, K. lived in a state governed by law, there was universal peace, all statutes were in force; who dared assault him in his own lodgings?

He is half-tempted to consider it a thirtieth birthday joke, but thought that dangerous: "if this was a farce, he was going to play along" (7).[12] K. looks for and eventually finds his birth certificate (though initially can only find his bicycle license!), as proof of his "identity." (Again, the suggestion is that K.'s identity is exhausted by his place in the bureaucratic institutions of the empire.) The guards are dismissive and claim they are lowly employees whose only strength is their "knowledge" that the higher authorities never err. The law is, after all, attracted by guilt and "informs itself" about the guilty. To K.'s claim that this "Law" exists only in their minds, they confidently and threateningly retort, "You will feel it eventually."[13] In a parody of the maxim, "Ignorance of the law is no excuse," they dismiss K.'s claims of innocence: after all, if he doesn't know the law, they reason, how can he be sure of his innocence![14] (And so here another theme is begun. Because we are in some ultimate sense fallen or sinful, and so "guilty," if there is no knowable law, we can be convinced that we have violated that unknowable law and our experienced "guilt" exploited against us.)

K. thought of just walking out, but was concerned that they might grab him and "once subdued he would lose any degree of superiority I might still have over them. Therefore he preferred the safety of whatever solution would surely arise in the *natural* course of things" (emphasis added).[15] Hannah Arendt observes, in her essay honoring the twentieth anniversary of Kafka's death, that to treat legal processes as natural and so inevitable leads in only one direction, as do all natural processes, to death.[16] Only human beings acting together politically can provide a new beginning in human affairs, a quality she calls "natality."[17] As we will see, the law is resolute in preventing that from happening.

An inspector summons him to the next room, where a typist, Miss Burstner, lives, and the guards insist that he wear a black coat for the hearing, a demand to which he acquiesces "to speed things up." (K.'s impatient desire to quickly get to the end of things is, throughout the novel, a factor in his getting to his own end.) "You're no doubt greatly surprised by this morning's events," began the inspector. When K. thoughtlessly says, "Not greatly surprised," the inspector repeats his statement as a question, "Not greatly surprised?" (taking K.'s statement as an admission of guilt). K. then tries clumsily to extricate himself from the inspector's twisting each of his statements with another accusatory question (13).[18] K. consoles himself with the thought that the matter must not be all that important because he "can't think of the slightest offense of which I might be accused." And he protests that he still doesn't know who is accusing him and is sure the matter can be easily cleared up. The inspector insists that K. is quite wrong and adds the truly shocking assertion: "These gentlemen and I are merely marginal figures in your affair, and in fact know almost nothing about it. . . . I can't report that you've been accused of anything, or more accurately, I don't know if you have. You've been arrested, that's true, but that's all I know." He then gives K. some overbearing "advice": "Think less about us and what's going to happen to you, and instead think more about yourself. And don't make such a fuss about how innocent you feel." In effect, the magistrate tells K., "there must be something you feel guilty about, not so?" and begins the steps by which the object of the "process" is forced back on his own psychological resources. (K.'s lawyer will tell him that this is precisely the goal of the process in which K. will find himself enmeshed.)

Then another vignette of verbal slapstick: when K. says he wants to call his friend the public prosecutor, the inspector tells him that it makes rather little sense to do so. K. is close to apoplectic: "What sense is there in telephoning a lawyer when I've supposedly been arrested? Fine, I won't telephone." "But do," said the inspector, ". . . please telephone." "No, I no longer wish to" (15).[19] A period of silence is followed by K.'s offer to shake hands and end on a note of reconciliation, an offer that the inspector declines, while telling K. he need not despair, "You're under arrest, that's all. I was to inform you of that, I've done so, and I've noted your reaction. That's enough for today, and we can take our leave, tem-porarily of course." He then tells K. that this "arrest" in no way prevents him from going to work and otherwise going about his business. In a fi-nal nightmarish surprise, it turns out that three other men who had been standing in the room admiring pictures were in fact low-level clerks[20] from the bank, whose presence the inspector claims to have arranged to aid K. to return to the bank inconspicuously. K. is shocked, "and stared at the three in amazement." K. catches a cab to the bank with the three clerks, though he notes, in another dreamlike touch, that he never saw the inspector and the guards leave, "the inspector had diverted his atten-tion from the three clerks, and now the clerks had done the same for the inspector" (19). Nightmare and paranoia join hands.

This summary doesn't begin to do justice to the details in the first scene and to the grim humor it contains. A reader often doesn't know whether to laugh or cry. It does, as we have noted, set some of the legal leitmotifs of the novel. One critic observed that the rhythm of Kafka's work is a rhythm of questions, not of assertions. Questions, never fully answered, yield other questions.[21] *Is* K. as innocent as he claims, a claimed innocence that, in its absoluteness and self-certainty, evinces a kind of thoughtlessness?[22] Is the guilt[23] that the law is drawn to just a universal sinfulness that a decent legal regime should have nothing to do with, a conclusion close to the heart of Arendt's interpretation of the novel. What is real here, and what is a dream? (These are questions that can be asked of both K. and the law.) Does the unreality of the law mir-ror K.'s unreality, his lack of inwardness, in his exhaustion by his role? After all, the arrest is not really an arrest,[24] the charges are not really charges, and the investigator doesn't seem to know what he is investi-gating. He "does his duty" without really knowing its purpose (17). His task is only to record K.'s reactions (16). Does K. have the ability to break out[25] of the maddening situation into which he is thrust, and if so, how? If he is unable, is it because of who he has chosen to become or is it an unavoidable human fate?[26] He continues to submit to the often-preposterous demands of the guards and inquiries of the inspector, pre-ferring "the safety of whatever solution[27] would surely arise in the natu-ral course of things."

K.'S FIRST (AND ONLY) PUBLIC "HEARING."   K. next hears by telephone that a "small inquiry" would take place on the next Sunday[28] in a distant and unfamiliar neighborhood and that he could expect similar events regularly. K. realizes that he didn't ask the time of the hearing, but tells the bank vice president that "it's not that important" and resolves to appear at nine, the time court is usually held.[29] K. resolves not to seek anyone's help in preparing for the hearing, keeping it all "in his head," so to speak (38). Another nightmarish touch: he is late, finds himself rushing, doesn't know the building number, and the tenements on the street, themselves teeming with urban life, are almost identical (38).[30] He enters a building with various courtyards and staircases without knowing where the courtroom is. As he ascends the stairs, he is, in a hellish way, clawed at by angry-looking children "with the pinched faces of grown tramps." After another set of bizarre and preposterous twists and turns, K. is finally led into a "medium-sized room with two windows," crowded by people "dressed in black, in old, long, loosely-hanging formal coats," surrounded by "an elevated gallery just below the ceiling that was likewise fully occupied" (42). They appear to be some kind of jury, or at least a lay audience.[31] Eventually, a "fat little man" addresses K., reproaching him for being an hour late. K. dismisses his own lateness, an act of assertion that is greeted by applause from people on the right half of the hall. "'These people are easily won over,'" thought K. as he contemplated how to win over those on the left side. (He believes initially, and foolishly, that he can actually be listened to, that the "other side" can hear and be heard.)

"So, said the examining magistrate," suggesting that the law had not quite so unerringly "informed itself" of the situation, "You're a house painter?" something K. indignantly denies (44), provoking riotous laughter from his allies on the right side of the audience.[32] K. then lectures the magistrate expansively that he himself doesn't take the proceedings seriously, is immune from injury at the court's hands, and is speaking only for others who may endure what has befallen him (47). Cheered by the applause of the crowd, K. then gives a speech recounting the "public disgrace" he has been forced to endure at the hands of the corrupt guards and the "mindless arrogance" of the inspector, while maintaining, in a gesture of aloofness, that the matter has caused him only "some unpleasantness and temporary annoyance" (48).[33] K. claims to be "completely detached from this whole affair, so I can judge it calmly," this after slamming his fist down on his table.

K. begins to believe that he is in control of the situation and is actually convincing the apparently responsive assembly (49). He decries a corrupt "extensive organization" arrayed against him with the only pur-

pose of senselessly prosecuting the innocent (50). His speech is interrupted by a shriek of a law student engaged in a sexual encounter[34] with
a washerwoman in the far corner of the assembly. The crowd prevents K.
from coming to her aid, and someone grabs him from behind. And then
we descend into nightmare again, as K. realizes the crowd was only pre-
tending to listen to him:

> The faces that surrounded him! Tiny black eyes darted about, cheeks drooped
> like those of drunken men, the long beards were stiff and scraggly, and when
> they pulled on them, it seemed as if they were merely forming claws, not pull-
> ing beards. *Beneath the beards, however—and this was the true discovery K.
> made—badges of various sizes and colors shimmered on the collars of their
> jackets. They all had badges, as far as he could see. They were all one group,
> the apparent parties on the left and right, and as he suddenly turned, he saw
> the same badges on the collar of the examining magistrate.* (51–52) (empha-
> sis added)

K. is shocked and shouts, "You're all officials, you're the corrupt band I
was speaking about; you've crowded in here to listen and snoop, you've
formed apparent parties and had one side applaud to test me, you wanted
to learn how to lead innocent men astray" (52). As K. tries to leave, the
examining magistrate steps in front of him, and warns him that "you have
today deprived yourself—although you can't yet have realized it—of the
advantage that an interrogation offers to the arrested man in each case"
(52–53). What advantage might that be? There is no jury of laymen here
to be convinced. As will emerge later, the only "advantage" would seem
to be the opportunity to confess and declare complete subservience to,
indeed absorption into, the law. (We will see that American suspects are
often told [falsely] that their only salvation lies in confessing.)

The initial hearing scene (which turns out to be the last semblance of
a public hearing K. receives) is a nightmare. It is not difficult to understand why Arendt thought *The Trial* a premonition of the totalitarian regimes to come, one where the bureaucracy invaded all spheres of life.
K. cannot get a hearing before ordinary decent people, the "good men
and true" of the Anglo-American jury, but only by members of a bureaucracy that plays deceitful and strategic games with him. The merging of nightmarish process into judgment is only one example of a fearful merging of everything into everything else that is a central motif of
the book. (That "each thing is what it is and not another thing" is an im-

portant regulative principle of a decent legal order and of a consciousness that avoids mental illness.[35]) The law holds court in the attics of tenements (64) throughout the city, and the protagonist leaves an apartment
to find himself in the lobby of the court. This is what he sees when he
searches for the courtroom:

> A few women held babies in one arm as they worked at the stove with their
> free hand. Half-grown girls, apparently clad only in smocks, ran busily back
> and forth. In every room the beds were still in use, with someone sick or still
> asleep in them, or people stretched out in their clothes. (40)

The law hovers over all and merges into everything.[36] Things lose their
specificity. To invoke Arendt's language, the spheres of life are not kept
distinct. Not being distinct, they cannot qualify and "redeem" each other
as they do in decent societies.[37]

K. returns to the same place the following Sunday to find the room
empty, but also to find several books on the examining magistrate's table. The woman who admitted him the week before (and who tries to se-
duce K. before he leaves) tells K. that he is prohibited from looking at
those books. "Oh, I see . . . they're probably law books, and it's in the nature of this judicial system that one is condemned not only in innocence
but also in ignorance"[38] (55). (K.'s assessment grants the law too much:
the only book K. eventually sees turns out to be a pornographic novel.)
K. tells the woman that he would laugh at a conviction, which he thinks
unlikely, and believes that the proceeding is going forward as bait for a
bribe, which he self-righteously asserts that he would never offer (59).
She then tries to convince K. that the magistrate is interested in her sexually and she may thus be in a position to help him, but then behaves in
a way that gives him reason to believe that she, too, is deceiving him.
She doesn't resist when the law student with whom she had interrupted
K.'s hearing literally carries her off, something her husband, the usher,
laments to K. as an insult that he cannot avenge because of the weakness of his own position (69). Once again, bureaucracy is suffused with
sexuality and with real power exercised without decorum, formality, or
publicity.[39] And there is a strong erotic undertow in a number of scenes.
K. will have sexually charged encounters with four or five women, usually initiated by the women. Some women promise to influence the law's
judges because of intimate relations with them. This dreamy erotic world
is a world of obsession and compulsion, not freedom. It reflects the "Her-

aclitian flow" of our inner world and mirrors the unfreedom of the bureaucratic world with which it is complicit. It, too, excludes *action* in favor of a form of submission. At the end of the novel, a priest will finally tell K. that he is much too willing to accept help from women, help that turns out to be no help at all. Sex is part dream, part organic necessity: it too promises salvation by "going with the flow."[40]

The usher escorts K. to the court offices. There they see rows of other defendants, all middle-class men: "never straightened entirely; backs bowed and knees bent, they stood like beggars in the street" (69). The first defendant K. addresses can't answer the simple question, "What are you waiting for?" The question serves only initially to confuse him; then he explains that he has submitted a petition to present evidence and was waiting in vain for some response from the court (69). The offices are a kind of dark maze ("the interior of this judicial system was just as repugnant as its exterior" [68–79]), and K. can't find his way out. The stifling hot air makes him dizzy, something that surprises him; after all, as he tells two officials who appear from behind the many doors that surround his room, "I'm an official myself and I'm used to office air" (75). The officials help him out, and one, a young woman with a rather severe appearance, explains, "Perhaps none of us is hard-hearted, perhaps we'd all like to help, but as court officials it can easily appear that we're hard-hearted and don't want to help anyone. That really bothers me" (77). Even among the officials there is some recollection of decency, but it is fully submerged in the duties of officialdom.[41] Or is this, too, a deception, designed to disarm a potential victim?

The other official, a public information officer, smoothly "handles" K. without really helping him at all (78). They half-carry K., who is increasingly dizzy and confused, to the front door where K. notices that "they were unable to bear the comparatively fresh air from the stairway, accustomed as they were to air in the offices of the court. They could hardly reply, and the young woman might have fallen, had K. not shut the door as quickly as possible" (79). The officials cannot bear fresh air and the light of day. The court offices are oppressively close, a bureaucratic warren. Their inhabitants are concerned to appear kind, but are clearly company men (and women). The defendants waiting in the halls are bowed over, obsequious, and thoroughly confused. The officials and their system cannot stand the fresh air of ordinary life.[42]

There follow two scenes that are not obviously concerned with K.'s interaction with the court. Things again merge into one another: K. dis-

covers in a junk room of the bank where he works that the two guards
who initially arrested him are receiving a whipping by a leather-clad
flogger. They appeal to K. and are sure that they would not have been
punished if K. had not complained *publicly* about their financial interest in taking his undergarments (82). The guards complain that their ca-
reers are ended and now they will never get to be floggers themselves![43]
The guards are forced to strip naked. K. tries unsuccessfully to bribe
the flogger, who refuses the bribe, explaining that K. cannot now be
trusted to keep the bribe secret. K. asserts that "it's the organization
that's guilty, it's the high officials who are guilty" (83), not the guards, a
comment the flogger ignores. One of the guards venally asks K. to save
only him and let the other receive the flogging, but to no avail. K. leaves
the room when the latter begins screaming, so as not be found with this
bunch by other bank employees. The chapter ends with another dreamlike scene: the next day K. again visits the junk room and finds the floggers and the guards still there, with the guards still fully clothed, a step
back in time.[44] The guards cry out to K., who slams the door and pounds
it with his fists (87).

K.'s uncle, a small landowner from the countryside, then pays him a
visit. (K. is a bachelor without immediate family. He does not seem to
have a warm relationship with any of his more distant relatives.) The uncle knows about K.'s trial and is concerned about the disgrace it may
bring to the family. The uncle implies that even to "have a trial" means
guilt. He brings K. to visit his old friend Huld, a criminal defense lawyer, whom he thinks to be a good "poor man's lawyer." It turns out that
Huld is sick, probably with a heart condition, and he is attended by a
"nurse" named Leni. Huld already knows something of K.'s trial from
the "associations" that he maintains and that are, he explains, in his clients' interest. In fact, there emerges from a dark corner of his room a
man who turns out to be the chief clerk of the court, and Huld invites the
clerk to join the conversation he is having with K.'s uncle, from which K.
is excluded (103). K. is drawn by a crash caused, as it turns out, by Leni
throwing a dish against a wall in the next room to get his attention. She
brings him to the lawyer's large study where there is a painting on the
wall portraying a judge on a throne, positioned "as if he were about to
spring up any moment in a violent and perhaps wrathful outburst to say
something decisive, or even pass judgment" (105). Leni tells K. that she
knows the judge portrayed, who is "so small he's almost tiny" but whose
vanity insisted on the portrayal in the painting. (Power makes tiny peo-

ple large in their own minds and, sadly, in the minds of the persons they can terrorize.) They flirt, K. puts his arm around Leni's shoulder; she plays with his fingers, and offers this advice:

> [Y]ou're too stubborn, the way I hear it. . . . [S]top making that mistake, don't be so stubborn; you can't defend yourself in this court, all you can do is confess. Confess the first chance you get. That's the only chance you have to escape, the only one. However even that is impossible without help, but you needn't worry about that, I'll help you myself. . . . "And if I don't confess, you can't help me" K. asked tentatively. . . . "No," Leni replied, shaking her head slowly, "then I can't help you." (106)[45]

Leni tries to convince K. to give up his current girlfriend for her and shows him a "physical defect" she has, a weblike fold of skin that connects the ring finger and the middle finger of her right hand. "What a whim of nature," K. says, and adds, when he examines her whole hand, "What a pretty claw!" Leni then pulls K. down onto the carpet. "Now you belong to me," she says (108).[46] As K. leaves the building several hours later, his uncle grabs him and tells him in anger that he has offended both the lawyer, whose mistress Leni is, and, even more importantly, the clerk of court and "damaged your case so terribly, when it was starting out so well" (109). We thus have another scene where the law in its concreteness, in the minds of those who are enmeshed in it, is a vaguely erotic reptilian swamp. The law lacks the energy and clarity to be anything other than a reflection of our darker fears and desires.

We next see K. at some undefined time later. It is winter, and K. no longer casually assumes that the trial is just a minor annoyance (111). In fact, "[t]he thought of his trial never left him now." He is driven to contemplating the ridiculous expedient of offering a written defense in which "he would offer a brief overview of his life, and for each event of any particular importance, explain why he had acted as he did, whether in his present judgment this course of action deserved approval or censure, and what reasons he could advance for the one or the other" (112). In short, he would set out to justify his entire life to the court! In part this was because he had lost faith in Huld, his lawyer, who made useless speeches and bragged about winning many "trials" that seemed (even if they weren't) "even more hopeless" than K.'s (though, since they were secret, he couldn't show K. any evidence of that).

There follows a truly hilarious, and truly grim, description of the procedural posture into which K.'s lawyer is thrust by the unknowability of the law, the charges, and the court. Comedy is close to the heart of Kafka's vision. In the text, he makes one assertion after another and immediately takes each one back, as do his characters. K.'s lawyer was almost finished with his first petition, which was "very important" because first impressions were important, but most petitions were misplaced or lost by the court, and even if they weren't lost, they wouldn't be read until just before the verdict (where, of course, they were likely to have no effect). The lawyer's task in the petition, however useless in practice, is virtually impossible because "the court records, and above all the writ of indictment, are not available to the accused and his defense lawyers, so that in general it's not known, or not known precisely, what the first petition should be directed against, and for that reason it can only be by chance that it contains something of importance to the case."[47] A soundly reasoned petition can only be prepared after the defendant's lawyer knows the nature of the defendant's interrogations and thus can "surmise" the charges (114). The narrator comments sardonically:

> Under these conditions the defense is naturally placed in a very unfavorable position. But that too is intentional. For the defense is not actually countenanced by the Law, but only tolerated and there is even some controversy as to whether the relevant passages of the Law can truly be construed to include such tolerance. In the strict sense, therefore, there are no court-recognized lawyers; all those who appear before the court are basically shysters. (114)

Then follows a wonderful description of the "lawyers' room," designed to express the court's contempt for the defense bar. The defense lawyers are prohibited from changing anything in the room, even at their own expense. The account is filled with imagined physical humor:

> Light enters the room only through a small hatch so high up that if one wants to look out, and incidentally get a nose full of smoke and a sooty face from the chimney just outside, he first has to find a colleague who will hoist him up on his back. For over a year now—to give just one more example of the poor conditions—there's been a hole in the floor of the room, not large enough for a person to fall through, but big enough that one whole leg can sink in. The Lawyers' Room is in the upper level of the attic, so if someone slips through, his leg hangs down into the lower level, right into the hall where the parties are waiting. (114)

The administration treats defense lawyers badly in order "to eliminate the defense as far as possible; everything is to be laid upon the defendant himself, . . . who, after all, is timid and disconcerted, and distracted by all sorts of cares" (115). Defense counsel, not present for the interrogations, may try to discern the nature of the charges by talking with the defendant immediately after.[48] More importantly, he can use his personal contacts to achieve "momentary and even surprisingly positive results" through well-placed bribes. The value of these bribes, however, is ephemeral. "Only honest personal contacts are of true value, and with higher officials, by which is meant of course higher officials from the lower ranks" (116). (*Real* power is impersonal and remote.) These contacts, K.'s lawyer, Huld, had in abundance, as the chief clerk's earlier visit demonstrated. Officials came to see him and freely discussed cases before the court and sometimes seemed to be convinced by his arguments, though (here again the retraction of every assertion) "one didn't dare trust them too far with respect to this latter trait; no matter how decisively they state their new intent, which is favorable to the defense, they may well go straight to their office and issue a decision for the next day that conveys the exact opposite, and is perhaps even more severe with respect to the defendant than that which they had at first intended, which they claimed to have entirely abandoned" (116–17). Judges who take bribes and engage in "ex parte communications" can't really be trusted to act otherwise than in their own shifting self-interest.[49]

These visits with the lawyers aid the officials, Huld explains, because the secrecy of the proceedings means that "officials lack contact with the common people; they are well prepared for the normal, average trial, which rolls along its course almost on its own and needs only a push now and then, but faced with very simple cases or with particularly complex ones, they are often at a loss; because they are constantly constricted by the Law both night and day, they have no proper understanding of human relationships, and in such cases they feel that lack keenly" (117). In philosophical language, much like our computers, they lack access to the experiential "background"[50] that renders evidence meaningful. They need it explained to them and those explanations, like the explanations of jokes, are never really successful. There are two aspects of continental procedure to which Kafka alludes here. On the continent, judges are chosen not from a cross-section of practicing lawyers, but from a self-selected group of high-achieving students who have been educated to be judges from the beginnings of their professional lives, a career path that isolates them even from other lawyers. Second, the Habsburg Unified Kingdom of Austria-Hungary abolished trial by jury in the 1860s, along with press freedoms. So, once again, Kafka paints the picture of an isolated bureaucracy that, at least at its lower levels, depends on marginally corrupt ex parte communications with those who happen to choose the "right" lawyer. Further:

> The gradations and ranks of the court are infinite, extending beyond the ken even of initiates. The proceedings of the courts of law are generally a mystery to the lower officials as well; therefore they can almost never follow the progress of the cases they are working throughout their course; the case enters their field of vision, often they know not whence, and continues on, they know not where. The lessons to be learned from the study of the individual stages of a trial, the final verdict and its basis, are lost to these officials. (118)

Each official can only do his job, play his role, without any understanding of the significance of that role in the life of the defendant or of society.

Kafka illustrates the pervasive "irritability" of the officials toward the parties and their lawyers with another bit of physical humor, the story of one quiet, industrious official, who unproductively studied the files of a case "for one entire day and night without a break," then "waited in ambush, and threw every lawyer who tried to enter down the steps" (118). The lawyers waiting on the landing below, who knew they had to get in but had "no real right to be admitted, so they can hardly start legal proceedings against the official, and as already mentioned, they have to be careful not to arouse the ire of the bureaucracy," hit upon the expedient of rushing up the stairs, one by one, each allowing himself to be thrown down, until "the old gentleman, who was already tired from working all night, grew truly exhausted and went back into this office" (119). The details of the individual cases that the lawyers want to offer simply get in the way of the autonomous ("autopoietic") operation of the internal imperatives of the system that are exhaustively discerned behind closed doors by the judge's lonely study of the "files of the case." As K. himself experienced in his earlier hearing, the officials have long since stopped listening.

The lawyers are by no means reformers, and Kafka's narrator offers some of the most truly dispiriting advice in the novel:

> [A]lmost every defendant, even the most simple-minded among them, starts thinking up suggestions for improvement from the moment the trial starts,

and in doing so often wastes time and energy that would be better spent in other ways. The only proper approach is to learn to accept existing conditions. Even if it were possible to improve specific details—which, however, is merely an absurd superstition—one would have at best achieved something for future cases, while in the process damaging oneself immeasurably by attracting the attention of an always vengeful bureaucracy. Just don't attract attention! Keep calm, no matter how much it seems counter to good sense. Try to realize that this vast judicial organism remains, so to speak, in a state of eternal equilibrium, and that if you change something on your own where you are, you can cut the ground out from under your own feet and fall, while the vast organism easily compensates for the minor disturbance at some other spot—after all, everything is interconnected—and remains unchanged, if not, which is likely, even more resolute, more vigilant, more severe, more malicious. (119)

The law is an organism, a system, impervious to human action, possessing a necessity that will thwart any attempt at change.[51]

Not only is the system itself impervious to change, even in individual cases it isn't clear that lawyers acting "informally" can have an effect, can break the iron law of necessity: "[T]here are always dark hours, everyone has them, when it seems as if the only trials that turned out well were those that were destined to do so from the beginning, without any help at all, while all the others were lost in spite of following them so closely, in spite of all the effort, all the small apparent victories that gave such pleasure" (121). And some trials enter a stage where "no further assistance can be given, where it is being handled by inaccessible courts of law, where even the defendant is no longer within reach of the lawyer" and the lawyer finds all his petitions returned, "worthless scraps of paper." It is no surprise, then, that K.'s visits to his lawyer remained frustrating, indeed "exhausting": "Progress had always been made, but the nature of this progress could never be specified. He was always at work on the first petition, but it was never finished, which generally proved at the next visit to have been a major advantage, since the last time, and there had been no way of foreseeing this, the circumstances had been quite unfavorable for its submission" (122–23). Because the real determinants of the ultimate decision are unknowable, the law creates or reflects a world in which an unknowable necessity makes effective human action at any level impossible.

After trying to absorb all that Huld has explained to him, K. vainly tries to assimilate his legal situation into the rationality of the business world.[52] He tells himself that he had to think of the trial as he would a business deal at the bank, where he "had managed to work his way up to a high position . . . in a relatively short period of time, and, respected by all, maintain that position; all he had to do now was turn the abilities that had made that possible partially toward his trial and no doubt everything could turn out well" (125). And so "all thought must be focused as clearly as possible on one's own advantage," and, with an institutionally sanctioned predator's innocence, no thought of guilt even entertained. He thus considers adopting toward his trial the stance of the pure arms-length hard bargainer that serves him well in the capitalist marketplace. But he can do no better than his lawyer. Because the law may choose to pass judgment on any aspect of his life, he finds the composition of his autobiographical petition impossible, as, of course, it was. If the law is ubiquitous, surely violations occur continually. K. now found himself deeply distracted at work, keeping important clients waiting for hours (125). He had by now resolved to represent himself, and his preoccupation with his trial made ordinary work, where he was increasingly concerned about his career, almost impossible (132).[53] Clients seemed to know about his trial. "So many people are connected with the court!" K. exclaims. Finally, one of his clients at the bank, a manufacturer, suggested that K. visit a man whose pseudonym was "Titorelli," a landscape painter from whom the client had learned about K.'s trial and who supported himself painting portraits of judges[54] and who might not have much influence himself, but might know people who did (135).

K. then goes off to visit Titorelli, who lives a in a dismal, rat-infested slum (140).[55] He climbs a set of stairs, particularly narrow, extremely long, and which ends directly at Titorelli's door, a kind of reprise of his earlier attempt to find his hearing room. He is confronted by a thirteen-year-old girl, a hunchback, who stares "boldly and invitingly" at K. She is joined by other girls who surround him and who "conveyed a mixture of childishness and depravity" (141). (Titorelli later informs K. that the girls, like the apparently lay jury for K.'s first hearing, also "belong to the court. . . . Everything belongs to the court" [150].) Titorelli, barefoot and dressed in his nightshirt, admits K. to his apartment and, in another slapstick scene, fends off the gaggle of girls who dearly want to enter. (142). Titorelli complains that they have a key to his apartment and they turn up, even in his bed, when he least expects it. They are an unwanted plague, or so Titorelli would have K. believe, of adolescent sexuality.

"I'm Titorelli, the artist," he declaims to K. Titorelli tosses aside the letter of introduction from the manufacturer: "Had the manufacturer not clearly spoken of Titorelli as someone he knew, a poor man dependent upon his alms, one might have easily believed Titorelli had no idea who the manufacturer was, or at least couldn't recall him" (144). (The artists, who have "the absolute point of view," are dependent upon the capitalists, who have the money. And the artists are not at all happy about that!) Titorelli shows K. the half-finished pastel portrait of another judge, much like the one in Huld's study. Titorelli confesses that he has never seen the judge, a lower court judge who really does not have such a throne, but paints him as his vanity demands, with the permission of the higher judges. Indeed, his claim to be the best of the painters of judges comes from his father's also having held that position. It was from him that Titorelli has learned all the "numerous," "varied," and "secret" rules for painting judges at all levels. "Everyone wants to be painted like the great judges of old, and only I can do that" (151).

The painting portrays the judge rising up threateningly from his throne, which this time is topped by a figure of "Justice," with blindfold and scales in hand, but, oddly, in motion and with wings on her heels. K. comments, "That's a poor combination. . . . Justice must remain at rest, otherwise the scales sway and no just judgment is possible." Ominously, it occurs to K. that it looked more like the goddess of the hunt (145). (In *Amerika*, when the protagonist sails into New York harbor, he describes the Statue of Liberty with a sword, not a torch, lifted high.) K. notices that the room, like the offices of the law, was becoming muggy and breathing again was difficult: "the room probably had not been aired for ages." In answer to Titorelli's question, K. exclaims that he himself is "totally innocent." Titorelli claims that this "simplifies matters." K. demurs, repeating what he has already learned about the court: "once it brings a charge, it is convinced of the guilt of the accused and that it is difficult to sway it from this conviction." Titorelli replies that it is, in fact, *impossible* to sway it, as it turns out, through "proof brought before the court." Titorelli, however, promises to get K. off on his own, in "behind-the-scene efforts, in the conference rooms, in the corridors, or for example even here in the atelier" (151).

This brings some hope to K.,[56] who finds the painter "simpler" and "more open" than his lawyer, and perhaps more likely to help. However, K. finds contradictions within Titorelli's claims (1) that the court is impervious to proof and yet an innocent man needs no help and (2) judges may be personally influenced and yet they can never be influenced to achieve actual acquittal. Titorelli smiles condescendingly and distinguishes what the law is said to provide (only speculation, of course, because no one has actually read the law), on the one hand, and his actual experience of it, on the other: the law on the books as opposed to the law in action, as we might say. In all his years around the court, he has never seen an actual acquittal; they exist only in ancient legends, tales that may not be literally true, but "they surely contain a certain degree of truth, and they are very beautiful; I myself have painted a few pictures based on such legends."[57] The suggestion is that real art's truth is on the same level of real guilt and innocence, which are nowhere to be found in the City of Man, in either public law or the marketplace.[58]

Titorelli then embarks on a truly amazing inventory of the possible resolutions K. may seek from the court. There were basically three possibilities: "actual acquittal, apparent acquittal, and protraction" (152). Titorelli explains that no one could help K. achieve actual acquittal, certainly the best result, and one that would depend on a finding of actual innocence. A final acquittal can be granted only by the highest court, which is "totally inaccessible to you and me and everyone else. We don't know what things look like up there, and incidentally, we don't want to know" (158). (Why don't we want to know? Because the actual process at that level is so terrible that we cannot look upon it? Because it is so out of our ken that we cannot return to the joys of ordinary life once we see it? See God and die? [158].) At K.'s urging, Titorelli moved on to the next possibility, "apparent acquittal." Titorelli explains a kind of vouching procedure whereby he himself first vouches for K.'s innocence in writing and influences a number of judges with whom he has contacts to vouch based on his "surety." The document with signatures is then presented to the judge to whom K.'s case is currently assigned, who will almost certainly acquit K. just to please Titorelli and his colleagues. Now this works temporarily and only with judges at the lowest level. In an apparent acquittal the charges continue to "hover over you and can be reinstated the moment an order comes from above." The files are not expunged, as they are in an actual acquittal, but are passed from hand to hand in the higher courts until a higher judge unpredictably orders an immediate arrest, which can occur as soon as the same day on which the apparent acquittal occurred (159). Unfortunately for the defendant, this can happen over and over again. This is unacceptable to K. who maintains the demand for absolute vindication that he has sought from the very beginning. He cannot live his life as a "sinner" or as "guilty" and insists on an immediate declaration of full innocence from the powers that be. He seeks what the law will not give. His pursuit of the law's full embrace will bring him only death.

K.'s understandable lack of enthusiasm for apparent acquittal leads Titorelli to explain protraction or postponement, which occurs "when the trial is constantly kept at the lowest stage," and is accomplished through constant contact with the court (160). It requires less effort than an apparent acquittal, but more vigilance and constant persuasion of the judge and often other judges as well such that the "defendant's future is less uncertain; he's spared the shock of sudden arrests," but there must be constant going through the motions, "spinning," of usually short interrogations and inquiries. While both methods prevent a conviction, they also, as K. sees as he prepares to leave, "prevent an actual acquittal" (161). The difference between the approaches is "only one of emphasis. In Ostensible [Apparent] Acquittal, it relies on effort and concentration; in Postponement the stress lies on observation and on mollifying the power that has arrested and continuously threatens one."[59]

What do these options mean? Like a "shyster" schooled in the most skeptical forms of legal realism, one must accept "a cynical dichotomy between what should be and what is, between the 'law' as idea and empirical reality. Experience and the law are 'two different things' and should not be 'confused.'" One must absolutely renounce the hope of real acquittal: "as there is no salvation and no justification for human existence without God, neither is there real acquittal without the Highest Court. However, it is only the renunciation of this hope which permits the trial to stay within the limits that make survival in it possible by virtue of the indefinite postponement of the verdict, the only kind of verdict known,"[60] that of guilty. A defendant must "stick to observation, and renounce the expectation of final answers." For example, judges are required to be impartial and above influence, but in practice one must "hold them in low esteem, realize their weaknesses, vanities, venalities, and play on their all too human character."[61] Titorelli tells K. how to survive through apparent acquittal in a legal world that has a distinctively modern cast:

> If survival is to be the central concern, Titorelli presents a picture of human existence which corresponds in essentials to the world view of the modern secularist. . . . Ostensible Acquittal is distinct from real acquittal by its to-

tally provisional nature. After he has been ostensibly acquitted, the accused must live in constant expectation of a new arrest. He must be extremely wary and utilize whatever changes might take place. . . . A complete lack of ultimate certainty, security, and freedom characterizes life under Ostensible Acquittal. No state of final harmony can ever be hoped for. Since no acquittal is definitive, the cycle of rearrests and ever renewed efforts for new acquittals must go on ad infinitum. It can end only arbitrarily with exhaustion or natural death. Life under Ostensible Acquittal . . . knows no ultimate finality and certainty, no definitive answers, no ultimate solutions, no permanent goal, and above all no justification of human existence, whose sole Absolute is survival.[62]

What can be lethal is the state's inclination to promise more than this, to simulate the Absolute.

Protraction cares much less about strategic play within the rules of the game. Instead, the defendant here tries to survive by acting outside the rules and appealing to those real, but "illegitimate" motivations of the court:

The accused and his helper must bend all their efforts toward assuring the permanent procrastination of the trial. The trial has to stay confined to its lowest stages. The means are constant observation of the lowest judges and never-tiring attempts to humor and influence them. The accused must never "lose the trial out of sight." . . . The lowest judges . . . have to be cajoled, flattered, and influenced . . . to prevent, not facilitate the entrance into the law. The method consists in trivializing the trial, in substituting the semblance of trial for its reality, "turning the trial around and around in the tiny circle to which it has been artificially contracted. . . ." One goes through the motions of a trial, but these motions are meaningless. They are not to achieve results, except the single one of not coming to any fruition. Meaninglessness is their sole meaning.[63]

The scene at Titorelli's apartment devolves into comedy again. As the girls continue to comment on events from outside his porous door, Titorelli tries to sell K. a series of his landscapes, which he describes as "companion pieces" to each other, but are, in fact, identical. K. offers to buy one after another of these mass-produced items, then eventually all, just to get out of the room. To allow K. to avoid the girls, Titorelli shows him another door, which K. has to climb over the bed to reach. K.

draws back from the open door when he sees what lies beyond: another set of law court offices like the ones he had seen before, with the same dim light and stifling air! After escaping the swarm of girls who came through Titorelli's door, K. finally escapes to a cab and to the bank, where he locks all the paintings in his bottom drawer.

K. then goes to inform his lawyer that he will handle his own defense. After he arrives, Leni introduces him to a merchant named Block, an old client of the lawyer, who confesses that he also has five other lawyers (*Winkleadvocaten*, "shysters").[64] It turns out that the merchant's case has proceeded under the lawyer's direction for more than five years and he has dissipated all of his wealth in the effort. He is, from the paramount point of view of survival, a successful protractor. (Indeed, it turns out that Block's life in his process has already lasted five times as long as will K.'s.) Block admits being present at the court offices, where he appears daily, on the occasion when K. visited and recounts an upsetting "superstition" expressed by other defendants that the shape of K.'s lips surely suggested that he would certainly be convicted soon. Block recounts, too, the imperviousness of the court to political action: "When a group occasionally begin [*sic*] to believe they share some common interest, it soon proves to be a delusion. Group action is entirely ineffective against the court."[65] Block tells of the uselessness, as well, of the quite scholarly petitions that his lawyers submitted early in his case, the uselessness of his documentary submissions to the court, the aimlessness of repetitious hearings, and the impossibility of getting a firm date for a dispositive hearing or convincing his lawyer even to try to get one (177). Leni tells K. in Block's presence that Huld has lost interest in Block's case: Huld is generally rude to Block and sees him only at his own convenience, one reason why Block is now actually sleeping in the maid's room in Huld's quarters (182)! Playing by the court's rules is necessary for survival, but leads to one indignity after another.

K. then tells Block that he is about to dismiss his lawyer, occasioning more slapstick, as the merchant runs around the kitchen with his arms in the air, crying, "He's dismissing his lawyer!" while Leni beats the merchant with her fists to get him out of her way. She takes off running after K., who has to escape her to enter the lawyer's room, locking the door behind him (183). K. then actually does dismiss his lawyer, explaining that the representation has only served to increase his level of anxiety about the trial, especially because nothing was happening, and he felt the trial "positively closing in on me in secret" (187). Huld then gives a long apologia, in which he explains that he now took only very interesting cases, impliedly like K.'s, but then exhausts K.'s patience by saying, in effect, that he would do nothing different in the future. For K.'s benefit, the lawyer summons Block, who is the object lesson on what "protraction" actually means, and proceeds to tantalize him with a claim to have learned something about his case and then to further humiliate him. There follows another internally contradictory conversation, echoing K.'s first conversation with the investigator, where everything goes round in circles. Huld tells Block, "[Y]ou've come at an inopportune time." "Wasn't I summoned?" "You were summoned . . . but you've still come at an inopportune time. . . . You always come at inopportune times." "Do you wish me to leave?" "You're here now. . . . Stay!" K. becomes enraged at Block's servility toward Huld,[66] which causes Block, in turn, to become angry at K.'s contempt. Block invokes "the old legal maxim: a suspect is better off moving than at rest, for one at rest may be on the scales without knowing it, being weighed with all his sins" (193).

Leni prompts Block to kiss the lawyer's hand, and then again and again; she strokes the lawyer's hair, tells him that Block has been "quiet and industrious."[67] It occurs to K. that this ritual of degradation has "occurred many times before, and would occur many times again, one that would remain forever fresh only to Block," like a religious liturgy (194). Attitudes that are traditionally appropriate for one's relationship with God are transposed to the law. K. feels "almost dishonored" to be present and sees that the lawyer's methods "resulted in this: that the client finally forgot the entire world, desiring only to trudge along this mistaken path to the end of his trial. He was no longer a client, he was the lawyer's dog. If the lawyer had ordered him to crawl under the bed, as into a kennel, and bark, he would have done so gladly" (195). The ritual of degradation gets worse, as the lawyer informs Block that the judge has spoken harshly of him, saying that though Block knew how to "protract" a trial, "his ignorance far outweighs his cunning." The judge's attitude is not surprising, given that Huld's "defense" of his client consisted in telling the judge, "It's true he's an unpleasant person, has bad manners and is dirty, but with regard to procedural matters, he's irreproachable." Huld then upbraids Block for showing a lack of confidence in him: "You're still alive, you're under my protection. It's senseless anxiety!"[68] The scene ends with Leni's ordering Block to stop running his finger anxiously through the fur of the bedside rug and to listen to his lawyer.

The great penultimate scene of the novel occurs in the city's cathedral. K. had been assigned the task of showing an Italian client of the bank "some of the art treasures of the city" (199).[69] It was a task he was reluctant to assume, because his growing fear of being undermined at the bank led him to rue every minute away. He fears now that "only success in the office could protect him" by allowing him some stable public identity (200). The Italian explains to K. and the bank president that he really only wants to see the city's cathedral, "but to take a really good look at it," and he agrees to meet K. there at 10:00 a.m. As he prepares to leave for the cathedral, K. receives a phone call from Leni, tells her that he is going to the cathedral, whereupon Leni warns, "They're hounding you." K. has to agree.

The day was dismal and rainy, making the cathedral, apparently deserted save for one old woman "kneeling before a painting of the Virgin Mary and gazing up at it," even darker than usual (206). The Italian was nowhere to be found, and the candlelight seems, in any event, inadequate to allow viewing of the altarpieces. K. is forced to use his pocket flashlight to see one painting, a conventional interpretation of the entombment of Christ portraying an armored knight leaning on a sword thrust into the ground (207). K. decides to linger in the cathedral and notices a small auxiliary pulpit, so cramped as seemingly constructed to "torture" the preacher, with the kind of lamp above it that usually signals a sermon about to begin. K. catches sight of a young priest "with a smooth dark face" about to ascend; K. crosses himself and bows, dismissing the possibility that a sermon would be given to him alone at 11:00 a.m. on a workday. K. tiptoes away down the center aisle of the cathedral; he almost makes it out of the church when he hears a "powerful, well-trained voice" cry out, "Josef K.!"

K. knows that he could simply walk out, but that if he turns he is "caught." He does turn, just as he accepted the authority of the guards in the first scene, and, obeying the priest's beckoning him to stand just below the pulpit, approaches to hear, "You stand accused." The priest tells K. that he was the prison chaplain and that he had K. "brought here" to speak with him.[70] "Your trial is going badly. . . . They think you're guilty. . . . At least for the moment, your guilt is assumed proved." "'But I'm not guilty,' said K. 'It's a mistake. How can any person in general be guilty? We're all human after all, each and every one of us.'" "'That's right,' said the priest, 'but that's how guilty people always talk'" (213).[71] Within the law, truthfully describing the human condition is evidence of guilt. The priest then advises K. to stop seeking additional help, especially from women, apparently to turn inward, as Franz and Willem had suggested at the beginning of K.'s ordeal.

The day darkens. Now no light penetrates the stained glass window, and the sexton begins to extinguish the candles. K. sarcastically demeans the "skirt-chasing" of the magistrates. "Perhaps you don't know the sort of court you serve." There is prolonged silence, broken by the priest's scream, "Can't you see two steps in front of you?" The narrator tells us, "It was a cry of rage, but at the same time it was the cry of someone who, seeing a man falling, shouts out in shock, involuntarily, without thinking." Mild criticism of the court's ordinary foibles evokes a rage that is also fear: rage at the danger of claiming the court is a merely human institution and fear that such criticism can only be self-destructive. K. believes that the priest has "good intentions," and hopes that, "if he would come down" from the pulpit, he might offer "some form of decisive and acceptable advice . . . something that might show him, for example, not how to influence the trial, but how to break out of it, how to get around it, how to live outside the trial. Surely that possibility existed" (214).

Religion alone, perhaps, may offer a way to transcend the compulsions embedded in institutions that themselves claim to be absolute. To offer this path, however, it would have to renounce its alliance with domination. It would cease lording it over the people from an elevated position and come down to ordinary people. Then it might offer us some compassion and light.

This is not to be: K. sees at once that the priest was "part of the court, and . . . when K. attacked the court, he had suppressed his gentle nature and actually shouted at K." (214). Even religion will not risk living freely without the support of the powers that be. The priest agrees to come down to K., explaining, "I had to speak to you first from a distance. Otherwise I'm too easily influenced and forget my position" (215). Pulpits, like the law's thrones depicted in Titorelli's paintings, serve to neutralize ordinary fellow feeling. Christendom, beginning with Constantine, has given up its promise of providing a "truth that will set you free" and now teaches resignation to the ways of the world. Religion's kindnesses seem only a largely deceptive interlude between its initial shouted condemnation and a final assertion of fidelity only to the law.

K. appreciates the priest's friendliness: "You're an exception among those who belong to the court. I trust you more than I do any of them I've met so far. I can speak openly with you." The priest corrects him, "Don't deceive yourself. . . . You are deceiving yourself about the court."

This sort of deception is described "in the introductory texts to the Law" (215).[72] And then the priest tells K. the parable, "Before the Law,"[73] in which many have seen the key to the entire novel. The parable "bursts out of its narrative shell in the novel," a part that is in some ways greater than the whole: "The terrible greatness of Kafka is absolute in the parable, but wavering in the novel, too impure a casing for such a fire."[74]

A man from the country wants access to the law, but his way is blocked by a doorkeeper, who wears a fur coat and has a large, sharply pointed nose and a long, thin, black tartar's beard. The doorkeeper tells the man: "I'm powerful. And I'm only the lowest doorkeeper. From hall to hall, however, stand doorkeepers each more powerful than the one before. The mere sight of the third is more than I can bear" (215). This doesn't seem right, thinks the man from the country, "the Law should be accessible to anyone at any time." The man from the country continually begs admission, but dares not enter without the permission of the doorkeeper. He never receives it. The man languishes outside until his own death. No force is deployed against him: he is kept in ignorance of the law, it seems, only by his own inaction. (K., too, has been told throughout that action is impossible.) Finally, the man from the country, as he dies, asks the doorkeeper why no one else has sought entrance through his gate:

> The doorkeeper sees that the man is nearing his end, and in order to reach his failing hearing, he roars at him: "No one else could gain admittance here, because this entrance was meant solely for you. I'm going to shut it now." (217)

The law seems to appreciate and accommodate each person in his individuality, but only if he has the courage to enter though what seems to be a very "narrow gate"[75] guarded by deceptive officials of all sorts, who falsely claim to be speaking in its name.

There follows a many-leveled discussion between Josef K. and the priest as to the meaning of the parable.[76] Has the doorkeeper deceived the man from the country, or has he not? The priest argues that the man from the country didn't *ask* whether he could enter after the doorkeeper only *initially* barred him and it wasn't the doorkeeper's duty to inform him that the entrance was meant for him alone. Indeed, the doorkeeper "exceeded his authority by holding out to the man the prospect of a future entry," and was otherwise an ideal servant of the law. If he were simpleminded and somewhat conceited, he also showed some compassion. When finally asked again whether the man from the country was

deceived, the priest says only, "Don't misunderstand me. . . . I'm just
pointing out the various opinions that exist on the matter. You mustn't
pay too much attention to opinions. The text of the parable is immuta-
ble, and the opinions are often only an expression of despair over it"
(220). Life and law are what they are, but we only have access through
the opinions we form. The priest then describes a range of contradictory opinions about the doorkeeper's actual knowledge of the law and
whether he has actually ever been "inside" his own door. Some are of the
opinion that the doorkeeper is himself deceived. He is "in a state of deception about the man from the country, for he is subordinate to him and
doesn't know it." After all, the man from the country is free to go where
he wants, and "he is in service of Law but the doorkeeper serves only at
this entrance, and thus serves only this man, for whom the entrance is
solely meant. For this reason as well he is subordinate to him" (221). And
there are a range of opinions about whether the doorkeeper can really
close the door. There is doubt too about whether the man from the country is superior in that he "sees the radiance which streams forth from the
entrance to the Law" to which the doorkeeper has turned his back. To
K.'s opinion that the doorkeeper deceives whether or not he is himself
deceived, the priest opines:

> [T]here are those who say that the story gives no one the right to pass judg-
> ment on the doorkeeper. No matter how he appears to us, he's still a servant of
> the Law; he belongs to the Law, and thus is beyond human judgment. In that
> case one can't see the doorkeeper as subordinate to the man. To be bound by
> his office, even if only at the entrance to the Law, is comparably better than to
> live freely in the world. (222–23)[77]

It's just another opinion, of course, and it contradicts the view that living freely in the world is superior to being bound to the law. Josef K. rejects this account, arguing that it implies that everything the doorkeeper
says is true, something the priest has already shown to be false. Not so,
responds the priest, "[Y]ou don't have to consider everything true, you
just have to consider it necessary."[78] "A depressing opinion," counters
K., "Lies are made into a universal system" (223):

> K. said that with finality, but it was not his final judgment. He was too tired to
> take in all of the consequences of the story; they led him into unaccustomed
> areas of thought, toward abstract notions more suited for discussion by the

officials of the court than by him. The simple tale had become shapeless; he wanted to shake off the thought of it, and the priest, who now showed great delicacy of feeling, allowed him to do so, accepting his remark in silence, although it surely is at odds with his own opinion. (223)

K. walks on with the priest "in darkness" and seems to perk up at the thought of his own public role at work, one that offers some hope of stability. He feels the need to leave a world where the truth about truth is a series of questions. "Of course, I have to go. I'm the chief financial officer of a bank and they're expecting me." K. seems disappointed that the priest's initial friendliness has turned to apparent indifference. The priest explains, "First you must see who I am." "You're the prison chaplain," says K.

"Therefore I belong to the court," said the priest. "Why should I want something from you? The court wants nothing from you. It receives you when you come and dismisses you when you go." (224)

On the evening of K.'s thirty-first birthday, two men in top hats who look like "old supporting actors" arrive at K.'s apartment. K. asks whether they are "meant for me," and they nod affirmatively. "They want to finish me off cheaply," he muses to himself. They seize K.'s arms from either side "with a well-trained, practiced, and irresistible grip," and the three of them walk forward together: "It was a unit of the sort seldom formed except by lifeless matter," a kind of molecular bond that belongs to the world of nature.[79] K. begins to resist, but then sees a woman who resembled Fraulein Burstner, a sight that, enigmatically, drains him of the will to resist further. His executioners allow K. to set the direction of their progress. K. sees a group of policemen, one of whom approaches the three men with his hand on the hilt of his saber. Rather than asking for their help, K. pulls his companions past the police and quickens their pace to a run.

They end their journey in an abandoned quarry, surrounded by some open fields, and an abandoned city building. The men remove K.'s jacket, vest, and shirt. He shivers in the night air, and his guards fold his clothes neatly. They sit him on the ground and prop him up against an altar-like block of stone. One of the men draws out a "long, thin, double-edged butcher knife, held it up, and tested its sharpness in the light" (230). The men pass it back and forth over K.'s body. "K. knew clearly now that it was his duty to seize the knife as it floated from hand to hand above him and plunge it into himself," but he could not "relieve the authorities of all their work." K.'s last moment is filled with unanswered questions:

> His gaze fell upon the top story of the building adjoining the quarry. Like a light flicking on, the casements of a window flew open, a human figure, faint and insubstantial at that distance and height, leaned far out abruptly, and stretched both arms out even further. Who was it? A friend? A good person? Someone who cared? Someone who wanted to help? Was it just one person? Was it everyone? Was there still help? Were there objections that had been forgotten? Of course there were. Logic is no doubt unshakeable, but it can't withstand a person who wants to live. Where was the judge he'd never seen? Where was the high court he'd never reached? He raised his hands and spread out all his fingers.
>
> But the hands of one man were right at K.'s throat, while the other thrust the knife into his heart and turned it there twice. With failing sight K. saw how the men drew near his face, leaning cheek-to-cheek to observe the verdict. "Like a dog!" he said; it seemed as though the shame was to outlive him. (230)

Thus the novel ends.

CHAPTER TWO

Institutional Perspectives on
The Trial

Kafka's so-called prophecies were but a sober analysis of underlying structures which have come into the open. . . . Just as a house which has been abandoned by men to its natural fate will slowly follow the course of ruin which somehow is inherent in all human work, so surely the world, fabricated by men and constituted according to human and not natural laws, will become again part of nature and will follow the law of ruin when man decides to become part of nature, a blind though accurate tool of natural laws, renouncing his supreme faculty of creating laws himself and even prescribing them to nature.
—Hannah Arendt

The Trial Is Centrally Concerned with the Justice of Institutions and Practices

It may be more appropriate to speak of perspectives on *The Trial*, rather than interpretations, and certainly rather than *an* interpretation. Still, it is clear that issues of justice and what we would call "institutional design" are at the center of Kafka's concerns. "Everyone strives to apprehend the law," after all, has a literal, as well as a metaphorical, meaning. This can be no surprise, given Kafka's daily immersion in the nitty-gritty of Austrian legal and bureaucratic institutions:

> Seeing that Kafka himself was a fully qualified lawyer and spent a good many years practicing as such, patiently and with immense conscientiousness, in a large assurance company concerned with compensation for industrial accidents, it is surely not surprising that he should have been not just "interested" in the exercise of justice but deeply concerned to show it at work in the world of his fiction. What most critics imply, by way of an unexamined premise, is

that somehow it is unworthy of the high seriousness of Kafka's art to see it concern itself "merely" with bureaucracy or the law.[1]

Kafka's world, like our world, is one of "unprecedented institutionalization," and he is able to intimate what evil means for us in the form in which it takes for us: "[J]ust so many critics proceed in the expectation that you can have a vision of pure desolateness without having to consider the very particular form under which that desolateness is presented. And the form this takes in a large number of Kafka's stories is the disfunction of an institution."[2] Kafka's own art shows the shabbiness of the "ferocious and despotic" legal institutions that Titorelli's "art" falsely glorifies. The latter serves to "overwhelm and humble the defendant" in a manner "inimical to human freedom, dignity, and life" by assisting, in a way I will explain below, "the hold of a wrathful authority over the longing hearts of men."[3]

In an essay written twenty years after Kafka's death, Hannah Arendt emphasized the importance of his work, particularly *The Trial*, for understanding the nightmare into which German legal institutions were plunged shortly after his death. It was only after the thirties, she notes, that we have appreciated that Kafka's story addresses the truly awful capacities of bureaucracy, especially when justified by some notion of historical or natural necessity: Only until the thirties, were "[p]eople more frightened by the tale than by the real thing":

> That *The Trial* implies a critique of the pre-war Austro-Hungarian bureaucratic regime . . . has been understood from the first appearance of the novel. . . . He knew that a man caught in the bureaucratic machinery is already condemned; and that no man can expect justice from judicial procedures where interpretation of the law is coupled with the administering of lawlessness, and where the chronic inaction of the interpreters is compensated by a bureaucratic machine whose senseless automatism has the privilege of ultimate decision. But to the public of the twenties, bureaucracy did not seem an evil great enough to explain the horror and terror expressed in the novel.[4]

A contemporary student of organizational theory, Malcolm Waner, sees Kafka, along with Max Weber, as the principal creator of *"organizational gothic*, with organizations as 'sites of darkness,' 'labyrinths with endless corridors'; and locked doors hiding evil secrets shifting from the 'dark street' to the 'cramped office' or the 'nightmare factory'"[5] Waner argues that Kafka "speaks directly to many of our contemporary concerns . . . the alienation of our times . . . the perverse bureaucracy ." The "profound religious doubt" that permeates the novels has a major effect in the inability of their heroes to recognize justice or injustice in institutions and to possess the conviction to act decisively against injustice.[6] Kafka portrays the fate of a "modern citizen who realizes that his fate is being determined by an impenetrable bureaucratic apparatus whose operation is controlled by procedures which remain shadowy even to those carrying out its orders and *a fortiori* by those being manipulated by it . . . under the guise of an apparent ethos of selfless public service."[7] For Josef K.'s enemies, whoever they are, "are in the service of injustice and a disorder that has donned the semblance of order. . . . In a word, they are mere functionaries."[8] "Because these functionaries are merely steps in the 'infinite hierarchy,' . . . they cannot have any opinions of their own, nor can they be depicted as personalities."[9] Recall the lament of the severe woman in the offices of the law that it can "appear" that officials are hard-hearted. It is only that "appearance" that "really bothers" her.

The first principle of procedural justice has been said to be *audiatur et altera pars*, let the other side be heard.[10] It presupposes opposed parties and an impartial tribunal to decide between them. By contrast, "[i]n Kafka's novels, one of the two parties is the hero, who is invariably alone. . . . He is a defendant or a plaintiff, defending counsel and witness, all in one person."[11] The opposing party is "the world of organized disorder—or seeming order. . . . But the third element is missing: there is no impartial authority to sit in judgment. Judgment has been usurped by those who oppose the hero."[12] And the opposing party is "invisible" presenting "no targets to hit. Their arguments are nullified by the sheer impenetrability of the mysterious systems that confront them." Thus Josef K. simply wears himself down opposing "an order that never actually shows its face" but which has taken an interest in him in a way that makes him "guilty in the eyes of the world."[13] *The Trial* is thus a "burlesque of the very legal procedure of which Kafka was a master." In sum:

> *The Trial* portrays the injustices of a subjective law as practiced in the Habsburg in *fin de siècle* and carried to its absurd extremes: *a system in which the preliminary investigation has displaced the other states of the procedure with*

its guaranteed protection for the rights of the individual. The preliminary in-
vestigation, in turn, goes to the extreme in ignoring the objective facts of the
case and focusing on the guilt of the accused. It carries out its activities, more-
over, in an atmosphere that abuses the rights of the accused both by violating
privacy and discretion in its hearings and by concealing from the accused and
his advisors the information needed for his defense. . . . Kafka's attitude vis-
à-vis the legal issues of the day is symbolized by a Justitia who would remove
her blindfold for greater clarity of vision but also forsake the wings on her an-
kles in order to hold her balances steady.[14]

In this world, even protestations of innocence provide, as the priest explains to K., evidence of guilt. For they are the "the talk of guilty men"
absorbed by "the process" as "the proceedings only gradually merge
into the verdict,"[15] inevitably a verdict of guilty.

The novel is also a commentary on disputes in legal philosophy not
completely accessible to us but with which Kafka was familiar and which
remain with us in a somewhat different key. Danger lurks for us in *both*
the impersonal operation of a mechanical legal system, on the one hand,
and the exercise of discretionary moral judgment by legal officials, on
the other. Our problem remains the achievement of an orderly, yet hu-
mane, middle way. Much of the debate in Austria during the first two
decades of the twentieth century involved the question of autonomy of
the legal system and its relationship, if any, to the moral order. Formal-
ists, most prominently Hans Kelsen, argued for a sharp discontinuity between the legal world and that of morality, at least in the modern world
where law, morality, and religion were no longer an integrated whole.[16]
Others, including Hermann Kantorowicz, who was a member of a discussion group in which Kafka participated, argued under the slogan of
"Free Law" that the law must in application reflect moral intuitions, and
that, "the particular circumstances in any given case were more important than written norms and that the judge should feel free to ignore positive law altogether, or to fill in its gaps, by applying his sense of right
and wrong . . . to the reality of the case before him."[17] (Note the completely unexamined assumption here that the adjudicator is a *judge*; the
notion that a jury might serve this function was not even contemplated
by the theorists Kafka knew.) The latter perspective, however, tended to
refocus the attention of a criminal court not on the specific act of which
the defendant is accused or of its wrongfulness, but rather on the mental state, indeed on the whole character, of the defendant. Later devel-

opments, when combined with a highly ideological notion of "right and wrong," applied by statist judges wholly committed to the regime, came to have truly grim consequences for Nazi "justice" where "character" came to be fully identified with ethnicity or political stance. There, too, the courts came to be "no more than the formal means of making it 'legal' for the police to pass and execute its sentence upon the prisoner."[18] The Nazis effectively "delegalized" the process created by the Weimar courts, effectively worked to "personalize it, to draw it away from impersonal and generally valid formulations" to vaguer and more politicized norms, inevitably endorsing the police's prior judgments.[19] These are consequences that Kafka anticipates in the novel. The issues concerning the character of law and legal judgment remain central for us. As a legal thinker, Kafka sought a middle position where he expresses

> a degree of discomfort with the Free Law movement that sought to liberate judges from the narrow constraints of the codified law. On the other hand, the conclusion of the novel, where K. is summarily executed "like a dog" . . . suggests an equal dissatisfaction with . . . [a] severe notion of punishment as retribution and its faith in law as an autonomous absolute. The opposition of the constitutional state of laws and the total, even totalitarian system of the Law, suggests that Kafka . . . was firmly on the side of society with its codified laws and safeguards for the rights of the individual.[20]

Kafka was thus centrally concerned with disclosing and satirizing, as Charlie Chaplin did in his movies, those "hidden structures" of his own public regime that posed a danger to a decent world built up "in accordance with human needs and human dignities, a world where man's actions are determined by himself and that is ruled by laws and not by mysterious forces emanating from above or from below."[21] In the midst of his grim satire of contemporary institutions, he "carried the image, the supreme figure of man as a model of good will . . . who can rid the misconstructions and reconstruct the world."[22] The novel is thus about institutions and practices. His art accepts "the ethical trajectory of the aesthetic."[23] Kafka's genius was to address institutions and practices as problems specifically for modern people with modern political, psychological, and religious sensibilities. We must then first take a short detour through Kafka's presentations of those sensibilities and then address briefly some of the broader issues of interpretation.

The Layers of Modern Experience

We see all of what occurs in *The Trial* through the eyes of Josef K., a bachelor, bank executive, and member of the modern middle classes with no apparent religious or immediate family allegiance. K. is conflicted in his attitudes toward and perceptions of the law, and those conflicts are crafted to allow the reader to *experience* at a heightened level the real conflicts that are part of our public world. Our novelistic encounter with K.'s experience reveals our world and, again to invoke Taylor, *realizes* contact with moral sources that may serve as a criticism of that world, without, of course, providing a blueprint for change.

What are these multiple levels—or tangled threads—of modern experience? We can experience primitive neurotic guilt that can devolve into full paranoia. It is pathological and inhabits the dream—or nightmare—world into which we can fall in our waking lives, that "Heraclitian flow" of our (semi)conscious lives. Primitive guilt may seize and disable us, or at least many of us. Freud's Oedipus complex was one attempt to account for it. This kind of guilt can be alternatively paralyzing or self-destructive. Kafka invests much of his genius in showing how the state can control and sometimes destroy us by deftly playing the keys that occasion that kind of guilt. Because we see almost everything through Josef K.'s eyes, we (and he) maintain a double perspective throughout: a deflating modern urbane satirical stance toward the court and its doings, combined with an increasingly desperate longing for an acceptance or vindication by the authority that exercises real power. Such acceptance would provide a declaration of innocence (or at least an absolution of guilt), the embrace of the estranged and threatening parent that is, in turn, a caricature of divine intimacy. To use our language, properly religious attitudes are "hijacked" in the novel by the law's exploitation of feelings of guilt. This "leads him into confusion, into mistaking the organized and wicked evil of the world surrounding him for some necessary expression of the general guiltiness which is harmless and almost innocent if compared to the ill will that turns 'lying into a universal principle' and uses and abuses even man's justified humbleness."[24] K.'s *educatione sentimentale*,"[25] conditions Josef K. to become utterly powerless before it. "In the case of K., submission is obtained not by force, but simply through increase in the feeling of guilt of which the unbased accusation was the origin in the accused man. This feeling, of course, is based in the last instance on the fact that no man is free from guilt."[26] K.'s feeling of individual guilt is the lever by which his trial "absorbs him, moves him further and further away from the everyday world of normality" so that he is "torn from the world of ordered society."[27] The fact that *The Trial* is, in part, "an embodiment of Kafka's own sensitive and troubled search for religious truth" does not mean "ordeals like K. endures" are illusory and cannot "break men down in much the way that K. is broken. . . . It is no new thing for an individual to find himself helplessly at the mercy of vast, and hostile, and morally inexplicable machines."[28] This is much of what Justice Kennedy means when he tells us that *The Trial* is "closer to reality than fantasy."

The first scene of *The Trial* opens in K.'s bedroom where he emerges into the fuzzy existence just beyond the dream world. K. tries to establish who he is by finding his identity papers, and, in a touch of humor, first finding only his bicycle license. The magistrate begins the process of forcing K. back onto his own inner resources: he orders K. to think about himself. Huld explains to K. that defendants are timid and vulnerable: the law "wants to eliminate the defense as far as possible; everything is to be laid upon the defendant himself" (115). The priest, who "belongs to the court," tells K. that he seeks too much outside help. K. himself realizes that he himself "chooses" to legitimize the process by engaging the guards and the magistrate and turning around in the cathedral in answer to the priest's first command, just as the man from the country himself "chooses" not to enter the door to the law. Neither really can "help himself."

Here the line between freedom of choice and servitude is blurred: "Kafka's characters usually do what they do—go to work in the morning, become lovers, commit crimes, obey laws, or whatever—not because they believe that by doing so they will improve their own well-being, but because they have been told to do so and crave being told to do so."[29] "[T]he distinctions between fate and choice, freedom and bondage, and power and servitude are blurred or nonexistent" so that "the powerful put themselves in servitude and slaves consent to their own bondage."[30] "There can be no other novel so thoroughly pervaded by the sense of nightmare and paranoia," one that presents "guilt as an Urphenomenon, an irreducible phenomenon." This carefully nurtured and manipulated sense of guilt has an important political consequence: "K. dies in a darkness that is never lifted from his trial, . . . he dies in a shame that results from total inability to discern an unambiguous reason for action"

against the forces that bear down on him.[31] And the neuroses that paralyze K. also function in quite a different way to provide much of the motivation of his oppressors and to paralyze *their* ability to act. The ways of
the totalizing state are rooted in an often irrational obsession with order
and security that the spirit of bureaucracy engenders.[32]

However, K. also occupies a place in the public world. There he has
a defined status and role. Late in the novel, when he is led to think of
nothing but his trial, he reflects that if he had to deal with his accusers
in the bank, it would be much easier. There everything is clear and subject to defined public conventions: problems are determinate and solu-
ble. In Orson Welles's film version of *The Trial*, K. manages a vast hall of
workers, all sitting at desks in long, perfectly linear rows, with a factory-
like din of typewriters in the background: the rationally organized, modern financial institution as factory. In *Amerika*, Kafka depicts the ad-
ventures of a young Central European exile in the United States whose
chilly Uncle Jacob comfortably inhabits the capitalist business world.
That world's hard edges provide the ego its best defense against the irrational forces of primitive guilt (but also against any human sympathy
for his nephew).[33] By contrast, "[i]n Josef K., Kafka presented a figure
in whom the will to live as economic man, secularized and self-reliant,
is not strong enough to prevail over the twin lures of self-transcendence
and justified existence, but too strong to permit what Leni calls 'the confession' of these needs."[34]

We, too, have our places in the public world. We each have some political authority to participate in government, the "liberty of the ancients,"
varying very much by the regime that we inhabit. We have a legal status
that can provide immunities and trigger defined consequences. We each
have a place in the economic system. These roles can serve, in Arendt's
terms, as the "stable worldly structure" that can benignly limit the destructive force of that "Heraclitian flow" of our (and others') inner lives
when it turns to fear and anger. That legal status holds the promise of
limiting, as well, the destructive force of mobilized state power. These
roles may also have an impersonal mechanical rigidity and inhumanity
that the word "bureaucracy" often suggests. In *The Trial*, Josef K. is a finance officer in a modern bank, a party in what appears to be a criminal
prosecution, and the victim of a largely unseen bureaucracy.

Finally, we may speak broadly of spiritual experience. Some moderns
seem wholly outside this experience and even claim "tone-deafness" to
this realm. Kafka's novel speaks elusively of the "radiance" that streams

through the door to the law. Charles Taylor describes the modernist tenor of this experience as involving a "subjective resonance" with a "something" that is not subjective. Taylor includes Kafka among those modern writers who struggle to articulate this intuition, largely in the absence of religious institutions that support it.[35] Because much of the novel, and its relevance for us, revolves around its portrayal of a malignant merging of the religious and the legal spheres, a few words about Kafka's religious sensibility are in order.

Within this dimension of experience, we may seek to "walk humbly before the Lord" and understand that the perfection it demands[36] is beyond us. The great humanist Wayne Booth provides what he calls a "common ground definition," one that is not narrowly sectarian, of what this religious perspective implicates. The definition has a number of elements, all of which, I believe, apply to Kafka. First, "insistence that the world is somewhat flawed" and, second, "that the flaws be seen in the light of the Unflawed":

> [T]o qualify as a religion, a belief system must relate the first mark to the second one: it must imply a story, a master narrative that says, "Something *went wrong with creation.*" It's not just "I don't like some things about it," but rather, "Some things are wrong when judged by what would be right, by what a fullness of rightness would demand, by what the whole of creation as I see it implies as the way things should be, but are not." In other words, there was, and in some sense still is, a fall, a brokenness, a decline from what would have been better to what is in fact at best a combination of the better—some ideal—and the worse.[37]

This engenders a kind of "double vision: a vision of a possible past or future order or cosmos superior to the way things actually work now, entailing an awareness that much of what we experience seems out of whack in that order; *the times are out of joint.* . . . I know that what's wrong about it is *wrong,* not just unpleasant." Third, and this turns out to be important for understanding *The Trial,* "*All whom I'm calling genuinely religious will somehow see themselves as in some inescapable sense a part of the brokenness.*[38] . . . Even the best of us . . . are inherently lacking, deficient or, if you prefer the words, we are sinful or guilty. I am an inseparable part of a cosmos that produced this flawed fraction of itself."[39] This feeling of participation in the fallen state of the world makes a moral and perhaps a political claim: "*Four, following inescap-*

ably from the first here: The cosmos I believe in, the cosmos I feel grati-
tude toward for its gift of my very existence and its implied ideals, the cos-
mos that is in its manifestations in my world in some degree broken—my
cosmos calls upon me to do something about the brokenness, to do what
I can in the repair job, working to heal both my own deficiencies and to
aid my fellow creatures in healing theirs."[40] Fifth, *I should subordinate*
my own immediate wishes to these remedial obligations.

The "guilt" or sinfulness in this vision is not neurotic. It is part of seeing the world steady and seeing it whole. This is consistent with a major stream of Western thought: with Plato, where life has to be lived under judgment; certainly in the Hebrew scriptures, where man calls "upon
God *de profundis,* loving the Law, but broken under its yoke"; and the
New Testament, which "calls upon men to know themselves under the
aspects of Sin, Righteousness and Judgment."[41] A. E. Dyson, a distinguished English critic, writes, "this knowledge has always been the path
by which European man has reasserted his dignity, saved his sanity,
when tempted to deny beauty, holiness, God from the depth of despair.
It is the man who knows himself vile and accepts guilt who is able to live
again."[42] For Kafka, Genesis reveals that we possess a clear understanding of good and evil. What we lack is the moral strength to honor this
knowledge. "We have lost Paradise from our sinfully being cast into the
world, but then we have sinned once more, this time against the world,
by not living in it courageously and abundantly."[43] The door to the law
remains open, and the guard never really blocks the entrance.

The religious aspect of the novel is maddeningly elusive. In the great
parable told in the cathedral scene, one may ask, "Does he actually perceive a radiance, or are his eyes perhaps still deceiving him? What would
admittance to the radiance mean? . . . Torah flickers uneasily near as a
positive analogue to the negation that is playing itself out. . . . Josef K.
then is . . . waiting for that new Torah that will not be revealed."[44]

Kafka, however, cannot be described as an "agnostic": "His life would
have been easy to live, and his task as a writer simple to accomplish, if he
had been an agnostic. He had an eminently analytical mind and saw no
reason to believe, and yet he continued to suspend even his disbelief and
inquire why it had become impossible for him to see the light."[45] And so
his "basic inflection is the cadence of questions[,] . . . left open as part of
his grand design. His very greatness lies in the endeavor to formulate his
questions ever anew although he could not hope that an answer could be
given—at least to him."[46] The contradictions within the novel, reflected

in K.'s conflicted attitudes, disclose "[n]ot hopelessness but struggle, not defeat but defeat contended against by hope."[47] And Kafka's novel, like his other novels, is really a series of parables, the cathedral scene and "Before the Law" being the greatest. The priest's rejection of any single interpretive hypothesis for the unchangeable scripture of the parable, like the unchangeable experience of ordinary life, implies that "only a theory covering all the facts is finally of any value, and this is what logic, if K. is ruthlessly honest, cannot provide."[48]

And so to speak of Kafka's "religious" view in any conventional sense is misleading. Indeed, the great parable serves as a critique of religions or "superstitions":

> The outlines of the "meaning" of the parable seem clear enough. The man from the country is the human pilgrim, engaged in his search for truth. The door-keeper is in some sense the theory or philosophy or religion which he finds, and accepts as his authority. The result of their encounter is that the man seems in the end to have been betrayed. His life has passed away in waste and unfulfilment, because he is either misinformed of the truth or has misunderstood it; and this because the door-keeper is either deliberately lying, or because he does not have the authority he claims, or because he does represent an authority but the authority is too strange to be understood.
>
> Each time K. proposes a theory, the Priest points out defects in terms of the actual wording of the Parable. His technique is that of the fundamentalist interpretation of scripture, but it is turned upon the data of life itself. The Priest insists that his business is not to provide a hypothesis of his own, but to bear constant witness to the evidence.
>
>> I am only showing you the various opinions concerning that point [he tells K. at one stage]. You must not pay too much attention to them. The scriptures are unalterable, and the comments often enough merely express the commentators' bewilderment.[49]

"We do not have to be able to understand something in order for it to *be*; indeed our very *need to understand* might prohibit such being from revealing itself to us."[50] Indeed, as Adorno learned from Kafka, "the purpose of art, like philosophy is to say what cannot be said." "Art flies around the truth, but with the definite intention of not getting burnt. Its capacity lies in finding in the dark void a place where the beam of light can be intensely caught, without this having been perceptible before."[51]

K., exhausted at the attempt to discern the meaning of the parable, drops into a Job-like silence. Kafka writes parables—and the unfinished novels really are a sequence of parables, or even the same parable repeated in rising keys—because "[t]he parable . . . acknowledges intellectual slippage, a failure of the mind to apprehend its object."[52] Kafka never uses the word "God," and the parable dramatizes "the impossibility of fully knowing." And yet, consistent with the Jewish mystical tradition, it provides the symbols "within which the unknowable shows and conceals itself."[53] A literary attempt to speak the ineffable must invariably criticize itself as it goes along, for since "literary language cannot avoid operating with some sort of metaphors, it is condemned to add one lie to another."[54] And so "[t]here is a certain justice in K.'s conclusion that the priest's tale has turned 'lying into a universal principle.'" But beyond the priest, the court, and the law, "it is language itself that stands exposed as the arch-liar."

We live, like Kafka's heroes, on different levels of experience. The possibility of the malevolent confusion and then exploitation of this "polymorphism of human consciousness"[55] is one of the central themes of *The Trial*. And so arguments about whether the book is "really" about religious or psychological or institutional matters are misconceived.[56] We need to heed Leibnitz's warning here: theorists tend to be right about what they affirm, but wrong about what they deny. Before we look more concretely at what the book discloses about a law that pretends to be what it is not, however, I should say a word about issues surrounding the interpretation of the text.

Interpretive Perspectives on *The Trial*

Novelist Joyce Carol Oates tells us that "[t]hough the words 'Kafkan' and 'Kafkaesque' invariably point to paradox and human frustration . . . Kafka's stories and parables are not at all difficult to read and to understand. . . . His unique and yet powerfully familiar world can be entered by any reader and comprehended *feelingly* at once."[57] Harold Bloom writes that Kafka is "evasive," though not ambiguous: he "writes between the lines," as Leo Straus put it. Kafka takes from the Jewish tradition a conviction that everything really makes total sense; it's just that he believes that it cannot be conveyed in a single univocal proposition. Kafka's novels—even *The Trial*, which, as arranged by his friend and editor Max Brod, comes closest to having a beginning, middle, and end—don't really conclude: the reader's desire for a conclusion must be confounded, as is the reader's desire for a single "meaning" of the text. The latter is impossible, in part, because contradictory scripts are built into the novel. After all, we see everything through the conflicted eyes of Josef K., who desperately seeks vindication by the court and yet does everything he can to provoke it. The contradiction is the truth of the situation.

This is consistent with Kafka's own approach to his writing. For example, he said that the significance of the doorkeeper story dawned on him only after writing it.[58] In composition, he was "guided by a valid intuition rather than a conscious design in writing his works. Yet it is a valid intuition; the meaning is there, and he himself perceived it *once technique discovered it*, once the creation was accomplished."[59] Again, the parable "indicates intellectual slippage, the failure of the mind to apprehend its object." In the novel, "[t]he door-keeper, like the Door itself, like the priest who tells the story, of which that story is a part, is on *this side* of the impenetrability" and yet, "[i]n the darkness he can now perceive a radiance that streams inextinguishably from the door of the Law."

Let us turn now to the actual characteristics of the legal system that Kafka describes in the novel.

The Characteristics of the Law

The Unknowability of the Law

A pervasive theme of *The Trial* is the unknowability of the law, the "substantive law," the procedural law (if there be any) controlling the process, and the particular charges being brought against Josef K. He initially protests his innocence while admitting that he "doesn't know the law" (8). The arresting officer offers the obvious retort to his colleague, "[H]e admits he doesn't know the law, and yet he claims he's innocent," and to Josef K.: "So much the worse for you. . . . You'll feel it eventually" (8). It turns out that the "bench books" used by the examining magistrates are initially unavailable as well: "Oh, I see," said K. and nodded, "they're probably law books and it's in the nature of this judicial system that one is condemned not only in innocence, but also in ignorance" (55). (Again, they turn out to be pornographic novels [57].) Josef K.'s comforters and advisors continually remind him that he will never meet the real judges, that they are out of sight, and wholly inaccessible. They "inform themselves" (8) about the case after being "attracted to guilt"

(8), especially of those who "attract attention." The law chooses which proceedings are public for its own purposes, and "the court records, and above all the writ of indictment, are not available to the accused and his defense lawyers, so that in general it's not known or not known precisely, what the first petition should be directed against, and for that reason it can only be by chance that it contains something of importance to the case" (113). Because K. is never informed of the specific charges against him, his lawyer is never able to complete even his first filing to the court:

> Truly pertinent and reasoned petitions can only be devised later, when, in the course of the defendant's interrogations, the individual points of the indictment and its basis emerge more clearly, or may be surmised. (114)

His ignorance of both the substantive law and the particular charges against him suggests the fully preposterous expedient of composing an autobiographical account that would fully exonerate him from all possible charges:

> The thought of his trial never left him now. He had often considered whether it might not be advisable to prepare a written defense and submit it to the court. In it he would offer a brief overview of his life, and for each event of any particular importance, explain why he had acted as he did, whether in his present judgment this course of action deserved approval or censure, and what reason he would advance for one or the other. (111)

In the parable "Before the Law," the man from the country is left musing helplessly that "the Law should be accessible to anyone at any time."

Another Legal Parable on the Unknowability of the Law: "The Problem of Our Laws"

A short essay, "The Problem of Our Laws,"[60] written shortly after Kafka finished *The Trial*, illuminates the notion of law woven into the novel. Not surprisingly it is filled with paradox, each assertion tending to be dissolved in qualifications. The most famous line in the fragment comes early: "[I]t is an extremely painful thing to be ruled by laws that one does not know." And this pain is endured in the narrator's country, for there "our laws are generally not known; they are kept secret by the small group of nobles who rule us."[61] The common beliefs about these laws are that they are very ancient and that centuries of interpretation have narrowed the range of potentially arbitrary "interpretive freedom." What seems reassuring, though, turns out not to be, for "the nobles have obviously no cause to be influenced in their interpretation inimical to us, for the laws were made to the advantage of the nobles from the beginning, they themselves stand above the laws."[62] And it also turns out the very existence of the laws being interpreted is "at most a matter of presumption," since the "essence of a secret code is that it should remain a mystery."[63] The narrator tells us that the common people have, over the centuries, tried to formulate "certain main tendencies" in the action of the nobles "which permit of this or that historical formulation," but when citizens attempt to order their present or future in light of "these scrupulously tested and logically ordered conclusions" then "everything becomes uncertain, and our work seems only an intellectual game, for perhaps these laws that we are trying to unravel do not exist at all."[64] There are a few skeptics who claim there are, in fact, no laws and that the illusion that they exist only serves to give "the people a false, deceptive, and overconfident security in confronting coming events."[65] But the majority urges that it will take "several centuries" before any conclusions may be drawn about the existence or nature of the law. This unhappy conclusion is softened only "by the belief that a time will eventually come when the tradition and our research into it will jointly reach their conclusion, and . . . when everything will have become clear, the law will belong to the people, and the nobility will vanish":

> This is not maintained in any spirit of hatred against the nobility; not at all, and by no one. We are more inclined to hate ourselves, because we have not yet shown ourselves worthy of being entrusted with the laws. And that is the real reason why the party which believes there is no law has remained so few—although their doctrine is in certain ways so attractive. For it unequivocally recognizes the nobility and its right to go on existing.[66]

The hope, then, is that the "secret code" will collapse into the very process of its interpretation by common people and its mystery will disappear and with it the transcendent lordship of the nobles. But the people haven't managed yet to take this responsibility.[67] If they had, it might have been possible for Josef K. to enter his gate to "true law," to be judged "according to conscience."[68]

The hope for what we might call democratic law remains utopian. It is not clear whether it is a true hope ("We have not *yet* eaten of the tree of life!"), or whether it is an element of an ideology that allows the elites to continue to rule in their own interest. It is also unclear whether, at the moment of decision, those elites are following "the law" or making wholly discretionary determinations in their own interest. And our attempts to formulate coherent "legal doctrine" that can reliably predict outcomes often seem to be a fool's errand.

The Law Is Not Only Unknowable: It Is Ubiquitous

Kafka dramatizes the ubiquity of the law throughout the novel. The courthouse appears in the tenements in the city's urban underclass, amidst women caring for their children and other signs of family life. When K. visits Titorelli in his "atelier," to use the latter's overblown description, he exits and finds himself in the halls of the court, peopled again by the confused defendants. Almost all the important characters in the novel with whom K. must interact in all sorts of contexts "belong to the Law." Surely the initial investigators, who appear uninvited in K.'s bedroom, do, and as it turns out, so do the apparently lay audience in K.'s first and only court appearance, all of whom turn out to be officials. The law's enforcers turn up in a closet in the bank, a place where K. might have thought his role in the rationalized economic system was protected by its internal rules and roles. K.'s distant relatives come to know about and be concerned with K.'s process. Psychologically, K. ends up obsessed with it such that he cannot clear his mind to concentrate on his work. In his own time, the thought of the process comes never to leave his mind. His obligations at the bank are used to lure him to the cathedral where, as Leni tells him, he is being hounded by the law. And, of course, the cathedral itself provides no escape: the priest is a prison chaplain and is himself an agent of and apologist for the law. The law is, like the God of the *Book of Revelation*, "all in all."

The Bureaucratization of Law and the Ascendancy
of Ideological Officials

Kafka's world of "organizational gothic" is populated, as we have seen, by pure functionaries. They are themselves not free, as we hear of the doorkeeper in the final parable:

The doorkeeper, insofar as he is an official, is unfree, impersonal, and subject to a necessity which neither he himself nor the others understand. . . .
Officials have no responsibility toward other people; their justification lies
solely in their function—their calling—with which they are completely identical. This mere facticity and functionality of the officials must be accepted like
the facticity of the material world. It detaches the officials from the sphere of
human judgment by classifying them with the world of objects, in which there
is no guilt and no responsibility.[69]

These functionaries have no idea of their place in the entire case against
Josef K.: "The proceedings in the courts of law are generally a mystery
to the lower officials as well; therefore they can almost never follow the
progress of the cases they are working on. . . . ; the case enters their field
of vision, often they know not whence, and continues on, they know not
where. The lessons to be learned . . . are lost to these officials" (118). K.
despairs of dealing with them and longs to deal with "someone of my
own sort" who, he hopes, "will make everything incomparably clearer
than the longest conversation" with the lower officials. Because there is
no responsibility in the bureaucracy, because it embodies, as Arendt famously put it, "rule by nobody," it is only the organization itself, whatever it is, which is guilty (83). Tribunals that appear to be staffed by
ordinary people, like the audience for K.'s only public hearing, are actually filled by officials, "the corrupt band I was speaking about; you've
crowded in here to listen and snoop, you've formed apparent parties and
had one side applaud to test me, you wanted to learn how to lead innocent me astray" (52).[70] They are members of "a great organization . . .
which . . . not only employs corrupt wardens, stupid inspectors, and examining magistrates . . . but also has at its disposal a judicial hierarchy
of high, indeed of the highest rank, with an indispensable and numerous retinue of servants, clerks, police, and other assistants, and perhaps
even hangmen."[71] Kafka "knew that a man caught in the bureaucratic
machinery is already condemned; and that no man can expect justice
from judicial procedures where interpretation of the law is coupled with
the administering of lawlessness, and where the chronic inaction of the
interpreters is compensated by a bureaucratic machine whose senseless
automatism has the privilege of ultimate decision."[72] Twentieth-century
history has shown, Arendt tells us, that what appears to be a nightmare
is a tale in which Kafka "adequately represents the true nature of the
thing called bureaucracy."[73] Kafka's heroes "move in a society where

everybody is assigned a role and everybody has a job. . . . And all of this society that strives at some kind of superhuman perfection live in complete identification with their jobs. They have no psychological qualities because they are nothing other than jobholders. . . . To err is to lose one's job; therefore, [a jobholder] cannot even admit the possibility of an error. . . . Jobholders whom society forces to deny the human possibility of erring cannot remain human."[74] Priests and judges who belong to the law speak wrathfully and *from above* and leave their ordinary human sensibilities behind.

Today, "[e]verywhere there is organization, everywhere bureaucratization; like the world of feudalism, the modern world is broken up into areas dominated by castles, . . . the castles of Kafka," and so he "speaks directly to many of our contemporary concerns."[75] And so it is true that "standing back, we can see that the contribution of Kafka may help . . . ourselves in the West . . . to better resist the sanitized versions of a 'brave new world' that are being imposed upon us."[76] As Primo Levi put it in 1989, "Kafka understands the world (his, and even better, ours of today) with a clairvoyance that astonishes and wounds."[77] Kafka "satirizes *dominance*, particularly the *authority relationship*."

> Kafka writes from the perspective of a "modern citizen who realizes that his fate is being determined by an impenetrable bureaucratic apparatus whose operation is controlled by procedures which remain shadowy even to those carrying out its orders and *a fortiori* to those being manipulated by it[,] . . . [a] *Kafka-esque* bizarre hierarchical timeless system that reflects the "golden rule" that it never makes mistakes. In an apparent ethos of selfless public service, there lurks a self-serving bureaucracy.[78]

Attempts at reform serve only to risk "damaging oneself immeasurably by attracting the attention of an always vengeful bureaucracy," which "remains unchanged, if not, which is likely even more resolute, more vigilant, more severe, more malicious." The officials are easily offended, for "[i]n many ways the officials were like children. They were often so hurt by seemingly minor matters" (119).

At another level, Kafka sees the roots of bureaucracy rooted more deeply in human nature than we might like to think. Indeed, in a letter to a friend written some years after *The Trial*, he laments that it is "the social structure most closely corresponding to human nature."[79] There is something deep in K.'s soul that identifies with the court, which makes submission to its lethal claims attractive to him. K. wants to belong, not to offend, although he cannot seem to help himself. The bureaucrats' lack of freedom expresses a part of the soul where obsessions and compulsions hold sway. This is an aspect of Kafka's anticipation of the totalitarian state. From K.'s point of view, which is the only point of view from which the events of the novel are seen and which we are asked to interpret and judge, "[t]he suggestion, indeed the insinuation, [is] that the exterminators and the law they enact are not wholly in the wrong, that there *is* a foothold for their authority in the victim's soul, as though their hold were somehow a matter not merely of might but also of right—that insinuation, too, is part of Kafka's anticipation."[80] On the other hand, and there always is another hand, the grim ending of the novel serves as a rejection of any such claim of right, such "political theology."

Critics have noticed how the women in the novel, such as the "severely dressed" official K. meets in the offices of the law[81] and, of course, Leni, are the spokespersons for the bureaucracy, and urge submission to it as the only way actually to live in this world. Kafka is toying here with the notion that power is the rule (and condition) of life and women understand this and express what one writer calls "Kafka's masochistic and sacrificial poetics."[82] Kafka suggests that controlling bureaucracy is not simply a matter of being more efficient, of rational institutional design, as we might say. It would require a kind of conversion that freed us from the profound sources of its power. This interweaving of spiritual and political issues means that we should not claim that Kafka is *only* a religious or *only* a political writer. Both perspectives are necessary to appreciate his achievement. And both perspectives may have something to do with our heeding his warnings.

Yet Another Short Parable: The Public Prosecutor

An unfinished story, "The Assistant Public Prosecutor,"[83] that Kafka wrote near the time of *The Trial* stands as a critique of the notion of an "apolitical" conservative prosecutor dedicated only to common good. The protagonist fantasizes himself publicly prosecuting judges before whom he practices. He recalls a case he prosecuted fifteen years earlier, at the beginning of his career. It was a prosecution of a politically active man who had allegedly uttered a "remark insulting to His Majesty" while in a drunken stupor, as reported by someone at the next table who was "probably even drunker . . . probably believing, in his befuddlement, that he was doing something meritorious" and who had "instantly rushed to a policeman and returned with him, smiling blissfully."[84] There was no doubt that the accused had, in fact, been drinking, and there did seem to be some ambiguity about what was said. One version had the defendant waving his wineglass at a picture of the king and shouting, "You low scamp up there!" (*Du Lump dort oben!*),[85] though there was some confusion about there being some kind of connection (*irgendeiner Verbindung*) with a vaguely similar line from a song, "so long as glows the lamp" (*solange noch das Lampchen gluht*),[86] "in this way obscuring the meaning of the explanation." Any trial lawyer would appreciate the confused nature of the purely factual evidence and the prominence of what we could call "character evidence" in the following:

> Almost every witness was of a different opinion regarding the nature of the connection between the exclamation and the song, and the denunciator even maintained that it was someone else, and not the accused, who had been singing. What gravely militated against the accused was his political activity, which made it seem at any rate very credible that he was *capable* of uttering the same exclamation in a state of complete sobriety and with entire conviction.[87]

As in *The Trial*, the facts are far less important than are more global judgments about the *kind* of person the defendant is. The assistant prosecutor recalled "how it was almost with ecstasy" that he prosecuted the defendant because, like other assistant attorneys, "he sincerely hated the accused and his cause." "Though without having any systematic political views, he was, however [an] out-and-out conservative" who valued "childlike" deference to the king and hated the defendant's sort. Untroubled deference to authority was "prevented from coming into existence by people of the accused's kind, people who, making their way up from some underworld or other, split up the solid mass (*die feste Masse*) of the reliable nation (*Volkes*) with their shouting."[88] The prosecutor worked on his case "for nights on end" and was convinced that it would make his career. It was clear that the defense counsel, "an unworthy opponent," had no real confidence in his case. At trial the prosecutor took the unusual step of agreeing with the motion of defense counsel to hold the hearing in public:

Everything was so clear and so well thought out, it was as though all the people round about were interfering in a matter that belonged to him alone, a matter that he himself could carry through to its conclusion in a way that was in accord with its nature, without any judge, without any counsel, without any accused. . . . [The judges, defense counsel, and the accused] realized that here one man was wresting the entire matter, with which they had this or that faint connection, from them and making it his own inalienable property. Each of them had thought he was going to be present at a small case of *lese majeste*, and now he heard the Assistant Public Prosecutor, in his very first speech, in a few words dispose of the insult itself as though it were something irrelevant.[89]

What was actually said and by whom disappears into irrelevancy. The "capacities" of the defendant loom large, as they threaten a "childish" psychology of identification with the *Volk* that lashes out against anything that looks like criticism of solidarity. Once again, law has lost its contact with the specific and the worldly and become the method by which larger forces, social and psychological, press down upon individuals through the operation of the bureaucracy.

Jettisoning Formality

Nothing happens in the court through formal procedures. As befits the bureaucratic world we have just examined, events occur through an almost physical pressure being exerted on the functionaries who inhabit it. In the very first scene, the guards clownishly explain that they are the better custodians of K.'s underclothes, because only bribes will pressure the prison officials to surrender them later. Huld explains that a lawyer's personal contacts are what really serve him and that the majority of lawyers operate by "bribing people and pumping them for information" (114). K.'s personally offending the chief clerk means that the latter has to be "crossed off the list" of officials who may be turned to for help. Titorelli claims to be of real help to K. because of the personal relations he has with many judges. When K. objects to Titorelli's offer of help that he himself had explained that the "court is totally impervious to proof," Titorelli retorts, "'Impervious only to proof brought before the court[,]' . . . lifting his forefinger, as if K. had missed a subtle distinction. 'But it is another matter when it comes to behind-the-scene efforts, in the conference rooms, in the corridors, or for example even here in the atelier'" (150). (As Lenny Bruce famously put it, "In the halls of justice, the only justice is in the halls.") And there is no actual progress in the proceedings as defined steps are taken. Rather "the final judgment comes unexpectedly from some chance person at some random moment" (197). The real determinants of decision at the highest level is completely unknowable: "We don't know what things look like up there, and incidentally, we don't want to know." From our side of the law, it appears that its wholly unfree machine is activated when some unknowable pressure builds up from we know not where. All we can do in the meantime is to apply some informal countermeasures temporarily to relieve that pressure and keep the machine from moving in its inevitably lethal direction.

The Ubiquity of Deception

It is not only that there is no transparency about the law's processes and motives. The law's agents engage in systematic misdirection and deception. The guards who appear in K.'s room steal his breakfast and warn him that his undergarments will surely be stolen by the prison bureaucracy, though K.'s "arrest" never leads to imprisonment at all. They tell K. that the higher authorities never err, though the magistrate in his first hearing gets so basic a thing as his occupation wrong. The inspector gives a wholly implausible explanation for the presence of the three clerks from K.'s bank at his initial interview. The audience for K.'s hearing is wholly other than it seems, filled with officials rather than an apparently lay audience. Half the audience seems to cheer K. on, though he concludes they are simply trying to "test" him in order to lead an innocent man "astray." Upon his return to the courtroom the next week, he finds what are apparently law books on the magistrate's desk, only to learn later that they are pornographic novels. K.'s offer of a bribe to the flogger in the junk room at the bank is refused only because the latter cannot, he says, trust K. to keep the bribe secret. Leni tells K. that the portrait of the imperious judge in Huld's apartment completely misrepresents what the judge actually looks like. Huld boasts of his prowess at winning many "hopeless" trials, though later concedes that it's not at all clear what effect his efforts have had on the outcomes. The court pretends that the written submissions of the lawyers have some effect, but most are lost or read too late to affect the judgment. K. is lured into composing a narrative that has to be false, one that shows, in effect, that he has lived a perfect life. Titorelli explains, in effect, that the law's promise of a result based on actual guilt or innocence is something that exists only in legends. The priest confesses that his own apparent friendliness is deceptive. One opinion is that the doorkeeper cruelly deceived the man from the country about the possibility of entry to the law. And, finally, K. understands the priest's injunction to consider the doorkeeper's statements not as true, but as necessary, as the acceptance of lies as a "universal system."

The Marginalization of Defense Counsel

We are told that "the defense is not actually countenanced by the Law, but only tolerated." And, in fact, it is not completely clear that they are even tolerated. The court does not really "recognize" them or their function. They are all thus "shysters." They are forced to gather in a shabby room that they are not permitted to fix up even at their own expense. They are thrown down the stairs by the elderly magistrate. None of this is accidental, for the goal is "to eliminate the defense as far as possible" so that all of the pressure of the law can be felt by the vulnerable individual psychology of the defendant. We hear, mainly from Huld, that most of what the lawyers do is ineffectual paper shuffling. The system is so little coherent that Block has several lawyers, each working his own "angles" in ignorance of the others' efforts. Titorelli suggests that his own more "personal" contacts with the lower judges whom his art flatters is more likely to do some temporary good than the more formal efforts of the lawyers. In sum, the law creates a situation where it may bring all of its force to bear on the defendant unconstrained by the binding formalisms of which we tend to think lawyers the masters. Their craft has no purchase on the elusive sources of real power.

The Irrelevance of the Facts of the Case

In the opening scene, K. is confidently informed that the court "informs itself" of the truth of the situation and is "attracted to" the certain guilt of the accused individual. Naturally, then, the court intentionally places the defense in a "very unfavorable and difficult position . . . [f]or the defense is not actually countenanced by the law, but only tolerated, and there is even some controversy as to whether the relevant passages of the law can truly be construed to include even such tolerance," something that, of course, can never be settled because no one has even actually read the law. Our confidence in the court's infallibility is rather shaken when the examining magistrate begins his conversation with Josef K. with the leading question, "You are a house painter, are you not?" And the court has so constructed its procedures that the "timid and vulnerable" defendants are unlikely aggressively to marshal the specific facts that may actually provide a defense. In Kafka's "In the Penal Colony," written about the same time as *The Trial*, the defendant is sentenced to an excruciating death without any semblance of due process at all. Because the officials are justified by an absolutely higher law, any defense would pose an affront to the majesty of that law, would suggest that it could be anything but infallible. (Arendt writes that simple factual truth is experienced as an irritating constraint in the willful world of politics, where "facts are purposes."[90]) In the "Assistant Public Prosecutor," discussed above, the actual details of the defendant's actions fade into irrelevance before the hostile attitudes that the prosecutor brings to people of "the wrong sort," those who threaten the solidity of the *Volk*. Kafka gives us an eerie premonition of his own legal world twenty years hence, when a doctrine "dominates all social life" wherein "certain people are classified and grouped, judged and condemned and eventually done to death, not because of what they do or the way they function in society, not [even] because of what they say or think or believe—in all respects it is virtually impossible to distinguish them from the rest of society—but simply because of what they are."[91] Jews were thus both Marxists and international capitalists, both "mere foreground manifestations of an unalterably (because 'naturally') depraved state of being which lies behind and beyond all doing, all inessential 'patter and opinion,'" about the actual facts.

> This is the situation Kafka anticipates in a number of his stories, most directly in those which are concerned with juridical matters. . . . An important aim of his remarkable prose patterns is to establish an all but unbreakable spider-web of insinuations which connects the guilt his "heroes" are involved in with the feeling of guilt they experience. Their punishment never fits the crime. The feeling of guilt is always greater than the guilt entailed by the action they are responsible for—a gap which insinuatory prose is intended to bridge. However, the gap remains. The ultimate justification for the verdict passed on his "heroes" which is always a verdict of "guilty," is that they are what they are. . . . The reason for Joseph K.'s peculiar arrest and apparently

inescapable involvement in the protracted trial is never formulated; what is significant is that guilt is ascribed to him the moment he acknowledges the jurisdiction of the court, and that "the trial" quickly becomes justified in the eyes of others simply by becoming "*his* trial."[92]

The German Penal Code adopted after the Nazi ascent to power in 1933 provided that the "sound sense of the people for right and wrong determines the content and application of the penal law." "Through an amendment of July 28, 1935, which was heralded as a 'revolution in penal law,' judges were given the authority to punish acts not specifically prohibited by law if they offended the 'sound sense of the people.'" The National Socialist Penal Code provided further that "[a]ny person shall be punished who commits an act that the law declares punishable or that according to the basic principles of the penal code and according to the sound sense of the people deserves punishment. If no specific penal law is directly applicable to the act, then the act is punished according to the law whose basic principle best applies to it."[93] Thus both liberal first principles were abrogated: there could be punishment imposed without an act that violated the law, and without any law that directly proscribed an act.

The Claimed Right Infallibly to Judge the Whole Person and Relevance of the Entire Character of the Accused

The guards who appear at K.'s apartment have absolute confidence in the global judgment that the higher officials have pronounced on K. After all, they tell him, "we are smart enough to realize that before ordering such an arrest the higher authorities who employ us inform themselves in great detail about the person they arresting and the grounds for the arrest. There's been no mistake. After all, our department, as far as I know, and I know only the lower level, doesn't seek out guilt among the general population, but as the law states, is attracted by guilt and has to send us guards out" (8). Given the unknowability of the law and the secrecy surrounding the charges, K. is forced into an impossible task: "[W]ithout knowing the nature of the charge and all its possible ramifications, his entire life, down to the smallest actions and events, would have to be called to mind, described, and examined from all sides. And what a sad job that was" (127).

The Merging of the Political into the Religious and Psychological

The court is, like God in classical theology, unchanging: "the vast judicial organism remains, so to speak, in a state of eternal equilibrium, and that if you change something on your own where you are, you can cut the ground out from under your own feet and fall, while the vast organism easily compensates for the minor disturbance at some other spot—after all everything is interconnected—and remains unchanged." The court judges K.'s entire *existence*. It implicitly claims the divine prerogative to be addressed as David addressed God: "O Lord, you have searched me and know me. . . . You discern my thoughts from far away. . . . Such knowledge is too wonderful for me. . . . Search me, O God, and know my heart . . . test me and know my thoughts." It is only appropriate, then, should K. be found wanting, "that the sentence eventually passed on Josef. K. will be absolute, as from a divinity: it will be a sentence of death."[94]

The most powerful revelation of what the law, the parable "Before the Law," is told by a priest in a cathedral. The priest, who "belongs to the law," tells K. that he had to speak to K. "from a distance. Otherwise I'm too easily influenced and forget my position." Religion, if offered not from "on high," from a pulpit, offers some promise of brotherly help to K., "something that might show him for example, not how to influence the trial, but how to break out of it, how to get around it, how to live outside the trial" (214). But that is a possibility that the court must decisively suppress, as it takes on the mantle of a despotic divinity.[95]

This usurpation of the divine is at the center of Arendt's interpretation of *The Trial*. We have already seen how the court effectively manipulates, through his *educatione sentimentale*, K.'s "religious" sense of humility to its own ends: K.'s "submission is obtained not by force, but simply through increase in the feeling of guilt of which the unbased accusation was the origin in the accused man. This feeling, of course, is based in the last instance on the fact that no man is free from guilt."[96] K. becomes increasingly confused, "mistaking the organized and wicked evil of the world surrounding him for some necessary expression of the general guiltiness which is harmless and almost innocent if compared to the ill will that turns 'lying into a universal principle' and uses and abuses even man's justified humbleness."[97] K. thus becomes "capable of entering the world of necessity and injustice and lying, of playing a role according to the rules, or adapting himself to existing conditions."[98] The court's agents aid in this enterprise. His lawyer "tells him at once that the only sensible thing to do is to adapt oneself to existing conditions and not to criticize them. He turns to the prison chaplain for advice, and the chaplain preaches the hidden greatness of the system and orders him not to ask for the truth, 'for it is not necessary to accept everything as true, one must accept it as necessary.'"[99]

> Kafka depicted a society which had established itself as a substitute for God, and he described men who looked upon the laws of society as though they were divine laws—unchangeable through the will of men. In other words, what is wrong with the world in which Kafka's heroes are caught is precisely its deification, its pretense of representing a divine necessity. Kafka wants to destroy this world by exposing its hideous and hidden structure, by contrasting reality and pretense.[100]

It is precisely Kafka's goal to "build up a world in accordance with human needs and human dignities, a world where a man's actions are determined by himself and which is ruled by laws and not by mysterious forces emanating from above and below."[101] (In the story "In the Penal Colony," it is the need of the officials to represent something higher that allows them to dispense with the ordinary mundane considerations of fair process and factual truth.) The fusing of the religious and the legal worlds allows Kafka's heroes to become collaborators in their own self-destruction, to satisfy "an unquenchable thirst for judgment and ultimately for punishment."[102] The last scene of *The Trial* rejects "the self's apotheosis through its submission to authority."[103] That scene "demythologizes Kafka's myth of redemptive dying. . . . The death of a dog robs not only K., but also the Court of all glamour." It rejects the "theocratization of bureaucracy in which the apparatus is accorded superior, mystical powers that precluded the assertion of autonomy."[104]

The Expansion of the Realm of Necessity and Inevitability

The bureaucratizing and theologizing of law has an important corollary. More of what it requires is necessary and inevitable, beyond the power of men to escape or to change. This is wholly acceptable to the priest. He tells K. that there are those who say that the doorkeeper is beyond criticism and possesses a transcendent dignity as a representative of the law. K. replies that he cannot accept that view, which would mean that he had to accept as true whatever the doorkeeper said. "No," said the Priest, "you don't have to consider everything true, you just have to consider it necessary" (222–23). "The force of the machinery in which the K. of *The Trial* is caught lies precisely in this appearance of necessity, on the one hand, and in the admiration of the people for necessity on the other. Lying for the sake of necessity appears as something sublime; and a man who does not submit to the machinery . . . is regarded as a sinner against some kind of divine order."[105] We have already examined Huld's account of the law as a vast organism, always in unchanging equilibrium, impervious to human action or change. In a reflective moment, the attorney confesses to melancholy moments when it seems that all lawyers' efforts really amount to nothing, as all results often seem wholly predetermined.

The agents of the law seek to return the human world wholly to the world of natural determinism, almost physical law, and with this consequence: "Just as a house which has been abandoned by men to its natural fate will slowly follow the course of ruin, . . . so surely the world, fabricated by men and constituted according to human and not natural laws, will become again part of nature and follow the law of ruin when man decides to become part of nature, a blind though accurate tool of natural laws, renouncing his supreme faculty of creating laws himself and even prescribing them to nature."[106] Predictability and necessity come at a cost:

> In so far as life is decline which ultimately leads to death, it can be foretold. In a dissolving society which blindly follows the natural course of ruin, catastrophe can be foreseen. Only salvation, not ruin, comes unexpectedly, for salvation and not ruin depends upon the liberty and the will of men. Kafka's so-called prophecies were but a sober analysis of underlying structures which have come into the open. These ruinous structures were supported, and the process of ruin itself accelerated, by the belief, almost universal in his time, in a necessary and automatic process to which man must submit. . . . But as a functionary of necessity, man becomes an agent of the natural law of ruin, thereby degrading himself into the natural tool of destruction, which may be accelerated through the perverted use of human capacities.[107]

Arendt notes as well that the twentieth century's "worst crimes have been committed in the name of some kind of necessity or in the name—and this amounts to the same thing—of the 'wave of the future.'"[108] We will consider below the ways in which our own forms of social ordering have become infected with beliefs that claim an often scientific necessity and how these beliefs threaten our abilities to "build up a world in accordance with human needs and human dignities."[109]

Conclusion

Kafka describes a legal order that amounts to a nightmare. I will turn next to an exploration of aspects of our own procedural ways wherein lurk some of those same qualities. I will then try to identify those resources within our practices and traditions that may be even now providing some immunity from the worst of what Kafka saw and that may provide the antidote to the worst consequences of the system of domination Kafka understood.

CHAPTER THREE

Echoes of Kafka Today

Today's justice system is more centralized, more legalized, more bureaucratized—and more devoted to the use of hard power. Like the constabularies of the European empires that nineteenth-century immigrants fled, urban police forces in late twentieth- and early twenty-first-century America are professional bureaucracies.—William J. Stuntz

It turns out that Kafka's visionary satire of domination applies all too often to our American regime. Features of our criminal process and "substantive" criminal law echo Kafka's nightmare and justify Justice Kennedy's claim that, for a person enmeshed in that process, that nightmare can be a reality. First, I will describe something of the social and political background that has brought a liberal democratic nation close to the bureaucratized hard power of the Central European empires. Then I will argue that the American criminal process has many of those same characteristics that Kafka satirizes in *The Trial*. This will allow me, in the final chapter, to ask whether we have the resources to halt the kind of slide that Kafka warned about.

Throughout I will try to keep our eyes on the dominant criminal process that we actually employ in the vast number of cases, the "law in action" rather than the law on the books. On the procedural side, we have seen that *The Trial* is on, one level, a "burlesque" of Austrian criminal procedure. In this parody, the preliminary investigation, which was conducted in secret before formal charges were leveled, "has displaced the other states of the procedure with its guaranteed protection for the rights of the individual." In *The Trial* we see a process, which "goes to the extreme in ignoring the objective facts of the case and focusing on the guilt of the accused."[1] It goes forward in "an atmosphere that abuses the rights of the accused both by violating privacy and discretion in its hearings and by concealment from the accused and his advisors of the information needed for the defense"[2]

It is now commonly understood that "our" criminal process is almost completely identical with the early stages of prosecution and that approximately 95 percent of criminal cases are terminated based on pretrial practices and without the procedural formalities of trial.[3] As Justice Stephen Breyer put it recently, "[O]ur criminal justice system is no longer the jury trial based adversarial system that it once was. . . . '[P]lea bargaining' is not some adjunct to the criminal justice system; *it is the criminal justice system*."[4] And in approximately half of American criminal prosecutions the police have successfully extracted a confession from the accused,[5] an event that greatly increases the likelihood that a plea bargain will be struck and often renders any trial that takes place a formality. Our criminal justice system in action is a system of police interrogation followed by plea bargaining and should be imagined concretely in those terms. In the account below, I will try to do just that. Additionally, as I will also show, the few cases that actually go to trial are often distorted by earlier interrogations, police perjury about them, and the procedural rules that allow these distortions to occur.

Introduction: Aspects of the Social Background

How could we have come to this point? We are a constitutional democracy where the people are sovereign and where power is dispersed and checked through a federal system. We lionize the rule of law and claim to have a "government of laws, not of men." We have an independent judiciary that is thought to be somewhat immune from political forces. And yet, as I will argue, we hear echoes of Kafka throughout our criminal justice system. Before we look hard at what we actually do in our *Process*, we need to widen the lens somewhat.

We have created a distinctive combination of neoliberal economics— like K.'s rationalized life in his bank—and angry, visceral neoconservative politics—the goddess of justice become the goddess of the hunt. The sovereign state's protection of the people, whose only common bond is vulnerability to crime, "will systematically favor vengeance and ritualized rage over crime prevention and fear reduction."[6] This is odd in

America, which is, as Arendt noted some time ago,[7] in many ways the most modern of societies. It seems that "modernizing processes that, until recently seemed so well established in this realm—above all the long-term tendencies toward 'rationalization' and 'civilization'—now look as if they have been thrown into reverse. The re-appearance in official policy of punitive sentiments and expressive gestures that appear oddly archaic and downright antimodern tend to confound the standard social theories of punishment and its historical development."[8]

On many measures, we have recently become a more punitive society. Some commentators have gone so far as to argue that we now very broadly "govern through crime." We all know that, judged by comparison with our own history or the experience of Western European democracies, our prison population is enormous. Between 1950 and 2000, the rate of imprisonment of whites rose 184 percent and that of blacks 355 percent. We imprison roughly four times as many people per capita as do the British and about six times as many as do the French and Germans.[9] As one investigator put it: "In the USA, the system that is taking form resembles nothing so much as the Soviet gulag—a string of work camps and prisons strung across a vast country, housing two million people most of whom are drawn from classes and racial groups that have become politically and economically problematic."[10]

In African American communities, our imprisonment rate can "fairly be called astronomical."[11] "The black imprisonment rate for 2000 exceeds by one-fourth the imprisonment rate in the Soviet Union in 1950—near the end of Stalin's reign, the time when the population of the Soviet prison camps peaked. If jail inmates are included, per capita black incarceration is 80 percent higher than the rate at which Stalin's regime banished its subjects to the Gulag's many camps."[12] Our prisons have largely abandoned rehabilitative goals and serve mainly to separate and warehouse inmates.[13]

There is little doubt that this relates to broader socioeconomic realities: "The disappearance of entry-level jobs for young 'underclass' males, together with the depleted social capital of impoverished families and crime prone neighborhoods, has meant that the prison and parole now lack the social supports upon which their rehabilitative efforts had previously relied" so that "imprisonment has become a long-term assignment from which individuals have little prospect of returning to an unsupervised freedom." Opening the lens even wider, we may see:

[O]ur practice of controlling crime and doing justice have had to adapt to an increasingly insecure economy that marginalizes substantial sections of the population; to a hedonistic consumer culture that combines extensive personal freedom with relaxed social controls; to a pluralistic moral order that struggles to create trust relations between strangers who have little in common; to a "sovereign" state that is increasingly incapable of regulating a society of individuated citizens and differentiated social groups; and to chronically high crime rates that co-exist with low levels of family cohesion and community solidarity. The risky, insecure character of today's social and economic relations is the social surface that gives rise to our newly emphatic, overreaching concern with control and to the urgency with which we segregate, fortify, and exclude.[14]

Toward the end of the Second World War, Karl Polanyi surveyed the collapse of nineteenth-century society.[15] That society was built, he argued, on a utopian conception of a self-regulating market based purely on freedom of contract. That economy collapsed in the Great Depression. The rise of European fascism was an attempt to impose order on the working classes who were beginning to resist the "sociological nightmare" that the nineteenth-century economy had imposed on them. There was an intrinsic link between the market economy in which Josef K. worked and the expedient of the centralized bureaucratic control that Kafka foresaw. We may be experiencing a so-far more limited version of the same dynamic. The enthusiasm for a "neoliberal" account of economics that accelerates the effects of a capitalist economy in labor and financial markets has brought with it a "neoconservative," authoritarian attempt to keep the (increasingly growing) "dangerous classes" under control. As the "greatest generation" has passed from power and our memory of the need for collective responses to the Great Depression and the Second World War have faded, we have reverted to an imaginary that is based on individual responsibility (and so often individual *criminal* responsibility) as the key to social control.[16]

We are one of few developed countries that retain the death penalty. We continue to execute people at the rate of one per week, though here again strong countercurrents have emerged. The politics of crime and capital punishment have become close to the center of our electoral regime. Support for capital punishment was an important factor in George H. W. Bush's victory over Michael Dukakis in the 1988 presidential election. Democrat Bill Clinton famously returned to Arkansas during the New Hampshire primary campaign to preside over the execution of Ricky Rector, a defendant with limited mental capacity, who had received a death sentence after killing a police officer. (Clinton placed a strong second in the primary.) Democratic governor Ruben Askew remained in office throughout the seventies and into the eighties (while Florida was moving toward the Republican Party) after he called the state legislature into special session and "enacted by near acclamation a statute that has proven highly productive of death sentences."[17] In New York, George Pataki won the governorship of a traditionally Democratic state away from Mario Cuomo largely on the basis of his stand on the death penalty. Gray Davis, another liberal Democrat, managed to win the governorship of California against a conservative Republican (Republicans had been governors for twenty years) by campaigning as a supporter of the death penalty. "Singapore is a good starting point, in terms of law and order," he proclaimed in a debate and otherwise invoked in campaign materials:

> I'm trying to let people know that I'm not going to tolerate violent crime. I believe strongly in the death penalty. I put it in all my ads . . .
> I think Singapore has very clear rules. . . . They don't fool around and they have very little violent crime. And if you don't like it, you can get on a plane and go somewhere else.[18]

In broad terms, a transformed political reality has prevailed in the United States:

> Simply put, to be for the people, legislators must be for victims and law enforcement, and thus they must never be for (or capable of being portrayed as being for) criminals or prisoners as individuals or as a class. To do so is damning in two distinct ways. First, it portrays a disqualifying personal softness or tolerance toward crime. Second, it means siding against victims and law-enforcement in a zero-sum game in which any gain for prisoners or criminals is experienced as a loss for law enforcement and victims.[19]

So the response to crime is very, very important in American society and politics. In many elections, it determines the outcome. We have developed criminological categories that are "sanctioned by social authorities and backed up by institutional power" and that should be considered "not as 'true' or 'valid' or 'scientific' knowledge but rather as effective truth producing categories that provide the discourse conditions for real social practices."[20] For political and institutional reasons, resort to criminal law and procedures has often become the default practice for addressing social problems. Unfortunately, "[t]he hardening of social and racial divisions, the reinforcements of the criminogenic processes; the alienation of large social groups; the discrediting of legal authority; a reduction of civic tolerance; a tendency toward authoritarianism—these are the kinds of outcomes that are liable to flow from a reliance upon penal mechanisms to maintain social order." In short, we increasingly resort to punitive means to address our social problems and seek ever greater dominance and control over the citizenry. And so Kafka's law lurks in the background of our justice system and threatens American law. It is especially likely to emerge whenever the state feels the need to express sovereign prerogatives and when it is most likely to surrender its own self-imposed limitations.

We saw in the first chapter how Josef K.'s process moved quickly and relentlessly, that it expressed irresistible force, a sovereign power, a force that was brought to bear on a single individual. This celebration of sovereign power has reappeared as one strand[21] in our response to crime. Elected officials in particular have been "escalating the penal response to crime and promoting what amounts to a strategy of punitive segregation," through strategies that "represent a positive symbol of the state's willingness to use force against its enemies, to express popular sentiment, and to protect the public by whatever means necessary."[22]

Arendt argued that under modern conditions, the people do not truly have opinions, but rather "moods." William Stuntz explains, in his comprehensive analysis of American crime policy, that "[c]hange as radical as the United States has experienced over the past eighty years, in both directions, suggests that criminal punishment is based more on political fad or caprice than on the moral quality of the defendant's conduct."[23] In America, of course, the people are said to be sovereign, though that sovereignty "circulates" among distinct sources of power:

> The multitude, infused with manifold particular traditions, come even more into the fore in a democratic regime. It helps to set the ethos in which official sovereignty is set. Better put, *in democratic constitutionalism, sovereignty circulates uncertainly among the multitude, the traditions it embodies, and constitutionally sanctioned authorities.* These elements can be specified more

closely, though never completely, according to need and context. Thus the police in American cities both express and help shape the ethos of sovereignty. They can find evidence or plant it, follow the spirit of Miranda or render it ineffective, intimidate a section of the populace or act evenhandedly depending on the unstable confluence of legal rulings given to them, the larger ethos in which they participate and the professional police ethos carved out of dangers, loyalties, and hostilities of the city. What would happen to a Court that "decides" that cops must walk without guns or, less dramatically, that they are free to shoot at any suspicious looking citizen? An unconscious context or the thinkable and the unthinkable, the habitually expected and the impermissible, the morally permissible and the morally outrageous enter into sovereign readings of constitutional texts.[24]

Fearful and then angry moods have been channeled by pollsters and mass media journalism such that our officials themselves are under a constant pressure.[25] The hydraulics of the system pressures prosecutors and police who are more or less eager to focus the pressure of "public opinion" on those who are "persons of interest." The point of greatest pressure occurs in the back rooms of police stations where, as we see below, detectives have learned how to move effectively against any psychological weakness of the potential defendant, to throw him back on his own resources, whether factually guilty or innocent, to remove him from society.

We will see shortly how the kind of pressure that Kafka described, an expression of an archaic sovereignty, plays out concretely. The expansive nature of our substantive law and the illusory protection of our procedural law, both of which I will examine shortly, contribute to it. The enormous discretionary power invested in the contemporary prosecutor, which allows for truly extortionate plea bargains,[26] threatening the death penalty or the prosecution of wives and children for those who refuse, expresses it. It is expressed as well by the lawlessness of some prosecutors' conduct at trial.[27] (One author describes an interview one of his students had in a local prosecutor's office where the student was asked whether he had ever "tasted blood in the courtroom." The stunned silence that followed ended when it was explained that the interviewer "wanted to hire lawyers who tasted blood and liked it."[28]) Prosecutors enjoy absolute "sovereign immunity" from damage suits for violations of defendants' rights,[29] their misconduct at trial almost never results in reversals, and they are almost never subject to disciplinary proceedings for ethical misconduct. "[W]henever state authorities wage 'war on crime,' flourishing penal powers to send law-breakers to their death, or to impose life-cancelling terms of imprisonment, they are deliberately employing the same archaic tactics as did the kings who sent offenders to the scaffold."[30] They are "sovereign acts" that have broad public support. The "cumulative outcome of such sovereign acts" in the United States "has been the emergence of mass incarceration of a scale never before witnessed in a modern democracy and the revival of a 'killing state' committed to the speeded-up execution of an increasing number of offenders."[31] Government can "respond to threats to itself by becoming a theater of punitive power."[32] And "the death penalty, today as in the past symbolizes the ultimate power of the state, and of the government of society, over the individual citizen. . . . The punishment is carried out in such a way as to give a spectacle not of measure, but of imbalance and excess; in this liturgy of punishment, there must be an emphatic affirmation of power and of its intrinsic superiority. The excessive sovereign power can thus assume a secular transcendence, coming from beyond, in its power over death."[33] In sum:

> The new penal policies that emerged during the 1980s, which combined pragmatic risk management of presumptively dangerous populations with populist punitiveness[,] belong to, and in many respects anchor a new political order. This new order stresses personal responsibility rather than collective risk spreading, and minimal protections against economic harm, with a harshly enforced, highly moralistic criminal law promising almost complete protection against crime, while emphasizing how dangerous the world is despite these much needed measures. What Garland calls a "crime complex"—a set of criminal justice principles that embody this mentality—not only determines crime policy and practice, but also influences the broader tone and direction of government, especially regarding other policies for managing the poor.[34]

The Trial shows that a process that is mainly the vehicle for bringing a mysterious, vast, unconstrained, and irresistible force to bear on an isolated individual has certain distinctive characteristics. Our system has too many of those same qualities.

The Unknowability of the Law

We have seen that Josef K.'s attempts to know the law he is accused of violating and the procedures it will follow in prosecuting him are all futile.

Indeed, the investigators initially tell K. that he cannot possibly claim innocence of a law he doesn't know. K. protests that he is to be condemned not only in innocence, but also in ignorance of the law, and Titorelli explains that the law in action is any event wholly discontinuous with the law as it appears to be. The investigators appear in K.'s apartment without his permission, and, throughout the novel, officials seek to extract a confession from him. Kafka's account mirrors the opacity of the procedural law that controls police investigation and interrogation in our system, the substantive criminal law that is said to determine criminality, and the law of evidence that controls the very few criminal cases that make it to trial. Americans can quite easily be condemned in ignorance.

Searches and Seizures

The popular view is that the law of criminal procedure that applies to police searches and seizures and police interrogation is specific and constraining, that it tilts toward the defendant and prevents the police from enforcing the law. This is almost wholly false. For a number of reasons the law that *actually* applies to searches and interrogations is virtually inaccessible. One reason is its extent and complexity. (It resembles a modern cruise ship, with a gleaming white superstructure that towers up and teeters precipitously up above the surface. It looks grand, but may occasion serious doubts about the ship's seaworthiness.) All constitutional criminal procedural rules applicable to searches and interrogations extracted from the Bill of Rights now apply equally to the states. However, there is almost no *worse* way to understand contemporary search and interrogation practices than to study the complex constitutional law that the Supreme Court has created and that lower federal state and federal courts apply.

The structure of this law is generally to announce what appears to be a rule that imposes demanding obligations on law enforcement and then watch it die a death by a thousand qualifications.[35] The text of the Fourth Amendment itself has been called, "brief, vague, general [and] unilluminating."[36] It fails to answer directly some of the most important questions of interpretation: to what items or events does it apply, what persons are entitled to protection, and, perhaps most vexingly, what is the relationship between the general prohibition on unreasonable searches and seizures and the "warrant clause," the obligation to seek out a warrant before search and seizures? During the twentieth century, the Supreme Court incorporated almost all of the protections in the Bill of Rights into the due process clause of the Fourteenth Amendment making them applicable to state criminal prosecutions;[37] announced the exclusionary rule, which made evidence resulting from unconstitutional searches and seizures inadmissible in federal[38] and eventually state[39] criminal trials; extended the applicability of the Fourth Amendment beyond the traditional physical trespass to property to include conversations;[40] and adhered to the general principle that all searches and seizures without warrants were presumptively "unreasonable" subject to narrowly defined exceptions.[41] The Fourth Amendment appeared to create strong protections against police intrusion into zones of personal privacy.

There followed the fairly rapid erosion of this law in the political climate described above. The protection of the Fourth Amendment does not apply to "open fields," to real estate outside the immediate surroundings of the house, even if the officers were there in violation of criminal trespass rules.[42] Conversations with government informers, "false friends" who agreed to wiretaps, were not protected because we all "assume the risk" of being betrayed.[43] Personal information, such as bank records, shared with one person or entity has no claim on protection from the government.[44] And so telephone company records of calls were not protected. Aerial surveillance of visible areas was unprotected, at least if not physically obnoxious. After all, we all know planes fly over our yards.[45] On the other hand, the owner or renter or an overnight guest in a house or apartment, but not a short-term invitee at least if present to act illegally,[46] continued to receive significant protection.[47] One sardonic account of what these rules amount to goes as follows:

> [I]t is instructive to imagine compiling the Court's holdings concerning when the Fourth Amendment applies or, more accurately, does not apply into an *"Accidental Tourist's Guide to Maintaining Privacy Against Government Surveillance."* The advice would be rather astonishing:
>
> To maintain privacy, one must not write any checks nor make any phone calls. It would be unwise to engage in conversation with any other person, or to walk, even on private property, outside one's own house. If one is to barbeque or read in the backyard, do so only if surrounded by a fence higher than a double-decker bus and while sitting beneath an opaque awning. The wise individual might also consider purchasing anti-aerial spying devices if available (be sure to check the latest Sharper Im-

age catalogue). Upon retiring inside, be sure to pull the shades together tightly so that no crack exists and to converse only in quiet tones. When discarding letters or other delicate materials, do so only after a thorough shredding of the documents (again see your Sharper Image catalogue); ideally, one would take the trash personally to the disposal site and bury it deep within. Finally, inspect them for any electronic tracking devices that may be attached.[48]

All these limitations simply go only to the preliminary question of whether police activity is a "search." But that's only the first step. The Fourth Amendment only forbids *unreasonable* searches and seizures and ambiguously refers to warrants. It turns out that searches are reasonable if they are supported by probable cause, which is rather misleadingly[49] said to exist "where 'the facts and circumstances within [the detectives'] knowledge and of which they [have] reasonably trustworthy information [are] sufficient in themselves to warrant a man of reasonable caution in the belief that' an offense has been or is being committed by the person to be arrested."[50] Whether there exists probable cause, which determines reasonableness, whether or not a warrant is required,[51] is determined by a holistic "totality of the circumstances test"[52] (if it can be called a "test"), the outcome of which is extremely hard to predict. Indeed, in the line of cases leading up to *Gates* and in the case itself, there were vigorous disagreements among the Supreme Court justices themselves as to whether or not probable cause existed. How could a policeman or a citizen know whether or not there was probable cause when the justices disagreed among themselves and refused to provide even an approximate metric of probability. In a recurring pattern of reasoning, Justice William Rehnquist in *Gates* argued that absent a relaxed standard for probable cause for obtaining warrants, police, who were, after all, engaged in the "competitive enterprise of ferreting out crime," were likely to forego the warrants and rely on a claim that residents had consented to a search. (And I cannot but discern a vague implication that they might forego consent, and then lie about it[53] later should there be a "swearing contest" between an officer and an individual with the low credibility that usually comes with criminality.[54]) Further, the existence of a warrant, even if constitutionally deficient, means that the evidence obtained through its execution, is not subject to exclusion: the involvement of a magistrate however indulgent to the police, immunizes the results of the seizure from suppression.[55]

Then we have the many exceptions to the warrant requirement,[56] which I will describe only generally. Exigent circumstances, including possibility of flight or loss of evidence (all drug arrests where there is a toilet available?), will excuse a warrant. A search of the person and the immediate area may occur pursuant to legal arrest,[57] and a "protective sweep"[58] of an entire house is permissible. (Notice how the loose rules compound one another: a weakly justified warrant for arrest will both justify a search of many parts of a house and immunize any evidence discovered from suppression.) Then there are another set of exceptions to the exclusionary rule based on unconstitutional search: "independent source," "inevitable discovery," and "attenuation."

The law with regard to automobile searches and seizure is even more inaccessible. First, it doesn't matter whether the stated reason for the stop is pretextual: officer motivation, including racial profiling,[59] is irrelevant.[60] The arrest of a person driving a car, for any reason including the existence of an outstanding arrest warrant for a nonviolent crime, permits a search of the entire passenger compartment, including closed containers therein, even when the arrestee is handcuffed, so long as he has not been transported to a waiting police car.[61] If there is no arrest, then the officer may still search any car, including the trunk, without a warrant, if he has probable cause (based on the totality of the circumstances) to believe that it contains contraband or evidence of a crime.[62] If officers lawfully stop a car, even if they do not initially arrest the driver, they may search the entire passenger area if they have a "reasonable suspicion" there may be a weapon in the car. Cars may, under some circumstances, be pulled over with no suspicion at all for a short interview.[63] And, in one of those exceptions that can completely swallow the more detailed rules that one may have painstakingly sought to understand, if the automobile is inventoried (after an arrest of its occupant or because it is parked illegally), then officers may search the entire vehicle,[64] including the trunk for the bureaucratic justifications that such a search may protect the owner from theft or the police from accusations of theft and to guard against bombs and guns (even if there is no evidence of such).

The paradoxical, we might say Kafkaesque, nature of this law may best be appreciated by contrasting two kinds of cases, in which the really important matter is covered over with a completely implausible factual assumption, and the other in which the constitutional rules are employed in a hypertechnically unpredictable manner. The latter makes the law look silly and reinforces the illusory notion that the police are wholly constrained in their law enforcement efforts. The important matter is the role of consent in search and seizure law. Any search or detention of one's person or search of his property can be justified by consent, so long as it is "voluntary," determined again by a vague "totality of the circumstances test." Whether there was consent is always a question of fact that, once again, will almost always be resolved in a "swearing contest" between officer and defendant. Even putting that huge matter aside, the Court always assumes that an ordinary citizen (for example, a young black woman disembarking a plane and confronted by drug enforcement officers in an airport[65]) is perfectly free to decline the officer's invitation to a search or a detention and just walk away.[66] (This is true even when, as is usual in litigated cases, the defendant knows that a search will reveal the contraband—drugs or weapons—which will send him to the penitentiary for a long time.) There is no obligation that the police inform the citizen of his or her right to walk away,[67] and it almost never happens. The Court's assumption is completely implausible, and consent is the basis for a very large percentage of the searches and seizures that occur.

By contrast, the Court can be hypertechnical in the other direction when there is relatively little at stake. In one case, officers were legally (because of exigent circumstances) in an apartment from which shots had been fired. Any contraband in "plain view" was subject to seizure. One of the officers noticed a set of expensive stereo components that seemed out of place in the very run-down apartment to which he had been called. He moved a turntable several inches in order to read its serial number, which he then conveyed to headquarters. He was not surprised to learn that it had been taken in an armed robbery. The Court ruled that moving the turntable even a couple inches constituted a prohibited search,[68] something the dissenters thought to "trivialize" the Fourth Amendment. A similar bit of unpredictable formalism occurred in the context of a so-called *Terry*-stop, a short on-street detention of a suspect. During such a stop, an officer is sometimes permitted to engage in a pat down for weapons, but only to the extent that the search can plausibly be for weapons. Any contraband identified during such permitted limited search is subject to seizure. In a case that reached the Supreme Court, an officer was conducting a legal pat down for weapons; he felt a small object whose nature was not immediately (through "plain touch") obvious to him, so he rolled the object between his thumb and forefinger until he was sure he was feeling drugs. The Court ruled that the trivial act of rolling the object constituted a prohibited search because it went beyond the permitted scope of the pat down for weapons.[69] The Court imposes a bizarre formalism in an area that is, from the real-world perspective, fairly trivial.

In *Terry v. Ohio*,[70] the Court addressed a matter that was far from trivial. The Court approved of short, warrantless detentions of individuals who police had an articulable "reasonable suspicion," short of probable cause, to believe were engaging in criminal behavior. It approved of limited pat downs solely for the purpose of determining whether the individuals were armed. In so doing, Chief Justice Earl Warren noted that he was deferring to "an entire rubric of police behavior" to which the requirements of warrants and probable cause did not apply. (Again, as in *Gates*, we see deference to actual police practices, perhaps as expressing a kind of popular sovereignty, in Connolly's sense, here in the very doctrine itself.) He likewise noted that the exclusionary rule was of limited value, that it could not deter pure expressions of police domination for its own sake. Therefore, the argument went, exclusion of evidence that was yielded by such expressions ought to be available in subsequent criminal prosecutions.

Terry was, in the twilight of the Warren Court, thought to be a police-friendly decision. It was thought to impose very modest limitations on street-level searches and seizures. At the end of the first decade of the twenty-first century, it is clear that those restrictions are systematically ignored in American cities, an issue that has come to be a subject of special controversy (and litigation) in New York City.[71] Police in minority neighborhoods systematically stop young black men without any articulable specific suggestion of criminal activity (other than who and where they are). They are subject to searches well beyond what *Terry* contemplates, often being required to empty their pockets. When the latter search turns up small amounts of marijuana or other drugs, they are arrested and charged with crime (allowing for an even more intrusive search[72]). And the arrestee can be drawn into the criminal justice system and given a criminal record. If the court resolves any credibility issues against the police and the defendant has competent counsel, the evidence might be excluded. And a weak possibility of exclusion seems, practically speaking, the *strongest* deterrent to apparently unconstitutional police practices. There is virtual consensus that civil rights suits, possible criminal prosecution, police internal disciplinary proceedings, and attorney disciplinary proceedings affecting prosecutors in the range of cases provide no effective deterrent and are very rarely successful.

The law on the ground in the area of search and seizure is in effect unknowable, and the law on the books will provide the weakest possible understanding of what officials are likely to do in any case. (It is often unlikely that even the most important actors in the criminal justice system know it either.) The jurisprudence here is, since the 1970s, "increasingly convoluted, result-oriented, and defensive."[73] As several authors have noted, the *more* rules there are, the less we have the rule of law, because there are more opportunities for result-oriented binary determinations. Intricate exceptions to the rule, the availability of consent extracted by the pure show of authority, the certainty that in most cases a court will resolve credibility issues against defendants, and wholesale disregard of the legal doctrine mean that the actual law of search and seizure—what officials are actually likely to do—cannot be realistically ascertained and is not really understood by ordinary citizens.

Interrogations and Confessions

In the area of interrogation and confessions as well, our general understanding of the law on the books is likely to obscure actual police practices, the law in action, rendering the law that is likely to be enforced truly unknowable. Our understanding of the law of interrogations is dominated by the *Miranda* warnings. One would think that they are universally offered and, at least where the arrestee had serious criminal exposure, often invoked. (Political discussions concerning the rights to be afforded accused terrorists almost always attack the notion that they be afforded *Miranda* warnings.) In fact, "almost no confession is ever excluded at trial because of a *Miranda* violation" largely because detectives "have developed multiple strategies to avoid, circumvent, nullify, and sometimes violate *Miranda*,"[74] methods that are enabled by the legal doctrine. Studies show as many as 96 percent of arrestees waive *Miranda* rights, the "scholarly consensus is that *Miranda*'s real world impact is, for the most part, negligible,"[75] and it belongs, with the search and seizure law described above, to the class of "mostly symbolic and largely ineffectual constitutional laws."[76]

Why is this so? First, *Miranda* has served largely to supplant an older analysis under which a serious inquiry could take place as to the coerciveness of concrete police methods. Now, in most cases, evidence of the formulaic reading of rights supplants further analysis. Second, the requirement applies only to *custodial* interrogations, so that important inculpating conversations outside the station house may precede the *Miranda* warnings. They apply only to *interrogations*, and the Court has been quite indulgent in excluding conversations from that category. In *Rhode Island v. Innis*,[77] for example, police officers arrested a suspect in the shotgun murder of a taxi driver and read him his *Miranda* rights, which he invoked. He was placed in the backseat of a police car separated from the front by a wire mesh. While transporting him to the station, one of the officers began a conversation with the other about the shotgun, saying that there was a school for children with disabilities nearby and that it would be a shame if one of them injured himself with the gun. The defendant directed the officers to its location. The Court ruled that, though the defendant was certainly in custody, there was no *interrogation*, because the officers didn't *know* that the appeal to the defendant's conscience would be successful.

Waivers of *Miranda* rights must be "voluntary," but an express waiver is not necessary: in effect, if, after reading the defendant's rights, he answers police questions, a waiver will usually be found.[78] (We will soon see the range of police tactics that are systematically found not to render a waiver involuntary.) It makes a lot of difference whether the defendant says, "I don't want to talk with you," as opposed to "I want to talk with a lawyer." If he says the former, the police may later resume questioning subject to another vague "totality of the circumstances test." If he says the latter, then the police must await his initiating the conversation. And if a defendant is in custody, but is not *aware* he is being interrogated (because the questioner is undercover), warnings are unnecessary. Finally, the "fruit of the poisonous tree" doctrine does not apply to *Miranda*:[79] for example, the police may introduce physical evidence they learn of through an unwarned interrogation and unwarned admissions are available for impeachment if the defendant takes the stand and testifies.

Substantive Criminal Law

As the reach of the criminal law has expanded, there has been a surge of what Stuntz calls "surprising criminal liability."[80] Americans find themselves in the same situation as did Josef K., facing a law that is demanding, but practically unknowable. There are at least three thousand federal crimes (and probably many more), hidden in the twenty-seven thousand pages of the US Code.[81] The Supreme Court has long approved of criminal convictions where the defendant would not have known that his actions were criminal, and absolutely no criminal intent was proven, "creating a crime . . . without a word of warning," as Justice Oliver Wendell Holmes Jr. put it in dissent.[82] The leading precedents in effect reject the proposition that "a central condition of a free society is the ability to stay out of prison—to avoid trouble if one is willing to comply with society's laws" and "made honest mistakes precursor to prison perms, meaning that even those who *try* to comply with the law might face serious criminal punishment, hardly the mark of a just criminal justice system."[83] All that is necessary to criminalize innocent behavior is that it serves the regulatory goal of the statute. It is increasingly the case that

> the general intent standard . . . , the standard that applies in the large majority of criminal cases, includes no requirement that the defendant intended to harm someone, to do wrong, or to break the law. Blackstone's classic dictum that criminal intent requires a "vicious will" forms no part of that standard. The defendant is guilty if he intended his physical acts and if those physical acts violate the conduct terms of a criminal statute. But save only those too intoxicated to know what they are doing, everyone intends his physical acts— and, under the governing law, intoxicated defendants are usually judged as if they were sober.[84] The upshot is that, in most cases, findings of criminal intent are automatic. The law of intent no longer serves the function it [once] served . . . : a means of ensuring that only those who understand that they are engaged in serious misconduct can be criminally punished.[85]

Other changes in the definition of crimes convert simple theft into robbery, remove the "breaking and entering" requirement for burglary, and convert previously civil claims for theft or larceny into crimes. Fraud no longer requires a material misstatement of fact relied upon to the victim's detriment but rather only the "loss" of "the intangible right of honest services."[86] Fraud crimes do not require a false statement of material fact: simple nondisclosure can be enough. The law of rape has been supplemented by different forms of "sexual battery."[87]

Hate crimes provide a growth area in civil rights legislation, and there are a growing number of crimes related to public safety.[88] Increasingly often, mutual accusations of criminal behavior, sometimes occasioning the involvement of the police, play a role in child custody disputes.[89] All these expansions of criminal liability make plea bargaining easier for prosecutors by eliminating "triable issues" from the possible case. Further, the criminal law now allows for charging under multiple overlapping crimes for the same act so long as each has a single element absent from the others. "Charge stacking" vastly increases the prosecutor's power in plea bargaining: the defendant faces *very* long consecutive sentences and a sometimes confusing trial where there are so many counts that conviction on at least one of them is likely.[90]

The ordinary citizen and even most professionals cannot know the reach of the criminal law:

> State and federal law have come to resemble the tax code, which is beyond the comprehension of lay-persons and can be navigated only with the assistance of a skilled attorney. All too often, expertise is unhelpful in fathoming the contents of the criminal law. Because of the phenomenal growth in the number of offenses, even professors and practicing attorneys who have spent most of their careers wrestling with the intricacies of the criminal law are familiar with only a fraction of the statutes to which we are subject. In the wake of this confusion and uncertainty, the need for a defense of ignorance of law becomes imperative—a defense that would be unnecessary if almost everyone could be expected to know the laws that apply to them. No reasonable person can pretend that this development is for the better.[91]

The notion of the rule of law implies that "the distinction between conduct that is and is not punished should depend primarily on the content of the laws that legislatures enact."

> No one, however, should hazard a prediction about who will be sentenced simply by examining criminal statutes. The *real* law—the law that distinguishes the conduct that leads for punishment from the conduct that does not—cannot be found in the criminal codes. . . . We are already well past the point at which statutes are the dominant factor in explaining who will or will not incur criminal liability. As a result, one might conclude that the substantive criminal law itself is not very important in the context of our system of criminal justice. As Stuntz bluntly concludes, "criminal law is not, in any meaningful sense, law at all. . . . If knowledge of the criminal law consists in the ability to make reliable forecasts about what conduct will be punished, it follows that no one knows the law."[92]

And, as Kafka tells us, "[I]t is an extremely painful thing to be ruled by laws that one does not know."

The Law of Evidence

Only about 5 percent of criminal charges result in trials. We will see that these trials can be distorted by different forms of official misconduct. But there need not be misconduct for trials to go wrong. One of the sources of potential injustice is the opaqueness of the procedural rules that apply at trial, in particular the law of evidence. Despite more recent liberalization, the law of evidence still serves as a set of exclusionary rules that may prevent either the state or the defendant from offering evidence believed to be relevant, important, and persuasive. Courts make decisions to include and exclude forms of scientific evidence in a chaotic, largely unprincipled, and result-oriented manner.[93] These decisions, particularly to exclude evidence, may distort the factual picture that a jury sees. I have in the past argued for continued liberalization of this law.[94] Here, however, I simply want to point out again that a fair reading of the rules of evidence will often fail to provide a picture of what really occurs at trial, and specifically, how little it ultimately limits the discretion of the trial judge, how the "real" law of evidence is beyond our knowledge.

We find ourselves in an odd situation in which inherited formalisms may have lost touch with the rationales that once supported them. Yet those formalisms continue to claim the authoritativeness of enacted law. And they continue sometimes to function as exclusionary rules whose hard edges have the force of positive law. They are regularly invoked by trial judges to exclude evidence that one or other advocate believes to provide considerations in support of a theory of the case.

There is, however, a good deal of illusion in this. The now generally accepted standard for the review of the trial court's evidentiary decisions is the abuse of discretion standard, one of the most deferential standards of review. This is indeed odd, because the determination of whether a particular basic fact—here a particular bit of evidence—falls within a general rule does not in the ordinary sense involve an exercise of what we usually call discretion. Indeed, administrative law usually distinguishes between the arbitrariness of an act of agency discretion and the sufficiency of the evidence to support an agency conclusion. In my experience, trial judges are generally reluctant, even when tempted by a provocative trial lawyer seeking to make a record, to go beyond an unelaboratcd "Sustained" or "Overruled." Least of all do they want to articulate clearly their understanding of an evidence rule, for fear of transforming an act of "discretion" into a question of law, subject to a more searching review. And because evidence often is supported by multiple theories of relevance and courts are happy to give the next-to-useless limiting instructions, an appellee is almost always able to identify a consideration that may support the judge's act of "discretion."

Thus the trial judge commits an "error" only when he abuses his discretion in admitting or excluding evidence. But, of course, not all error is reversible error. First, there are procedural obstacles. The requirement that error admitting evidence be preserved by timely and specific objections and error excluding evidence be preserved by complete offers of proof serves to insulate many evidentiary decisions from appellate review. By sharp contrast, there is the doctrine that allows the appellate court to identify any theory of admissibility or exclusion that may support the trial judge's decision, even though it never occurred to anyone in the trial court at all.

Then there is the expansive doctrine of harmless error. We often hear that a litigant is entitled to a fair trial, not a perfect one. Even if the trial judge has, in the view of the appellate court, abused his discretion, committed a particularly significant error, we still will not have a reversal unless, for nonconstitutional error, the appellant can convince the appellate court, by a preponderance of the evidence, that the error would have affected the result. If one reads the cases in which this question is considered (particularly, in my view, when the error involves permitting prohibited prosecutorial argument), one often comes away with an uneasy feeling that appellate courts are too quick to find the evidence "overwhelming." In my opinion, a large percentage of the cases that actually go to trial are "triable" cases, as lawyers like to say. Otherwise they should settle. Though there may be explanations in some cases, it seems strange that so many of them turn out to have been "overwhelmingly" tilted in one direction. Finally, I believe that appellate courts are very much inclined to overconfidence in their ability to divine the counterfactual significance of evidence that the jury never saw.

The effect of all these layers of deference is a strange combination of often relatively detailed exclusionary rules where admissibility turns on binary, razor's edge determinations of foundational elements, sometimes where the proponent bears the burden of proof by evidence sufficient to support a finding,[95] and sometimes by a preponderance of the evidence, the latter most significantly in the hearsay exceptions.[96] On the other hand, the trial judge will rarely be reversed for exercising his discretion to admit evidence that falls outside the most obvious meaning of an exclusionary rule or to exclude evidence that seems to fall outside it. It can easily occur that a trial judge who has never been reversed[97] for an evidentiary ruling may consistently have made many rulings that are just wrong.

It is not too far wrong to say that we mainly have just an inchoate balancing of probative value against perceived prejudicial effect,[98] with quite some number of more or less vague guidelines for its application. Only now and again will a formalistic bolt from the blue render some important piece of evidence inadmissible. The bolt may fall in the trial court or occasionally in the court of appeals, though the selection of cases in which it happens is far from predictable. To echo Stuntz's comment on the substantive criminal law, if our ability to predict outcomes is the metric for the existence of law, one might conclude that there is no law of evidence. Institutionally, all the rules beyond Rule 403 serve to give the appellate court some residual power to reverse some cases on evidentiary grounds, without the somewhat uncomfortable and rather uncollegial holding that the trial judge lacked "sound discretion." (Would you want to tell a colleague that his judgment was "unsound"?) Former judge Irving Younger said a long time ago that appellate review of a trial court's evidentiary rulings involves a kind of holistic "smell test": reversal occurs where the aggregate weight of debatable rulings falls too heavily and unfairly on one side, if then.

The law of evidence does not effectively prevent our trials from going wrong.[99] Some go wrong because of eyewitness misidentification abetted by faulty lineups and evidentiary rulings that deny juries the benefit of the social science learning about eyewitness misidentification. Others are the result of police or prosecutorial misconduct. Some occur because of coerced confessions. Some may be the result of unreliable "forensic science" often admitted for reasons of habit rather than science. The bulk of the law of evidence does not address the market and bureaucratic sources of error in the criminal justice system.

The Ubiquity of the Criminal Law

Kafka's criminal law exists everywhere in his city. It invades the tenements of poorer neighborhoods and appears when one opens the door of an artist's studio. No sphere of life seems outside its reach. It reaches the conduct of the respectably middle-class gentlemen who are waiting, bowed over and confused, in the law's offices. Its ubiquity is part of what it means to call it "totalitarian." This ubiquity is, as we have seen, accompanied by its unknowability: K. is quite right that one may be condemned in innocence as well as ignorance.

A few statistics suggest the reach of the criminal law into the activities of large numbers of Americans:

> [A]bout 90 million living Americans have used an illicit drug, an activity for which many could have been sent to prison if detected and prosecuted. Even occupants of our highest offices have engaged in felonious drug use....[100] Second, astronomical numbers of young adults have engaged in music piracy. According to some estimates, 52 percent of Internet users between the ages of 18 and 29 commit this crime by illegally downloading approximately 3.6 billion songs each month. . . . Internet gambling provides my final example of the ubiquity of criminal behavior. . . . [T]he Unlawful Internet Gambling Enforcement Act of 2006 prohibits American banks from transferring money to Internet gambling sites. Moreover, the very operation of these casinos is unambiguously prohibited. . . . The ownership of offshore Internet casinos that do business in the United States includes many of the most prestigious investment firms in the world: Fidelity, Merrill Lynch, Goldman Sachs, Morgan Stanley and others. Only prosecutorial discretion prevents criminal liability from extending to the highest reaches of mainstream society.[101]

And so, "almost everyone has committed one or more [offenses] at some time or another. . . . Perhaps over 70% of living adult Americans have committed an imprisonable offense at some point in their life."[102] Although the law on the books is a poor guide to the "real law," "we are steadily moving 'closer to a world in which the law on the books makes everyone a felon."[103] Part of this stems from the criminalization of common practices, and another part is the criminalization of innocuous behavior (using reptiles in religious services, playing three-card monte, training a bear to wrestle, etc.) in a way that fails the "laugh test."[104]

The growth and current extent of imprisonment must itself be strong evidence that the criminal justice system has increased its broad reach. "If present trends continue, nearly one in 15 Americans born in 2001 will serve time in prison during their lifetimes. . . . [O]ne in three black men, one in seven Hispanic men, and one in 17 white men."[105] It is more likely that an African American man will go to prison than that "he will to college, get married, or go into the military." The kinds of police practices of surveillance and search that prevail especially in minority neighborhoods and the illusory protection afforded by the Fourth Amendment mean that young black men are far more likely to be searched and evidence of crime more likely to be found.[106] Until recently federal drug laws treated the form of cocaine more likely to be found in black neighborhoods much more harshly than the form favored by whites. The "War on Drugs" itself increased the general priority of drug enforcement, and legislatures generally engaged in a bidding war to increase the punishment for drug infractions. Gun laws, including those making it a federal felony punishable by a long prison sentence for someone with a previous conviction, inevitably affect neighborhoods where a larger portion of the population carries guns for self-defense. The complexity of the welfare rules and the eagerness with which welfare fraud is vigorously prosecuted makes it increasingly likely that welfare recipients will, with varying levels of awareness, violate the criminal law.[107]

Stuntz describes what he calls the "strategic" character of American criminal law. In order to evade constitutional limitation on federal crimes, Congress "ceased to define the conduct and intent that prosecutors actually sought to punish, and instead treated crime definition as a means of facilitating arrests, prosecutions, and convictions."[108] The motivation for the Mann Act, for example, was moral outrage at the sin of prostitution. The act, however, was written very broadly, and its language prohibited transport of women in interstate commerce "for the purpose of prostitution *or debauchery, or for any other immoral purpose.*"[109] The broad language, probably designed with prostitution in mind, could be used to prosecute an engaged couple traveling together from Pennsylvania to Alabama to find work or an unmarried couple from New Jersey taking a vacation in Miami, or, more famously, Jack Johnson, the first black heavyweight champion, for sleeping with his white future wife.[110] Relatedly, it appears that a good deal of the target for the "War on Drugs," with all of its discriminatory and otherwise negative consequences, was originally the violence that accompanies drug trafficking. In order to make the criminal statutes most strategically effective in generating arrests, prosecutions, and convictions, however, harsher sentences were imposed for nonviolent crimes as well. The lowered level of criminal responsibility meant that knowing proximity to drugs could generate liability.[111] In one case decided by the Seventh Circuit Court of

Appeals in Chicago, a young woman went along with her boyfriend on a road trip. While on the trip he picked up a couple thousand dollars' worth of marijuana from which the woman smoked one joint. Although she in no way furthered the transaction or stood to gain through it, her conviction for possession with intent to distribute and conspiracy was affirmed because there existed "some nexus between the defendant and drugs." Our drug laws as written "make both convictions and draconian prison sentences nearly automatic. All plausible mitigating arguments . . . are ruled out of bounds. No wonder the rate of imprisonment for drug crime has multiplied *tenfold since the early 1970s; today's rate exceeds the total imprisonment rate in 1975.*"[112] In other ways as well the "War on Drugs" has manifested "massive denial" and has "utterly transformed law enforcement in the USA, as well as filling a hugely expanded prison system with disproportionate numbers of poor blacks."

> This massively expensive and largely futile attempt to change a widespread and deeply entrenched pattern of behavior by means of criminal punishments has all the hallmarks of a sovereign state dealing with its limitations by denying they exist. Motivated by the politically urgent need to "do something" decisive about crime, . . . the war on drugs was the American state's attempt to "just say no." Disregarding evidence that the levels of drug use were already in decline, that drug use is not responsive to criminal penalties, that criminalization brings its own pathologies (notably street violence and disrespect for authorities), and that declaring a war on drugs is, in effect, to declare a war on minorities, the US government proceeded to declare such a war and persist in pursuing it, despite every indication of its failure. Why? Because the groups most adversely affected lack political power and are widely regarded as dangerous and undeserving; because the groups least affected could be assured that something is being done and lawlessness is not tolerated; and because few politicians are willing to oppose a policy when there is so little political advantage to be gained by doing so.[113]

The Bureaucratization of American Criminal Process

Ninety-five percent of American criminal cases are effectively resolved through police interrogation and/or plea bargaining.[114] Those are activities carried out by bureaucracies. A police department is clearly a bureaucracy. Though the head district attorney still runs for office, prosecutors' offices are increasingly bureaucratic. By the mid-twentieth century "they were becoming more the creatures of the bureaucracies—and the legal profession to which they belonged than of the voters whom they represented."[115] In place of an earlier order in which criminal process involved many jury trials, and locally elected prosecutors responsive to poor and working class constituencies, we created prosecutors' offices characterized by "[b]ureaucratic detachment, legal procedure, and symbolic politics. . . . The consequences were poor crime control, rapidly changing punishment practices, and massive inequality."[116]

I will not attempt here anything like a comprehensive definition of bureaucracy, something that may not be possible. I simply want to point out a number of characteristics of bureaucratic governance. Hannah Arendt famously called bureaucracy "rule by nobody." Bureaucratic practices permit the abdication of individual human responsibility for actions taken in systems that seem to operate independently of human moral judgment. (Recall the severe official whom K. meets in the court offices who protests, "Perhaps none of us is hardhearted, perhaps we'd all like to help, but as court officials it can easily appear that we're hard-hearted and don't want to help anyone. That really bothers me." It does not, of course, "bother" her enough to do anything about it.) Within bureaucracies, the "officials," as Kafka put it, exercise only a "role morality" consistent with their function. In Arendt's terms, they are pure "functionaries." Often, though not necessarily, this takes place through a mechanical application of preexistent rules regardless of consequences (and so understandings of legal decision making that are "formalist," that would limit judges to such a "mechanical jurisprudence," assimilate legal decision making to bureaucratic judgment). Bureaucratic processes are instrumental—in their ideal type they are rigorously designed solely to further a goal outside the process itself, a goal set by a sovereign authority of one sort or another. "Bureaucratic rationality is the rationality of matching means to ends economically and efficiently."[117] Kings employed bureaucracies at a time when no "rule of law" ideal existed.[118] Although bureaucracies may operate in an instrumental fashion through discretionary judgments without mechanically following a detailed set of rules, "formalistic and literalistic methods" allow for a higher degree of top-down control by higher bureaucrats and, ultimately, sovereign authorities.[119] For example, substantive criminal laws that specify empirically determinable elements without the need for contextual moral evaluation and sentencing guidelines that contain measurable variables both allow control "from afar." And the advantage of mechanical rules for lower level bureaucrats is precisely the flip side of Arendt's criticism: since there is no discretion, there is no responsibility; since there is no responsibility, there can be no (individualized) criticism. The bureaucrat can always say when taking the most Kafkaesque action, "My hands are tied."

And so in the American criminal justice world, prosecutors have sometimes argued for rules that limit their own discretion: "The heightened political cost of discretion means that decision makers themselves will opt for rules over standards, if only to protect themselves against charges of making the wrong judgment."[120] Even in extreme cases, where a notice of appeal was erroneously filed three days late led to a prisoner's execution,[121] prosecutors and courts can simply explain that they are merely following the rules. "Those officials who serve . . . the state with their reason and will are pressed by organizational imperatives to substitute the state's instrumental rationality for their own moral wisdom: 'Most legislators, politicians, lawyers, ministers, and officer holders . . . serve the state chiefly with their heads; and as they rarely make any moral decisions, they are likely to serve the devil, without *intending* it, as God.'"[122] Or, as Chesterton put it in his eloquent tribute to the jury,

> Many legalists have declared that the untrained jury should be altogether supplanted by the trained judge. . . . [However], the more a man looks at a thing, the less he can see it, and the more a man learns a thing the less he knows it. [T]hat the man who is trained should be the man who is trusted would be absolutely unanswerable if it were really true that a man who has studied a thing and practiced it every day went on seeing more and more of its significance. But he does not. He goes on seeing less and less of its significance. . . . Now it is a terrible business to mark a man out for the judgment of men. But it is a thing to which a man can grow accustomed, as he can to other terrible things. . . . And the horrible thing about all legal officials, even the best . . . is simply that they have got used to it.[123]

The almost complete dominance of plea bargaining in America is itself the result of prosecutors and courts responding as bureaucracies to financial and mass political pressure. In his magisterial history, George Fisher tells us that "plea-bargain's power" is a "derived power, for the power of plea bargaining is the power of the courtier—the influence it has gained by serving well the interests of those in high places."[124] He shows in intricate detail how only those procedural innovations that furthered plea bargaining survived, while those that hindered it fell by the wayside. A key element of this story was the enormous number of industrial accidents that overwhelmed the courts in the unregulated industries of the late nineteenth and early twentieth centuries and gave the judiciary a good reason to avoid criminal trials. Plea bargaining was good for elected prosecutors because it drove up conviction rates. Once legislatures understood that it provided an "efficient" means of dealing with enormous caseloads without additional resources that would only provide something so politically ephemeral as "individualized justice" to the less advantaged, plea bargaining was frozen into place.[125] The developments in the nature of the criminal law and sentencing described above simply expanded its reach. Like so much in American criminal process, mass politics combined with bureaucratic self-interest set policy.

And by all these measures the American criminal justice system is increasingly bureaucratic. The language used in police departments, prosecutors' offices, and, increasingly, courts, speaks of "clearances, caseloads, and dockets," and safeguards its referents from ethical evaluation:

> Among societal achievements in the sphere of management of morality one needs to name: social production of distance, which either annuls or weakens the pressure of moral responsibility; substitution of technical for moral responsibility, which effectively conceals the moral significance of the action; and the technology of segregation and separation, which promotes indifference to the plight of the Other which otherwise would be subject to moral evaluation and morally motivated response.[126]

The increasingly lengthy sentences in our criminal codes together with the triumph of plea bargaining has led to our shocking levels of imprisonment. Stuntz argues that traditionally American criminal law was narrow and vague, consciously inviting contextual moral judgment[127] in the frequent jury trials that we held. It has increasingly become broad and specific, both invading broader areas of life, as we saw above, and disabling the jury trial from fulfilling its contextualizing and moderating function. In those few cases that get to trial, juries are frequently deprived of evidence that is morally significant in the case under the doctrine of "materiality," when a judge thinks it is really appealing to part of the jury's moral universe that is beyond the "law of rules." And juries are almost always kept in the dark about the often mandatory sentences that will follow a conviction, preventing them from deciding what the concretely appropriate resolution would be. (And they are sometimes shocked to find that they have occasioned a result they did not intend.[128]) Defendants, or their lawyers, are aware of these developments, which lead to more pleas, thus more imprisonment.

The police can be placed under strong institutional pressure to make an arrest and get a conviction. "Flawed systems of police accountability lead to extreme pressures on police officers, investigators, and supervisors to solve crimes, make arrests and reduce the crime rate in their jurisdictions."[129] It is not an accident that mistaken eyewitness identification evidence, which is the most prominent cause of false convictions and which can be enabled by a whole range of improper police practices, is more likely to occur "when the police have a strong interest in solving the crime, typically because it is serious or involved and the police have developed a strong interest in getting a conviction."[130]

In the rare case when plea bargaining fails, "a host of institutional, political, and psychological forces converge to pressure prosecutors to strive for convictions," including individual performance evaluations based on conviction rates.[131] Some offices publish "individual conviction rates in the form of batting averages or list . . . attorneys on a bulletin board with stickers next to each name, green for wins and red for losses." The Arapahoe County District Attorney's Office in Colorado gave "year-end bonuses to felony prosecutors who tried at least five cases and earned convictions in 70 percent of them." And "[t]he desire for—or, rather the *expectation* of—a conviction as the result of a criminal trial has become so entrenched with prosecutorial agencies that, in at least one office as of 2000, any assistant who tried a case that yielded an acquittal had to file a report with the chief prosecutor explaining 'what went wrong.'"[132] And, as I mentioned above, prosecutors are often even more tenacious in defending convictions already obtained in the face of mounting and finally overwhelming evidence of innocence. To use the term of which economists are fond, their rationality in these matters is decidedly "bounded."[133]

This has been true in the South for a long time. In the famous "Scottsboro Boys" cases in the thirties, nine blacks riding a freight train going from Tennessee to Alabama were accused of raping two white women in Alabama. The primary evidence was the testimony of the alleged victims, who had every reason to lie to avoid Mann Act prosecution for "interstate" prostitution, and who recanted their testimony after the first trials.[134] Most of the defendants were sentenced to death after a lynch mob surrounded the courthouse and defense counsel was assigned only the morning of trial. The case became a cause célèbre on the American left and a showcase for the failures of the justice system in the deep South. The Supreme Court, which, of course, would very rarely ever review such trial outcomes, twice reversed the cases on procedural grounds:

> [P]ublic opinion outside the South held, almost certainly correctly, that the defendants were innocent. Even so, Alabama prosecutors stubbornly continued to convict, Alabama juries stubbornly continued to convict, and Alabama appellate courts stubbornly continued to affirm the inevitable convictions. All the defendants who were initially sentenced to death were spared execution—but all served substantial prison terms.[135]

Prosecutorial decisions usually occur in courts that remain "places of *mass* processing." Felony courts "often docket 60 felony indictments in a day. Court business is conducted in a swirl of activity as judges seek to 'move' crowded calendars."[136] "Accused persons come and go in the court system schema, but the structure and its occupational incumbents remain to carry on their respective career, occupational and organizational enterprises."[137] As Packer put it some time ago, "[A]n assembly line conveyer belt down which moves an endless stream of cases, never stopping, carrying the cases to workers who stand at fixed stations and who perform on each case as it comes by the same small but essential operation that brings it one step closer to being a finished product."[138] The "officials" who staff that conveyor belt bear a strong resemblance to the lower functionaries in Kafka's novel.

Prosecutors controlled by these organizational imperatives have "enjoyed an enormous expansion of power at the expense of judges, paroling authorities, and defense lawyers."[139] Laws that allow the prosecutor, rather than the juvenile court judge, to decide whether a juvenile should be charged as an adult, effectively make him the "gatekeeper determining access to the juvenile process itself."[140] In earlier times, it was the lay jury that exercised discretion and determined whether the defendant's actions were "wrongful" in a more fully moral sense.[141] Today "prosecutors decide who deserves a trip to the nearest penitentiary. Thanks to substantive law that makes convictions easy to obtain and acquittals much harder, prosecutors' decisions tend to stick. More broadly and specifically defined crimes have helped to reinforce the rule of discretion, not the rule of law."[142]

This may seem rather abstract. And so perhaps the best way to understand Justice Kennedy's conviction that Kafka's *Trial* is a reality for participants in the American criminal justice system is to consider another case, that of Kevin Fox. On June 5, 2004, Kevin Fox dropped his six-year-old son, Tyler, and his three-year-old daughter, Riley, off with his wife's mother in the small Illinois town of Wilmington and drove to Chicago to attend a concert with one of his wife's brothers.[143] His wife, Melissa, had earlier driven to Chicago to attend a breast cancer walk. About 1:00 a.m., Kevin returned to his mother-in-law's house, picked up the children, and drove home. He laid the children down to sleep in the living room, locked the front door, and went to his own room. Around eight in the morning Tyler came into his dad's room and said, "Riley's gone." Kevin searched the house and then called the Wilmington police's nonemergency number, where he was given a reassuring message that "in a lot of cases" a child simply wanders off and is found after a short while. Kevin described Riley's white T-shirt with a pink flamingo on it and pink capri pants to the police. A search by hundreds of townspeople began. Melissa learned of Riley's disappearance and raced back to Wilmington. Two searchers found what they hoped they would not: Riley's body, duct tape over her mouth, floating in a tributary of the Kankakee River. She was wearing no pants, and an autopsy revealed she had been sexually abused and drowned. DNA samples were sent to the state crime lab who ruled the sample "inconclusive." The police picked up Kevin and Melissa and brought them to the police station, but would tell them nothing. They were separated, made to wait for forty-five minutes, and then told about the death of their daughter. "Kevin began to pound the walls. He turned to Lyons [a detective to whom Kevin had delivered newspapers as a child], incredulous that the detective hadn't told him earlier. 'Todd, what the hell! Are you kidding me?'"[144] Kevin was close to collapse.

The Will County Sheriff's Office detectives took charge of the investigation, and Will County State's Attorney Jeffrey Tomczak had responsibility for filing charges. The investigation seemed to drag on through the summer, and the detectives seemed more interested in asking questions than providing explanations of their progress. Some of Kevin's relatives advised him to see a lawyer. Kevin rejected that suggestion, saying that he knew he could trust the detectives: "I felt like I had nothing to hide. . . . I was raised with the idea that authorities were good people and that they should be respected."

The Foxes consented to an interview of six-year-old Tyler by a "forensic interviewer." A tape of the interview showed the interviewer asking a series of leading questions, distorting his answers, and rejecting his attempts to deny that his father was involved with his sister's disappearance. Detectives' notes made after an hour of suggestive questions ("Where did he take Riley? You can tell me.") recorded that Tyler "took Riley somewhere." By October, Kevin was the prime suspect. He insisted that he didn't need a lawyer. "The DNA will clear me," he claimed. After the inconclusive testing by the state lab, the DNA sample had been sent to the national FBI lab, which was backlogged by nine months.

That fall Tomczak's reelection campaign was running aground on allegations that his father has been indicted in a city truck leasing scandal and had made illegal contributions to his son's campaign. The *Chicago Tribune* endorsed his opponent. A Will County detective called Kevin to say that they had news and asked the Foxes to come to the station. They were separated when they arrived, and Melissa was locked in a room by herself.

A group of detectives began interrogating Kevin. For the first time, they confronted him with Tyler's statements and claimed that they had a videotape of his car in use in the early morning of June 5, something that was a distortion of what the tape actually showed. They criticized him for calling the nonemergency number the night Riley disappeared. Finally, they turned hostile: "We think you know more than you're telling us. . . . We think you were involved." Kevin responded, "Are you kidding me? You guys are nuts." Melissa, who had been kept alone for three hours, began kicking the door until a detective arrived. He told her "that there were some red flags that are making us look at Kevin" and revealed Tyler's statement and the exaggerated claim about the video of their car.

We will see below that interrogators are taught to offer a suspect a "scenario" that falsely appears to lessen his guilt and that may be an attractive way out to someone who feels trapped. The detectives followed that playbook bit of manipulation here. A detective told Melissa that he "suspected that Kevin had bumped Riley's head, perhaps while opening the bathroom door, and had panicked when it appeared she was dead. The detective surmised that Kevin had applied to duct tape and committed the sexual assault to make it look as if the little girl had been kidnapped."[145] Melissa was both completely incredulous and disoriented, beginning not to know what to believe.

Kevin's requests to see a lawyer were ignored. When he tried to leave, he was told, "Sit your ass down." The police insisted that a polygraph would show Kevin to be lying, and so he volunteered to take one. The detectives told Kevin that he had failed the test. (At trial in the Foxes's civil rights claim, the polygraph operator admitted that the results were fabricated, a common ploy in police interrogation.) When Melissa expressed her confidence in her husband's innocence, he responded, "I swear to God I didn't do it." Enraged at the strength of her conviction, one of the detectives, Edward Hayes, "got right in [her] face." He yelled, "Your husband's a fucking liar, and he's a fucking murderer. He never loved you or your fucking daughter, and he killed her, and you need to learn to fucking get over it." Melissa testified that he felt that "she was terrified and felt like Hayes had 'crushed the spirit out of her.'"

The questioning of Kevin resumed. The detective who had yelled at Melissa told Kevin that he would make sure that Kevin would be jailed and "fucked every day unless he told them what they wanted to hear." They showed him pictures of his dead daughter and claimed she was present in the room and needed "closure." They again lied to him, claiming to have fiber evidence that implicated him. They claimed without reliable evidence that they had videotape of the Fox family car on the road between the house and the place where Riley's body was found. "Your family doesn't love you," one shouted, "So just say you did it." One of the detectives rushed into the room and proclaimed that he was bringing Tomczak's last offer for a deal if he signed on to the bathroom door accident scenario he had described to Melissa. But it had to be right then and there. That would mean a two-year sentence for involuntary manslaughter, rather than a life sentence for murder. And even more alluring, after being up for twenty-four hours and being questioned for twelve, he was made the offer that he could go home on bond right then.

At eight thirty in the morning, the detectives videotaped Kevin who repeated the accident scenario, mainly in response to leading questions. He provided no information that only the killer would have known. At several points the detectives insisted on his changing his account to make it more consistent with the physical evidence. Kevin testified that he gave the confession because he thought it was the only way to get the detectives to stop threatening him. He renounced the confession almost immediately.

As the state's attorney's election approached, Tomczak publicly alluded to evidence that Riley had been sexually abused before, something the Department of Children and Family Services found no evidence of and that was roundly denied by Riley's pediatrician. The prosecutor sought the death penalty. (Tomczak lost the election.)

Kevin's lawyer's investigation found a series of implausibilities in the story the detectives had created. The bathroom door, for example, was so thin that it could not have delivered a lethal blow. But then came a major disappointment. The FBI lab would be returning the DNA sample within a week, apparently because there was insufficient material to conduct the test. But what defense counsel did not know was that the FBI had not tested the sample because they had received, a day after the election, an instruction "from the Will County Sheriff's Office halting any testing of DNA in the Riley Fox murder." The instruction came from the detective who had shouted obscenities in Melissa's face. After further bureaucratic mix-ups, defense counsel finally got the DNA sample tested by a sophisticated lab. It concluded that the sample was barely large enough to test, but the test conclusively excluded Kevin Fox as the assailant.

The new state's attorney dismissed the charges against Kevin. He had spent about eight months in jail. The spokesman for the Will County detective's office expressed unhappiness about Kevin's release: "I'm not saying he shouldn't have been . . . but we firmly believe, and the sheriff firmly believes, that [the detectives] did a good job . . . and we stand beside them."[146]

After Kevin's release, the Foxes filed a civil rights case against the detectives and Will County. The jury found in their favor. The Seventh Circuit Court of Appeals affirmed the judgment, reducing the multimillion dollar verdict by about one-third. Soon after, Scott Eby, a thirty-eight-year-old sex offender, was matched with the DNA from the Fox case. He soon confessed to the crime and pleaded guilty. (It turned out that the police had responded to a suicide threat at Eby's house on the day of Riley's disappearance and had found him vomiting and asking about "that little girl," evidence they did not connect with the Fox investigation.) Kevin's defense attorney blamed the detectives' obsession with their first theory of the case on their unwillingness to see important evidence as it emerged.

The case thus ended with legal vindication of the innocent and punishment of the guilty. But consider how close Kevin Fox came to the death penalty. A little less DNA would have prevented a competent lab to reach a conclusion. The police foot-dragging about supplying the evidence could have prevented the clearly exonerating evidence from emerging. An overworked public defender may not have been able to keep up the relentless pressure on the police and prosecution to supply the evidence. Kevin may well have been subject to the death penalty because a confession had been manufactured without real concern for the truth through a system that was responding to its own bureaucratic and political imperatives.

The Jettisoning of Formality

It is obvious, I think, that the American criminal justice system (operating through its "system imperatives") has embraced informal methods, primarily interrogation followed by plea bargaining. Half of cases involve confessions, and 95 percent end in plea bargaining. The triumph of plea bargaining has been long in coming, but has been accelerating over the past decades (to the point where it can, because of the small number of trials, hardly increase any more).[147] I described the interpretation of *The Trial* that sees it as a caricature of Austrian procedure created by imagining criminal process solely as pretrial process without any formal trial. We have adopted in reality something that, in the majority of cases, resembles that caricature. I have offered some of the attempts at historical explanation of why it "triumphed," largely because of the interests of bureaucracies that often sought to justify themselves to legislatures and executives who themselves sought to "govern through crime." These officials engaged in an ever escalating bidding war to appear tougher and tougher on crime, as portrayed in the mass media, and have been the agents of that development.

To echo Titorelli, when it comes to what actually goes on in police interrogation, the police are well aware that we don't know and most of us probably don't want to know. They go to some lengths to keep us from knowing:

> Detectives understand that police interrogation in the American adversary system is inherently morally problematic. . . . Because it often involves behavior—psychological manipulation, trickery and deceit—that is regarded as unethical in virtually all other social contexts. Perhaps it should not be surpris-

ing, then, that interrogation remains one of the most secretive of all police activities, despite the fact that police solve more crimes with interrogation-induced confessions than they do with virtually any other type of evidence.[148]

The logic of police interrogation and plea bargaining is continuous: "both are based on creating resignation, fear, and the perception than the only way to mitigate punishment is by accepting the state's deal."[149] It may be, however, that interrogation presents "the more serious problem for adversary theory because it is not only potentially coercive but also routinely fraudulent. Thus police interrogation (like plea bargaining) risks not only eliciting involuntary and unreliable evidence, but also corrupting the integrity of the very adversary procedures that are intended to protect legal rights, check state power, and ensure truthful fact-finding."[150]

The trial is designed to protect legal rights, check state power, and ensure truthful fact finding. Those three goals are closely related. Formality embodies a respect for the person who sits in the defendant's chair that is completely unknown in the interrogation room. Legal representation at trial, when competent, ensures the assertion of the rights that the law confers. Truth, paradoxically simple factual truth more than any other, stands as an affront to the sovereign power that runs from popular moods to legislative enactment to prosecutors' interest in conviction and incarceration.[151] A forum within which it can effectively be asserted, as at trial it can be, can frustrate public moods embedded in bureaucratic judgments in individual cases. After all, as Hobbes put it, only "such truth, as opposeth no man's profit, nor pleasure, is to all men welcome," and "I doubt not, but if it had been a thing contrary to any man's right of dominion, or to the interest of men that have dominion, that the three angles of a triangle should be equal to two angles of a square, that doctrine should have been, if not disputed, yet by the burning of all books of geometry, suppressed, as far as he whom it concerned was able."[152]

One way to empower the will of officials, increasingly discretionary, is to continually raise the price of going to trial until a plea offer becomes an "offer you can't refuse." Additionally, one can disable the capacity of the trial to insist on inconvenient truths by previously extracting unreliable confessions from the defendant under coercive circumstances that are difficult to expose. And both of those things have occurred.

This has occurred not consciously in a kind of conspiracy, but through the hydraulics of political and economic pressure as it is brought down on an individual defendant. Part of that pressure is the result of a public mood that wants public safety and the satisfaction of feelings of revenge or retribution, but is uninterested in paying the taxes that ensure that rights are respected, state power is checked, and truthful fact finding occurs. As Frank Zimring put it in the context of the imposition of the death penalty:

> the political units that maintain criminal justice systems with capital punishment are unwilling to make the heavy investment in defense services that faster, high-quality justice would require, and this is particularly true of the states where death sentences are most common. Massive investments in the defense at trial and initial appeal of capital cases would be required in states like Texas, Georgia, Virginia, Florida, Arkansas, and Alabama. Nothing could be further from the priorities of most of those who hold executive and legislative power in such places.[153]

Because confession leads so inexorably to either plea bargaining or, much more rarely, conviction at trial, there is pressure on police to extract confessions by whatever means, pressure on police to lie about the means, and pressure on courts to (1) resolve credibility issues to support conviction and (2) stretch doctrine to allow deception and threats. All that has occurred. The less trials are protective of a defendant's rights and the more he will be punished for choosing one, the more often a defendant will choose the bargain offered him. And it has led to the dominance of informal methods over the formal and protective rituals of our trials.

The Ubiquity of Deception

Alasdair MacIntyre set out the distinguishing mark of a morally justifiable interaction, one that treats another as an end and not solely as a means, in the following terms:

> To treat someone else as an end is to offer them what I take to be good reasons for acting in one way rather than another, but to leave it to them to evaluate those reasons. It is to be unwilling to influence another except by reasons which that other he or she judges to be good. It is to appeal to impersonal criteria the validity of which each rational agent must be his or her own judge.

By contrast, to treat someone else as a means is to seek to make him or her an instrument of my purposes by adducing whatever influences or considerations will be effective on this or that occasion. The generalizations of the sociology and psychology of persuasion are what I shall need to guide me, not the standards of a normative rationality.[154]

What could such high-minded thoughts have to do with our bureaucratic, interrogation-centered, informal methods of exclusively pretrial criminal process? Surprisingly, given where we have come and given the grim reality of the third degree in the first half of the twentieth century, our doctrine on the voluntariness of confessions and consequent limitations on the means permissible in interrogation was once quite exacting. Over the last fifty years, our doctrine has "caught up to" our practice: another example, along with "stop and frisk" law and the newly "holistic" standard for probable cause, in which doctrine has followed, rather than led, the expression of sovereignty to be found in police practices. Early doctrine valued the freedom with which such a confession was made. In a matter so personal and so close to the core of the human personality as confession, government should stand back and avoid inserting even the most refined of coercive methods into its dealings with a citizen. To choose only one example, in *Spano v. New York*,[155] the Supreme Court addressed the "delicate nature of the constitutional determination" involved in the review of a murder conviction, based largely on a confession. Vincent Spano, a twenty-five-year-old American citizen of Italian birth, got his revenge upon a man, a former heavyweight boxer, who had viciously attacked him sometime earlier in the evening. Spano called an old friend who was in training to be a police officer, one Gaspar Bruno, and told him what had happened, found a lawyer, and gave himself up to authorities. He strictly followed his lawyer's instructions not to say anything to the police. During his interrogation he asked to see his lawyer, a request that was denied under the pretext that the police could not find his telephone number. Finally, the police arranged for him to him to meet with Bruno, who was instructed to tell Spano falsely that the latter's call to him had endangered his career with the police department and the livelihood of his wife, three children, and unborn child, and to implore him to confess. After holding out for a long time, Spano finally gave in and confessed.

Chief Justice Warren, writing for the Court, reversed the conviction and ruled that "life and liberty can be as much endangered from illegal methods used to convict those thought to be criminals as from the actual criminals themselves." In this case, the combination of the length of the interrogation, the denial of Spano's requests to see his lawyer, and the manipulative use of a trusted friend rendered the confession involuntary and inadmissible.

The case, and earlier cases where even less pressure was brought to bear on the suspect,[156] evinces respect for an almost Kantian form of citizen autonomy. It may be true that offering a suspect a truthful account of the negative consequences of continued silence (accompanied by an account of its advantages?), which would allow the suspect a self-interested prudential calculation, is acceptable. But, sometimes as in the *Spano* decision, the Court seems to imply that a confession is voluntary only when the confession emerged spontaneously, as Kant might say, as an expression of the suspect's moral freedom to do what is right. When the government offers any incentives or brings pressure to bear on the suspect, it undermines his freedom to speak or not to speak in this ultimate sense. We have now moved very far from that world.

Richard Leo has argued that "American police interrogation is strategically manipulative and deceptive because it occurs in the context of a fundamental contradiction. On the one hand, police need incriminating statements and admissions to solve many crimes; especially serious ones; on the other hand, there is almost never a good reason for suspects to provide them."[157] Given that contradiction, it is not surprising that "American interrogation is designed to create a number of illusions: that the suspect has no meaningful option other than to comply with the interrogator's wishes and demands; that the interrogator's motivation is really to help the suspect and that the suspect is better off admitting some version of guilt than by denying culpability or terminating the interrogation. To persuade a suspect of these illusions, American police regularly rely upon psychological interrogation techniques that involve deception, trickery, and manipulation."[158] All these activities, combined with the ability to isolate the suspect, "in some other contexts would be regarded as criminal fraud."[159] Police lie about the evidence: fingerprints and other evidence found at the scene and statements made by alleged witnesses. They lie about the law: implying that shaking a baby until he or she dies will be regarded as an accident. They lie about the consequences of a confession: that it will allow the juvenile suspect to go home or be prosecuted in juvenile court rather than adult court. Courts are indulgent: "American courts almost always find that police lying during interrogation does not render a confession involuntary."[160]

The second kind of fraud that can occur during interrogation looks outward, toward the possible audiences of a confession, notably a jury in a subsequent trial. (Though a trial is unlikely once a confession has been obtained, the *imagined* trial greatly increases the state's bargaining leverage in the plea bargain that is likely to resolve the case.) "Police engage in impression management . . . by representing the interrogation process as little more than a noncustodial interview whose benign but noble purpose is merely to advance the public's interest in truth finding; they attempt to shift the focus away from their interrogation strategies and toward the suspect's incriminating statements which are usually unrecorded." Unbeknownst to the suspect, the detectives are writing a script for a play that the suspect cannot even imagine: "Confessions are constructed, not discovered."[161] Most dramatically, the postadmission stage of the interrogation often involves a process in which the detective and the suspect together reconstruct the events surrounding the crime, "ideally" in a way that demonstrates that the suspect knows details about the crime that only the perpetrator could know. In the significant number of cases in which false confessions have led to false convictions, as demonstrated to a high level of certainty by DNA pointing away from the suspect and toward a definite alternative later proven to be the perpetrator, the confessions of the system are larded with specific facts that must have come from the detectives. In some of the cases, the detectives subsequently misrepresented the source of details in their testimony at trial.

Again, consideration of specific cases should make these notions more concrete.[162] On July 27, 1981,[163] someone cut the screen on the back door, broke in, and raped Arta Kroeplin in Ogden, Kansas. She was unable to give any description of her attacker. The police fixed on Eddie Lowery, who was then in the army, and who had been in a small car accident near the Kroeplin home that night. The officers gave him a polygraph that they said he failed, denied his request for a lawyer, and interrogated him in an unrelenting and aggressive manner over two days, refusing to accept any of his claims of innocence: "We're going to lay the hardest conviction at you that we can, send you to prison as long as we can."[164] They told him that if he cooperated, "everything would go a lot easier, and I said okay." "Eventually Lowery broke down, cried, and began to agree with the officers' allegations. He believed that they would not let him leave the interrogation room unless he told them what they demanded to hear. . . . 'I didn't know what to do and I just wanted to

get away from it all.'"[165] Through the postadmission portion of the interrogation, the officers, using leading questions and other means, fed
him the details of the crime, something they denied in their testimony.
They also concocted a motive and described his guilt and remorse at the
crime. Lowery's jury was hung at the first trial, but convicted at a second. "He served ten years before being released on parole and register-
ing as a sex offender. In 2002, DNA testing excluded him as the rapist,
and based on that the District Court of Riley County vacated his conviction in 2003."[166]

In the summer of 1986, two rapes occurred in the same housing complex in eastern Pennsylvania.[167] The adopted sister of Bruce Godschalk,
who was twenty-three, called the police to say that a composite sketch,
which had been disseminated in the media, resembled her brother. One
of the victims identified Godschalk in a photo array, and a three-hour
interrogation ensued. The police falsely claimed to have witnesses and
fingerprint evidence, raised their voices, and told him "the sooner you
tell us what happened, the sooner we will take you home."[168] "Frightened, upset, crying, and believing he was not free to leave, Godschalk
eventually succumbed to the detectives' pressure and admitted to the
rapes." After the admission, the detectives fed many details of the rapes
to him (including facts that had not been made public), provided him a
motive, and had him practice his statement before turning on a tape re-
corder, where he also gave the apology they had practiced. At his suppression hearing, the detectives denied supplying him with any of the details and offered his account of the apology:

> When his eyes welled up, it wasn't because of any kind of attack by us or any-
> thing even verbal or anything. He had come to the realization, in my opinion,
> knowing what the conversation was at the time and reading his actions, that
> he was now facing the truth that he did it, and he was finally getting it off his
> chest and it was like, "I'm letting everything go here," and it was like, "I've
> done it," you know, "I'm glad I've got it over with," and he was emotional
> about it. There's no question about that.[169]

In 1987, Godschalk was convicted of two counts each of rape and burglary and sentenced to twenty years. "In January 2002, however, DNA
testing conclusively determined that the semen from each of the two rapes
had come from the same individual, but that person was not Bruce Godschalk. In February 2002, his conviction was vacated and he was released

from prison after serving fifteen years."[170] He could not have known any of the details of the crimes that he described in the confession.

In some ways these cases pale by comparison with that of Earl Washington Jr.[171] because in Washington's case, the complete lack of credibility in his admissions was apparent from the start. In the summer of 1982 a young woman, Rebecca Williams, was raped and murdered in her apartment in Virginia. The victim lived long enough to say she had been assaulted by a single unknown black man. About a year later, the police arrested Earl Washington, a laborer who is intellectually very limited, for the assault and burglary of a neighbor. Early in his interrogation he confessed to the assault and burglary "and to everything else they asked him about" including three other rapes that he could not have committed. He then confessed to the Williams murder (but not to the rape, since the detectives didn't then know about the rape). The statement, which was written up by the detectives and signed by Washington, contained numerous gross errors, such as the number of stab wounds, the race and size of the victim, and a false claim to forced entry. He could not supply any facts of which the interrogators were ignorant or lead them to the crime scene. Nonetheless, because the statement did contain eight details "only the perpetrator would know,"[172] and which the detective testified originated with him, he was convicted and sentenced to death. He spent ten years on death row, "once came within nine days of being executed," and "five different appellate courts (including the United States Supreme Court) upheld his conviction eight separate times."[173] Two rounds of DNA testing first lead to the death sentence being commuted to life imprisonment and then to an absolute pardon by the governor of Virginia (and identified the true killer as another convicted felon). He was released after serving seventeen years for a crime he did not commit.

These cases involve deception of the suspect and then deception of the courts:

> [L]egal scholars have opposed police lying during interrogation on multiple grounds: it is not necessary to solve most crimes; that it infringes on the suspect's dignity and autonomy while breaching social trust; that it corrupts the integrity of the fact-finding process and thus may diminish public confidence in the criminal justice system; that it has a tendency to expand into other areas of police work (i.e., it inevitably leads to police lying in other contexts, such as at trial); and that it does produce false and unreliable confessions.[174]

The Marginalization of Defense Counsel

Kafka parodies the plight of defense counsel throughout *The Trial*. Of course, because it is doubtful that the law even countenances a defense, they should expect little better. And so counsel are consigned to warrens with holes in the floor through which they continually fall and come away with soot on their faces if they try to get a bit of fresh air. One magistrate simply throws them down the stairs every time they try to address him on a matter of law. Huld himself was left to play a guessing game on what the court was likely to do, and a painter of kitschy and flattering scenes probably knows more about the law than do the lawyers.

Our criminal defense lawyers of course do better. (I expect Austria's defense lawyers did better.) But there remain many limitations on defense lawyers' ability to represent their clients, many of which we have seen in passing. As usual, the most important one has nothing to do with legal doctrine and stems from the overwork of the public defenders who represent most of those who appear in criminal court, making it extremely difficult for them to fulfill their professional responsibilities. (The doctrine is relatively indulgent in upholding convictions in the face of ineffective assistance challenges.) Evidentiary doctrines allow an overbearing trial judge to prevent a trial lawyer from presenting important evidence. There is the absence of the most effective pretrial discovery tool—deposition practice—which is available in civil cases. As we saw, there exist in some places a culture of resistance among prosecutors even to providing the discovery that is legally required.[175] There are the range of doctrines and practices that make it unlikely that a suspect will confer with a lawyer before police interrogation and have the assistance of a lawyer during the interrogation. And on and on.

The Irrelevance of the Factual Details of the Case

We have seen that Kafka's law "informs itself" of the facts of the case but that there seems to be good reason to think it gets those facts badly wrong, at least in part because the officials are uninterested in those facts. They seem most interested in who the defendant is and his attitude toward the court. The law's claim to semidivine status exempts it

from the small-gauged all-to-human burden of determining precisely
and carefully what it is that the defendant has done.

There is in the United States today no systematic and effective attempt
to obtain and present the very most reliable evidence in criminal cases.
This is shocking, given what is at stake. One obvious comparison, that
between criminal cases and commercial cases, where well-funded liti-
gants and expansive methods of discovery lift the quality of the evidence
considerably, is particularly dispiriting. The inflation-adjusted per-case
spending for defense lawyers for indigent defendants "fell by more than
half from the late 1970s to the early 1990s" while the number of felony
prosecutions increased two and a half times:

> More so than any other aspect of American government, the prosecution
> and punishment of criminal defendants grew dramatically more efficient.
> The justice system became, more and more, an assembly line in which cases
> are processed, not adjudicated.
>
> Assembly-line adjudication is not known for its accuracy. The greater the
> ratio of cases to personnel, the smaller the opportunity to examine carefully
> the evidence on which the government's case rests. And that opportunity was
> already small: even before the huge run-up in felony prosecutions, the ten-
> dency was for plea bargains to be struck early in the process, before either
> side had a chance to do much investigating. That tendency is even stronger in
> today's justice system because pleading cases out quickly is a necessity, not
> a convenience. The upshot is that noninvestigation is the norm in American
> criminal litigation, careful gathering of evidence the exception.[176]

We assume the suspect[177] is guilty "and focus on the task of creating
a fair fight between the prosecution and the guilty defendant"; no current doctrine insists on the "availability of the most accurate information concerning the crime and its investigation."[178] Given this approach,
it is not reassuring that, as measured by DNA evidence from the crime
scene, approximately 25 percent of those the police initially believed to
be the perpetrators were not guilty.[179] The scope of discovery in criminal cases, although improved over what it was fifty years ago, is ane-
mic compared to civil discovery: most importantly, in all but a couple
states, there exists no deposition practice in criminal cases.[180] Because
witnesses have no obligation to speak with defense counsel before trial[181]
(and witness statements found in police reports can be written in a stra-

tegic and unhelpful way), it is not unusual for defense counsel to be surprised at important details that emerge for the first time at trial.[182] In my own geographically limited (Chicago) experience of trying criminal cases, the entire discovery phase of the case has a chaotic, hit-and-miss, hard-elbowed character. Obtaining documents feels like pulling teeth. Prosecutors, even when they do not clearly withhold important evidence, treat discovery as a contact sport,[183] as one of my colleagues put it. The discovery comes out in dribs and drabs, and often quite late. Finally, prosecutors who see their work as a competitive game are likely to take advantage of the generally quite indulgent rules[184] concerning witness preparation, particularly in the preparation of detectives and police officers, which can take place with all police witnesses present, allowing for the coordination of testimony.

The forensic evidence offered at trial, largely developed in police-related labs far from universities, can be profoundly unreliable, in effect junk science.[185] George Thomas at Ohio State Law School, who has been deeply critical of the casualness with which issues of actual innocence are treated by the courts, describes the action of the Arizona courts in a murder case.[186] The case involved the murder of a female bartender, and the only evidence against the defendant was his "evasiveness" about his relationship with the victim and a bite mark on the victim's body that was compared to an impression made by the defendant for the police. The defendant's conviction and death sentence were initially reversed because, in an instance of prosecutorial foot-dragging on discovery, a key videotape used by a "forensic odontologist"[187] to show a match was only revealed just before trial. The defendant was retried and convicted again:

> This time, though, the judge sentenced Krone to life in prison, "citing doubts about whether or not Krone was the true killer." This borders on the unbelievable. A trial judge who had "doubts about whether Krone was the true killer" *sentenced him to life in prison.* Krone served over ten years in prison before DNA testing conducted on the saliva and blood found on the victim excluded him as the killer. The DNA matched a man who lived close to the bar but who had never been considered as a suspect in the killing.
>
> Ray Krone's case is an example of how the current system fails innocent defendants. Police seized on the first plausible suspect and looked no further. The prosecution built a case on a Styrofoam bite impression and mumbo-jumbo scientific evidence.[188]

There are hundreds of cases that parallel Krone's, though their details vary. In addition to the inclination of the police to lurch toward the first suspect, prosecutors tend to do very little investigation before charging.[189] And once the case is charged, the enormous pressure to obtain a plea bargain begins.

In a parallel civil context, related to criminal prosecutions, the Supreme Court has upheld the eviction of wholly innocent public housing tenants whose family members have committed drug or gun crimes, even if the tenant was unaware of the crime, and even if the perpetrator is no longer living in the apartment. One of the arguments that the Court accepted is that "in a situation of severe scarcity in which a large population of homeless families and families with deficient housing are on long waiting lists for any public housing, the one strike rule is a useful and appropriate way to eliminate large numbers of people without a case-by-case determination of either their threat to public safety or their needs."[190] And Anthony Amsterdam has pointed out that the often angrily expressed willingness of the US Supreme Court to vacate stays entered by lower courts in death penalty cases reveals an impatience with facts: "Fast-paced adjudication is conducive to mistakes; and mistakes made in vacating a stay will ordinarily be fatal."[191]

This inattention to careful fact finding extends to cases of incarceration based on group association. Historically, the detention of thousands of foreign nationals in the Parmer raids and the internment of Japanese Americans without evidence of wrongdoing reflect that attitude, as does the detention for long periods of time at Guantánamo of persons for whom there was likewise no evidence of criminality or threat to national security. In some cases, detectives have begun their interrogations with a strong presumption of guilt supported by virtually no evidence, identified a psychologically vulnerable person, and actually convinced that person that he committed the crime, though lacking any memory of it. And in case after case, prosecutors have refused to concede that they have obtained a false conviction, even when DNA evidence strongly demonstrates, sometimes to a moral certainty, that they convicted the wrong person. In cases such as these, we see bureaucratic imperatives casting aside a basic concern for factual truth.

We saw that *The Trial* is a kind of parody of the entire pretrial phase of continental procedure in a system where the more formal adjudicatory phase is never reached. (The one event that *seems* to be a trial turns out to be a gathering of officials alone.) Because an adjudication involves two adversaries and a truly impartial tribunal, K. simply flails away without effect. By making the trial an unusual event, our defendants are reduced to pleading their cases to the police and to prosecutors, both of whom understand themselves to be engaged in a *prosecutorial*, not an *investigative* function. In the 95 percent of cases that do not go to trial, a defendant never has a chance to plead his case to a truly impartial tribunal.

This is not accidental. Over the past twenty years, we have come to lodge more and more trust in the police and prosecutors over judges: "The traditional prosecutorial model called for deference to judges, but the new prosecutor understands that she has replaced judges and the more trusted agency of the public interest."[192] Prosecutors are thus more "willing to use the media and speak as a voice for the crime victims of the community and to advocate politically for tougher sentences, more prisons, and getting rid of judges who are not sufficiently tough on crime."[193] They have always "liked to campaign on the low rate of acquittals."[194] More fundamentally and more continuously with the world of *The Trial*, where, after all, the goddess of justice looks more like the goddess of the hunt, "[i]t is not [judges'] neutrality and judgment that have come to be mistreated, but neutrality and judgment themselves":

> The very virtues that made courts an attractive solution to many twentieth century governance problems—their relative autonomy from normal political and market pressures; the role of argumentation, deliberation, and interpretation in shaping judicial decisions; and the ability to consider different voices and many kinds of information—have come to be seen as flaws that bespeak a lack of alignment between judicial judgment and the common good.[195]

Echoing Kafka's "hunt" metaphor, one student of prosecutorial culture puts it this way: "[I]t is hard for young prosecutors to shun the hunt mentality of an aggressive institutional culture and pursue justice. That the object of the hunt is considered a threat to society fans the flames of many a prosecutor's indignation. . . . For many prosecutors, losing track of their prey is simply unacceptable."[196]

Some doctrine actually encourages the partisan withholding of information. So called *Giglio* material, which relates to the credibility of the prosecution's witnesses, need not, under current law, be turned over before plea bargaining. This, of course, makes it more likely that the defense will overestimate the strength of the prosecution's case and plead the case out. It has been held by some courts that *Brady* material, evidence favorable to the defense, does not have to be turned over during postconviction proceedings.[197] When the misconduct occurs at trial, it is rare that an appellate court will reverse, in almost all cases finding the error to be "harmless."[198] Studies have shown that the most aggressive prosecutors are the most "successful," and, as one former prosecutor put it, "Prosecutors are not part of a non-partisan priesthood purified of all base motives. Many are political actors who are more attentive to their own interests than those of the institutions they serve."[199]

Nor do suspects find an impartial ear in the interrogation rooms of our police stations. "By definition . . . interrogation is a guilt-presumptive process, a theory-driven social interaction led by an authority figure who holds a strong a priori belief about the target and who measures success by his or her ability to extract a confession."[200] Detectives "treat interrogation as a game. As in other games, the aim is to win."[201] Because of the power of confession evidence, "the legal rights that the adversary system seeks to protect at the trial stage [in those few cases that reach trial] may be rendered meaningless by what occurs at the pretrial stage."[202] "Interrogations are best understood therefore as social encounters fashioned to *confirm* and *legitimate* a police narrative. In this sense they are similar to the trial—the event which interrogations traditionally lead up to and feed into, but which they increasingly *replace*."[203] They are *dissimilar* to the trial in that there is only one effective narrative presented.

This lack of attention to the truth of an individual situation has also appeared in sentencing. Minimum and maximum sentences have grown longer, and sentencing guidelines have limited the ability of judges to individualize punishment. Indeed the popularity of guidelines was precisely that they prevented the judge from paying too much attention to the facts of the individual case and the real culpability of the defendant. They reflect a defiant and adamant refusal to allow those facts to qualify the punitive and self-protective goals of the criminal justice system itself. This results in "punishment at a distance, where penalty levels are set, often irreversibly, by political actors operating in political contexts far removed from the circumstances of the case."[204] This reflects a conviction, embedded more in a mood than an explicit belief, that there *cannot* be much to say on behalf of "those people" who end up being sentenced. And so "legislatures and government ministers have acquired more direct and unimpeded means of shaping practical outcomes. . . . There is, as Nils Christie might put it, a *more streamlined system of pain-delivery, with fewer intervening obstacles between the political process and the al-location of individual punishment.*"[205] The facts of the individual case do not get in the way of the will of the distant "highest court."

The Claimed Right to Infallibly Judge the Whole Person

The policemen who appear at Josef K.'s apartment are sure that he is guilty. After all, the "higher authorities who employ us inform them-selves in great detail about the person they are arresting and the grounds for the arrest. There's been no mistake."

Detectives "tend not to be skeptical about the possibility of the type of error that the adversary system in theory is designed to prevent: the wrongful prosecution and conviction of an innocent person," and so they believe that they "rarely make any sorting mistakes"[206] between the inno-cent and the guilty. Some detectives who conduct the interrogations that lead to the confessions that lead to the guilty pleas that define Ameri-can criminal process have actually "publicly asserted that they did not [could not!] elicit any false confessions because they interrogated only the guilty."[207] Suspects are often informed (sometimes falsely) that they had failed a polygraph and were, therefore, "beyond all doubt" "scien-tifically" or "100% certainly" proven to be guilty. This is simply untrue, and an innocent person is just slightly less than 50 percent likely to fail the test. John Larson, an early practitioner of the polygraph said, "I orig-inally hoped that instrumental lie detection would become a legitimate part of professional police science. It is little more than a racket. The lie detector, as used in many places, is nothing more than a psychological third degree aimed at extorting confessions as the more physical beat-ings were. At times I'm sorry I ever had any part in its development."[208] And given the level of certainty they claim, interrogators strongly im-ply, in a way that recalls Josef K.'s futile attempt to justify his life, that it is the suspect's duty to prove his innocence before the interrogation will cease.[209] Sometimes, at least, the detectives may believe their own "sci-ence," leading to even greater psychological pressure. This is because the manuals used to train them are "replete with false and misleading claims—often presented as uncontested fact—about the supposed behav-ioral indicia of truth-telling and deception. At least one prominent po-lice trainer . . . continues to insist 'we don't interrogate guilty people.'"[210] This level of certainty about what is often among the most elusive of questions is inconsistent with the "tentativeness and scrupulousness of democratic politics and democratic respect for persons."[211]

There is a kind of suspicion that pervades *The Trial*, one that Josef K. increasingly accepts, that there is something about him that the law in its wisdom knows, and that may justify his punishment. And in the world that Kafka "foresaw," one's guilt was established first when the charged action's "general tendency in the judgment of jurisprudence does more harm than good to the state and its members" and then finally, under the Reich, "[m]aterially unlawful activity is activity counter to the German National Socialist world view."[212] Once the criminal law was, additionally, considered as a "law of war," one was "led to the conclusion that 'obviously the goal of this law is not merely to resist the opponent, but to annihilate him.'" The emphasis in criminal law was less on whether a law had been broken than "whether the wrongdoer still belongs to the community," and scholars set about creating categories of "characteristic criminal types" to identify "habitual criminals" or "juvenile criminals" or "antisocial parasites" who all would be subject to the death penalty for homicide.[213] "Anti-social outsiders" were said to be liable to punishment for being a "burden to the community" and to "merit punishment not so much on the basis of single actions as for their antisocial . . . existence." The rationalization was that they were not being punished because they are antisocial but because they had become so through "culpable conduct of their own." The focus was on "motives, general tendencies, previous convictions, and character" of a defendant rather on the "objective and verifiable circumstances of a particular act."

Today, the criminology invoked by the "sovereign state strategy" of crime control is "one of essentialized difference. . . . Some—particularly 'paedophiles,' 'sexual predators,' or juvenile 'superpredators'—are evoked in ways that are barely human, their conduct being essentialized as 'evil,' 'wicked' and beyond all human understanding. . . . The only practical and rational response to such types, as soon as they offend, *if not before*, is to have them taken out of circulation."[214] "The open, porous, mobile society of strangers that is late modernity has given rise to crime control practices that seek to make society less open and less mobile: to fix identities, immobilize individuals, quarantine whole sections of the population, erect boundaries, close off access."[215] This strategy is "value-rational," not managerial, "the expressive mode is more overtly moralistic, uncompromising, and concerned to assert the force of sovereign power."[216] Recidivists in particular, including drug dealers, are "wicked individuals who have lost all legal rights and all moral claims on us."[217] And so repeat offenders have been sentenced under "three-strikes laws" to life in prison for writing a bad check for $88.30 or stealing three golf clubs.[218] And it has been suggested that the refusal of prosecutors to concede that DNA evidence has exonerated currently incarcerated persons, often leading to continued legal battles and years more in prison is the fact that many of those prisoners have criminal records (which is why their photographs are in the mug books from which the victim identified them):

> Post-conviction prosecutors may dwell on these backgrounds and infer that, even if the prisoner is innocent of the crime for which he is currently locked up, he did other bad things for which he never paid the price. In other words, *he is not "innocent" in a karmic sense.* The presence of a rap sheet may also convince prosecutors that the inmate poses a risk of causing *future* harm. Keeping him in confinement, then, at least incapacitates him from committing new crimes against the public.[219]

The Merger of the Legal into the Religious and Psychological

Arendt's interpretation of Kafka focuses on the way that his fiction criticizes the exploitation by the law of religious sensibilities and the at least implicit claim of the law to derivation from and legitimation by a mysterious transcendent realm. It is no accident that the most persuasive and subtle apologist for the law is a priest who speaks to Josef K. in a cathedral. *The Trial* enacts the relationships between the "really sacred" and the totalizing power of the law as we experience it. These religious sensibilities often cluster around feelings of guilt and sinfulness that are a hairbreadth away from primitive pathological patterns. Kafka's own religious thought struggled with his understanding of a godhead beyond human comprehension and language, on the one hand, and the ethical God of history and law, which, in concrete forms, is largely a human creation that bears the marks of the human *libido dominandi* (lust for domination) and that can find a comfortable home in the criminal law.

Winnifred Sullivan has noted that America is distinct from other advanced democracies in two ways: "in the extent to which they profess attachment to religion and in the high rate at which they incarcerate their fellows." By the usual measures, "the United States is a place where religion proudly and independently flourishes" and "also a place where a higher percentage of the population is incarcerated than in any other country in the world." "Both of these distinctions have become more marked in the last thirty-five years."[220] Sullivan describes as well the ironic[221] dependence of some forms of American Protestantism on the state for providing the concrete norms and institutions claimed to be divinely sanctioned:

> The American Protestant rejection of worldly power has, ironically, increased its dependence on secular institutions. Other institutions over the past five hundred years have gradually taken on certain traditional functions of the church. The structures of the military, the market and government provide the institutional bones of the Protestant movement. Because all authority is understood to come from God, however, and because evangelical churches do not have institutional superstructures, obedience to civil authorities often stands in for obedience to God.[222]

The criminal law in America has often been understood as expressing a kind of "political theology," a place where a quasi-divine sovereignty endures in a secular world. "[C]ivil religion does not replace religion as such: the two complement—even enable—each other by virtue of religion's very disestablishment and free exercise."[223] "[A] democratic state that seeks to honor the rule of law is also one in which a sovereign power both inside and above the law is also brought into play."[224] As we saw above, prosecutors and governors (who are often former prosecutors) have convinced electorates in many states that their role in enforcing punitive policies best expresses the people's sovereignty. Neoconservative partisans of an increasingly punitive and "anti-modern" criminology have invoked religious themes and metaphors: the upholding of order and authority, the assertion of absolute moral standards, the affirmation of tradition and common sense. It is also deeply illiberal in its assumption that certain criminals are simply wicked, and in this respect different from the rest of us.

> The criminology of the other . . . wants to punish more than understand. Aware, perhaps, that the death penalty and mass imprisonment depend upon our refusal to comprehend the human beings we so completely condemn, it

reinstates an older metaphysical conception that depicts the offender as an evil-doer, and the criminal act as unconditioned evil choice.[225]

The American religious right, which enjoys significant political influence, joined by secular neoconservative thinkers, who like Leo Strauss generally considered religion to be a useful illusion, was "implacably opposed" to the culture of the sixties and raised calls for "more discipline in schools and families, an end to 'libertarian license' in art and culture, condemnation of the new sexual morality, and a generalized return to a more orderly, more disciplined, and more tightly controlled society."[226]

Conservative thinkers were not simply wrong about all this. As Karl Polanyi saw long ago, they saw that the free market, which they also tended strongly to support, could not supply everything society needed: "[S]ocial arrangements of this kind pose acute problems of social order and call for the creation of governmental institutions and civic associations that can build social solidarity and ensure moral regulation. Complex societies need more organization, not less, and while markets can organize economic efficiencies, they do little to bring about moral restraint, social integration, or a sense of group belonging."[227] Religion literally provides the ties (*religio*, "ligaments") back to tradition and horizontally through present day society.

On the other hand, this religious function can easily be claimed by a state in the hands of neoconservatives. William Bennett, the first "drug czar" (talk about sovereign power!), argued "that all deliberate use of illegal drugs is harmful because it undermines the legitimacy of the government's authority to decide what citizen can and cannot use to alter their moods."[228]

> In this view, taking or selling drugs is a species of treason, and the specific physical harms and benefits of the drug being taken are unimportant. So all illegal drugs are from this perspective not only harmful, but equally harmful. The high-functioning drug taker may be even more dangerous than the devastated crack fiend on a public sidewalk because the high-functioning user is more likely to be admired and emulated.[229]

Kafka often tells us that the strategy of the law is to isolate the individual and drive him back on his own psychological resources, which are likely to be weaker than one might imagine, even for a worldly capitalist like Josef K. We have seen that this too is the strategy of American interrogators: the training manuals for police interrogation stress the importance of isolation and relentless questioning, always expressing the unshakeable conviction of the guilt of the suspect. The question is always how he did it, not whether he did it. Sometimes explicitly religious themes are invoked. Sometimes there is a somewhat vaguer appeal to the importance of "owning up" to what the suspect has done. In the postadmission phase of questioning, when the detectives are trying to construct a story that will appear plausible to a jury, they often invoke religious motivations for the confession, such as the suspect's felt need to "expiate" his sin. From the point of view of the interrogators, these invocations of the religious are as likely to be cynical ploys as not, but can be intertwined with the psychological confusion of the suspect. In documented cases of "persuaded false confessions," that is, confessions where the suspect has actually come to believe falsely that he committed the crime, the psychological process seems to be as follows:

> At some point . . . the suspect realizes that [the detectives] are not going to credit his assertions of innocence. He may then begin to experience dissonance because he cannot reconcile the obvious contradiction between his knowledge that he is innocent and his [false] belief that the police are truthfully reporting unmistakable evidence of his guilt. The asymmetry of the situation puts the suspect at a psychological disadvantage of which he is unaware. The interrogators may simply invent false evidence of his guilt to refute his assertions, but the innocent suspect, who does not realize the police are lying to him, cannot simply invent false evidence to refute their assertions. Instead, the suspect offers up the remaining basis for his belief in his innocence: that he has no memory of committing the crime.
>
> The interrogators, however, continue to press forward with their onslaught of accusations and challenges.[230]

Like Josef K., who finally accepts his guilt, the suspect, with the prompting of the interrogators, comes to embrace his own guilt. With the help of the detectives he goes on to construct a narrative of events. His story is likely to be less than perfect, but the detectives may be able to supply the details of which they have knowledge and avoid those areas where no one has knowledge. Again, in about 80 percent of cases, a confession (which, in these cases is likely to be repudiated) leads to conviction.

The Expansion of the Realm of Necessity and Inevitability

Stuntz argues that the political forces that led to the tsunami of increasing punishment were forces that neither the police who made the arrest nor prosecutors who brought and plea-bargained the cases nor the legislatures that authorized the building of the prisons really understood or controlled. It was "a failure of democratic governance."[231] It was facilitated by the fact that local government, who employed police and prosecutors, did not have to fund the prisons, which were funded at the state level, and the local governments that controlled the police and prosecutors could shift their costs to the states. But what really drove the increase were public moods of fear and then punitiveness that politicians at all levels chose not to resist. They acted like the characters in *The Trial*, officials and citizens, who lived under the law's sway: there was no perceived possibility of conscious political action. All they thought they could to do was to go with the flow of short-term political advantage.

At the microlevel, in the interrogation rooms in American police stations, we also saw the appeal to necessity. The detectives are trained to project a level of certainty to the suspect that does not allow contradiction. They are taught to project the unavoidable *presumption of guilt*, a heighted presumption the defendant then carries into his criminal trial, in the unlikely event that a criminal trial takes place. The detectives *enact* the relentlessness with which the cases will move forward into conviction and attempt to overwhelm the ability of the suspect to suggest another alternative. They also appeal to levels of "scientific" knowledge of physical evidence that simply cannot countenance the unreliable claims of the defendant's memory. The hydraulics of the system run from popular mood, partially created by opportunistic politicians, to elected officials' short-term interest, including elected prosecutors who cannot be "too" tough, to line prosecutors subject to bureaucratic controls. A parallel hydraulic has often controlled the police.

Whether these pressures are resistible is a real question, one that cannot be moralized away. I will address that question in the last chapter.

CHAPTER FOUR

Spaces of Freedom in American Law?

The jury is, above all, a political institution, and it must be regarded in this light in order to be appreciated. . . . He who punishes the criminal is the true master of society.
—Alexis de Tocqueville

We have the last remnant of active citizen participation in the juries.—Hannah Arendt

A Vast Unchanging Judicial Organism?

Huld the lawyer tells K. that imagining reforms in the system is a colossal waste of time, both futile and likely to "draw the attention of an always vengeful bureaucracy." Huld describes the law as a "vast judicial organism" that remains "in a state of eternal equilibrium, and that if you change something on your own where you are, you can cut the ground out from under your own feet and fall, while the vast organism easily compensates for the minor disturbances at some other spot—after all, everything is interconnected—and remains unchanged, if not, which is likely, even more resolute, more vigilant, more severe, more malicious" (119). One might say we have institutionalized vengefulness: anyone who exercises his Sixth Amendment right to ask a jury of his peers to decide his guilt will, if convicted, be assessed a "trial tax" of additional years of imprisonment for interfering with the ordinary workings of the system. If you looked at our criminal justice system as it actually functions with the compassionate clear eyes of an artist, one might conclude that we were close to the world of *The Trial*.

Does our legal system have this unreformable quality? William Stuntz, for one, tells us that reforms are possible, but unlikely. Stephanos Bibas tells us that "the gap between historical ideals and criminal-justice reality has never been greater" such that "[r]eforming a system so broken seems hopeless." He can only say that "I will not hold my breath" until the resources necessary to bring some sanity to the system become available and generally "[o]ne faces immense difficulty in beginning to reform a system as broken as our punishment factory."[1] These dark expectations are rooted in pessimism about the likelihood of action within what Arendt calls our "spaces of freedom"—here appellate courts and legislatures—that have not acted with real freedom in the recent past.

Of course, Kafka's law emanates from mysterious heights over which those ruled have no control and were enacted "from the beginning" in the interests of the nobles who enforce them. The people can only hope without hope that the nobles really are deciding cases by interpreting the law, something that will not really be known for centuries. It is hoped as well that the day will come when "the law will belong to the people, and the nobility will vanish." This is said without an animus against the nobility: "We are more inclined to hate ourselves for we have not yet shown ourselves worthy of being entrusted with the laws," and as Kafka puts it so elusively, "it [the doctrine that there really is no law] unequivocally recognizes the nobility and its right to go on existing." We, the people, will continue to be ruled through an elusive "law" until we deserve to rule ourselves.

Our legal texts are, of course, public and the people are sovereign[2] in the United States. We must accept that the law is ultimately and inevitably supported by force, as indeed it is.[3] If we feel individually unaffected, we can put it out of our minds, leave it to the "nobles" (our elites and bureaucrats). Kafka shows us what domination becomes if left on its own, we might say. To the extent we want to live in a decent society, our inevitable threat and use of force must not be left on its own; it must be constrained, channeled, and structured. But how and by whom?

Before we identify qualities of our regime that offer some hope, we must first consider the question, "Is our law an organism impervious to change in the way Kafka describes?" Plausible accounts of how we reached the place where we find ourselves emphasize the haphazard nature of our story, which nonetheless has significant elements of determinism in it. Small-bore descriptions of this or that aspect of our legal culture have that kind of "organic" quality. One of the most despicable aspects of the culture of judicial corruption that prevailed in Chicago until recently involved the need of judges who had been paid off to find some defendants not guilty to find others guilty (regardless of the evidence) so that the percentage of cases with acquittals did not draw attention.[4] And in the Social Security Disability administrative appeals system, there was an effort some years ago to impose "quotas" on the determinations of the judges to reverse denials of benefits by bureaucrats below them. Of course, that would mean that in some number of cases the determination would not really be "on the merits," but only a means to maintain the equilibrium of the organism set from outside. A similarly "organic" result in that system has recently been achieved simply by delays in adjudications, once the Supreme Court,[5] with an Olympian naïveté, approved a regime in which payments could be discontinued pending final adjudication.

But a deterministic picture of our criminal justice system as an organism whose apparent changes maintain an unchanging equilibrium can be written much more broadly. Why is one out of every hundred Americans incarcerated? Here is the merest outline of one deterministic story, one in which our current approach is the result of vast forces over which we have no conscious control. Our economic system was losing large numbers of industrial jobs just as the "great migration" sent millions from the rural South into the cities. Because of the opposition of southern Democrats at the time of the creation of the major American welfare system, no federal "non-categorical" income support system, such as a negative income tax, had been politically viable. (Southern politicians wanted state control over benefit levels and wanted to avoid "distortions" of the low-wage agricultural labor market.) Only a "dependent child" and his single parent were eligible for benefits, something that created disincentives to the formation of two-parent families. The level of unemployment in inner-city neighborhoods rose as did the number of families where no fathers were present. The approval of the separation of the cities from the suburbs and an important Supreme Court decision[6] meant that the well-to-do could spend their educational tax dollars locally. (In Illinois, affluent suburban districts spend perhaps 35 percent more per pupil than does Chicago.) This produced a large number of unemployable young people to whom the black market in drugs and the excitement of gang activity was appealing. The level of violent crime in our inner-city neighborhoods exploded. Those neighborhoods lost much of the "social capital" that would allow at least some "community-based" social programs that might counter these pressures to prevent, or at least remediate, criminal behavior.

Some social theorists (on the left and the right) tell a still broader story, arguing that the "neoliberal" policies of the last thirty years, the reliance on the self-regulating market in finance, and the general economy undermined the community bonds on which moral commitments depend for their plausibility and transmission. This makes the likelihood of criminal activity—think of cocaine use—relatively great throughout the society, not only in impoverished communities. So, the logic that one can find in our practices over the past thirty years: we have too much crime; its level is increasing; yes, to put it bluntly, poverty of a certain sort makes crime much more likely; our economic system is structured to deliver increasing levels of both inequality and poverty; for ideological and structural reasons, our political system has not taken the steps that would moderate inequality and poverty; for ideological and structural reasons, our political system *can* address the predictable increase in crime that we have experienced through mass imprisonment; therefore mass imprisonment is the most eligible, some might say inevitable, result.

At the very broadest level, important sociological studies of the American criminal justice system find it to be organically linked to more fundamental institutional structures. Loïc Wacquant, for example, argues that neoliberal economic policies are closely intertwined with the rise of the "carceral state." This has occurred not through any grand conspiracy, but, much as Stuntz suggests, but through a "rough *post-hoc functionality*, born of a mix of initial policy intent, sequential bureaucratic adjustment, and political trial-and error and electoral profit-seeking at the point of confluence of three relatively autonomous streams of public measures concerning the low-skill employment market, public aid, and criminal justice."[7] Although the linkages are tight, they are not the result of some "structural hyperdeterminism," but have emerged from past struggles in the political realm and in the bureaucracy. Our neoliberalism, in his view, has four elements, all seeking to "remake the nexus of market, state, and citizenship from above" and broadly administered by an elite of business leaders, politicians, and "cultural-technical experts in their employ (chief among them economists, lawyers, and communications professionals)" (Kafka's nobles!). The first element is economic deregulation, advancing out of the business world, into the provision of "core public goods, on putative grounds of efficiency (implying deliberate disregard for issues of justice and equality)."[8] The second is a retrenchment of the welfare state and the drive to "submit reticent individuals to the disciple of desocialized wage labor via variants of 'work-fare.'" The third operates on the cultural level and involves an elevation of the notion of individual responsibility and the "spread of markets, and legitimation for the widened competition it subtends, the counterpart of which is the evasion of corporate liability and the proclamation of state irresponsibility (or sharply reduced accountability in matters social and economic)."[9] And finally, *an expansive, intrusive, and proactive penal apparatus* which penetrates the nether regions of social and physical space to contain the disorders and disarray generated by diffusing social insecurity and deepening inequality, to unfurl disciplinary supervision over the precarious fractions of the postindustrial proletariat, and to reassert the authority of Leviathan so as to bolster the evaporating legitimacy of elected officials." The result is a "centaur state": "while it embraces laissez-faire at the top, releasing restraints on capital . . . , it is anything but laissez-faire at the bottom. . . . The results of America's grand experiment in creating the first social of advanced insecurity in history are in: *the invasive, expansive, and expensive penal state is not a deviation from neoliberalism but one of its constituent ingredients.*"[10] Wacquant concludes that "the linked stinginess of the welfare wing and the munificence of the penal wing under the guidance of moralism . . . are profoundly injurious to democratic ideals." "In short, the penalization of poverty splinters citizenship along class lines, saps civic trust at the bottom, and sows the degradation of republican tenets. . . . [N]eoliberalism is constitutively corrosive of democracy."[11]

How did these developments become eligible in the political system? Some portion of the "sovereign" people were honestly concerned, afraid, about what was a real increase in violent crime in the second half of the century. (For example, the murder rates between 1950 and 1991 went up 950 percent in Boston, 850 percent in New York, and almost 1,000 percent in Detroit.[12]) They wanted something done and looked to the political system and law enforcement for help. Beyond addressing in a pragmatic fashion a growing problem, some further portion of the population was also possessed by an indignant rage against lawbreaking and an enthusiasm for punishment regardless of costs and benefits. When the murder rate, and the general crime rate, went down in the 1990s (65 percent in Boston, 70 percent in New York, 31 percent in Detroit), levels of imprisonment declined only mildly.[13] Sensing this public mood, "prosecutorial" politicians specifically ran on "get tough on crime" platforms.

The mass media were friendly to politicians who aligned themselves with the victimized public, criminal law was the "go to" solution for a broad range of public issues, and the tsunami of imprisonment began. This was going on against the background of the ascendency of neoliberal political philosophy and a sense that economic developments either were or should be out of conscious "centralized" political control. This part of the story can thus be told as a confluence of economic developments, public moods, and political expediency such that the result seems inevitable.

This result would not have been quite possible were it not for the earlier triumph of plea bargaining. As Stuntz explains, plea bargaining's triumph assured that cities and counties, who paid for police and prosecutors but not prison beds, could quickly and efficiently remove from the community those charged with crimes. The growth in the number of crimes, the more mechanical definition of crimes, "charge stacking," and the vast increase in sentences allow prosecutors to make offers that can't be refused. On a short-term basis, removal from the community behind prison walls was both "punitive" and, if the sentences are really long, effective on a cost-benefit basis, at least if the costs of imprisonment were borne by someone else. Plea bargaining, remember, was the result of economic pressures on the courts and the strategic self-interest of prosecutors and judges. (A whimsical section heading in a law review article was entitled "The Repeal of the Sixth Amendment by the Courthouse Crowd."[14])

We have considered aspects of Kafka's law and seen how they lurk in the background of our criminal law. Kafka's law expresses an aloof sovereignty designed to bring irresistible pressure on the individual. It prefers to operate through plastic rules the application of which the citizen cannot really know ahead of time. It allows intrusions into zones of individual privacy and expands to reach into ever broader regions of ordinary life. The law operates with a casualness about the facts of the individual case, but makes claims to infallibility once it is committed to a course of action. It puts great emphasis on global judgments of character. It operates through bureaucratic methods where officials are fully identified by their role (as Josef K. himself is) and prefers informal methods to the formality of public proceedings. It relies on deception in its dealing with the individual. It merges the legal realm into both the religious and the psychological. It operates as the instrument of unplanned social and political forces and systematically seeks to marginalize the defense counsel whose role really doesn't fully fit into its own self-understanding.

It is surely true that the ultimate source of the force of law is different in the novel and in our regime. In the novel it is an utterly unknowable transcendent source that, as manifested (or distorted) by the officials,[15] brings lethal force to bear on an ultimately compliant Josef K. In our regime, it is the sovereign people and the other agents of sovereignty, "circulating," as Connelly put it, among the court, legislatures, prosecution, and the police. Notice the ideal and fall from the ideal in both the book and in our practices. In the novel, there are hints of a benign radiance emanating from the law and of an (ineffectual) fellow feeling and compassion from the woman who reaches out to K. before his execution. In the generation after the founding, there was great confidence that the judgment of ordinary citizens, allowed to deliberate in town hall meetings and juries, would represent commonsense morality, the common law with which it was identical, and even natural law manifested as "true law" in the individual case.[16] But the dark side of popular sovereignty can be seen recently in the "moodiness" of the mass political will as shaped and channeled by politicians, their advertising agencies, and media giants. The aspects of Kafka's law that we have found in the novel are simply the qualities of any law that seeks solely to be the channel through which the tsunami of sovereign power rushes forward without constraint. Popular sovereignty, the inchoate general will, so to speak, in a mass plebiscitary democracy can generate unconstrained power as well as any monarch who rules by divine right. The important variable is, as we will see at greater length below, the nature of the *process*. The sovereign people can resort to bureaucratic governance or it may proceed democratically, in the full sense that it proceeds through practices, like the practices of the jury trial, which actually realize the practical reason of the people. As we will see, this requires the participation of citizens (whom Josef K. failed to find in his first hearing) who are not bureaucrats. And it requires as well the participation of professionals who are the trustees of normative practices to which they can subordinate their own self-interest and which realize commonsense judgment.

I have largely been speaking of developments in American criminal practices over the past thirty years or so. That is, after all, where we are now. Much of this story describes the system by which popular moods can be brought to bear on the individual through a law that has the characteristics of *The Trial*'s law. But we shouldn't expect that every act of domination, always Kafka's topic, has this sort of pedigree. In earlier eras, state actors enforced the law without the level of bureaucratic pressure from above that prevails today, and still there were abuses. Although not alone in this, state actors can succumb to what Augustine called the lust for domination. Writing well out of our context, political theorist Judith Shklar described cruelty as the "deliberate infliction of physical and, secondarily, emotional pain upon a weaker person or group by stronger ones into order to achieve some end" and "when we think politically, we are afraid not only for ourselves but for our fellow citizens as well."[17] "It is this first principle," she argued, that has always led liberals to be wary of the state, "an assumption, amply justified by every page of political history . . . that some agents of government will behave lawlessly and brutally in small or big ways most of the time unless they are prevented from doing so."[18] The distinctive pleasure of "my boot in your face" will always be with us.

But some of the darkness in the criminal justice system does stem from public attitudes that have been mobilized and then given force by bureaucracy. It is a mobilization more attractive to politicians who cannot keep wages from going down, for example, or jobs from disappearing. At least the state can do *something*. It can punish, so long as it does not promise that punishment does anything more than segregate the convicted. *That* kind of punishment cannot fail in a way that embarrasses the officials, just as a "successful" plea bargain will always net the prosecutor a conviction. The moods of the Leviathan really are like Kafka's court, save that they are (for all we know, because we don't anything about the forces that move Kafka's court) subject to different sorts of forces. Social scientists can only make some guesses as to what those forces are, what causes the Leviathan to twitch his great tail. (Depending on your taste for economic determinism, it may be that the better analogue for Kafka's very highest court is the seat of finance capitalism, Wall Street. It surely operates at a great height removed according to rules that even its most sophisticated players do not understand. Many of its "officials" have turned out to be quite venal. And its doings have effects on ordinary people that are, in their concreteness, both serious, sometimes lethal, and pretty much off the screens of the major players.)

Glimmers of Possibility

The American jury trial is a space of freedom that can realize a democratic practical judgment on matters of criminal law and must remain the "central institution" of the criminal law, even if most cases are resolved through other means. The jury trial provides a path between bureaucratic discretion, on the one hand, and mechanical application of formal law, on the other. These were the only two options that Kafka's world could envision. It is obvious, however, that the jury trial's recovery and flourishing depends on other institutions. Ironically, appellate courts and legislatures will have to prove *themselves* to be spaces of freedom in the creation and fostering of processes that allow the jury trial to realize its potential. And the bureaucracies, police, and prosecutors will have to act in a manner that does not undermine the potential of the criminal trial.

With regard to the legislative action, at a certain point we must fall back on that suggestion always, at least since John Dewey died, offered with slight embarrassment and lowered voices: "public education" in the realities of the criminal justice system. For Dewey, "the democratic way of life is . . . identical with the process of continuing education, experimental valuation, moral growth and liberation" and "to have faith in democracy means, then, to pursue the life of freedom and growth as an individual and to work to accomplish a democratic reconstruction of all institutions."[19] That education would elevate the likelihood for a balanced and moderate judgment in matters of criminal justice:

> The massive decline in criminal punishment that began in the Northeast in 1950s and spread to the rest of the nation in the 1960s and early 1970s was a social catastrophe; it contributed to disastrous levels of urban violence and disorder and made a destructive backlash inevitable. The still more massive increase in criminal punishment that followed was likewise catastrophic, inflicting deep wounds on the neighborhoods where crime and punishment are concentrated. Now the need is for something more than (not less than) another swing of the pendulum. The justice system has seen enough extremism and excess. Justice and moderation, not alternating periods of lenity and severity, must be the system's lodestars now.[20]

It is only an educated public, one invested with the "spirit of magistracy," as Tocqueville put it, that can make such moderate judgments. And it can do that only if politicians present the issues in a less clichéd way (or if the public comes to disregard clichéd presentation of difficult issues). But why should they, if clichés (like negative advertising) "work," and the process for democratic judgment debases, rather than elevates, our common sense? We have some institutions that elevate judgment, but they are fragile. Most proposals for improvement will cost money, and legislators will have to convince their constituents that it is money well spent. That money will have to be spent on the kind of "process values"—more trials and fair trials—that the writers and readers of *The Federalist*—initially published as newspapers articles—understood, but the appreciation of which requires a kind of political sophistication among citizens that is often missing in our media-saturated culture. If we cannot regain that sophistication, we have every reason to believe that our criminal justice system will be the plaything of those distant forces that Kafka parodied and that provide the pessimistic and deterministic account of our current situation that I have given. The winning strategies in the game of electoral politics in the area of criminal justice, given the rules within which that game is played, mean that we simply may not be able get there from here. That's why we may have hope, but not optimism:

> For genuine reform to happen, it is not enough that those who live with crime and punishment demand it. Some of the demand must also come from those who see both crime and punishment at a distance and who decide, at long last, that they don't like what they see. That attentive and altruistic style of voting is not unknown, but it is not the historical norm either, certainly not in this context. Hope seems justified. Optimism, not so much.[21]

Large-bore changes "are far easier to dream about than implement" as they would "collide with entrenched institutional barriers."[22] If large changes reflect a utopian aspiration, given the realities of electoral politics and mass media, then reform will depend to some extent on the twitches of the sovereign Leviathan's tail. Unanticipated events may create unexpected opportunities. The unpredicted (and only partially explained) fall in the crime rate in the 1990s made some benign actions politically feasible: the 1994 law that subsidized police hiring and authorized injunctions against police forces with "a pattern of violating citizens' constitutional rights," George Ryan's moratorium on death sentences, laws banning racial profiling in two dozen states, and some actions in financially strapped states to reduce prison populations.[23] More recently, Eric

Holder, the attorney general of the United States, announced policies that would require local federal prosecutors to charge nonviolent, low-level drug offenders in such a way as to avoid federal mandatory minimum sentences, the effects of which are still uncertain.

> The greatness of the great crime drop of the twentieth century's last decade is yet underdetermined. The drop's size was substantial: a major social achievement, at least in the short run. Its long-term consequences are less clear. If, a couple of decades hence, the crime drop appears only to have reinforced the criminal justice status quo, if American prisons remain overstuffed and American cities underpoliced, it will amount to little more than a missed opportunity. On the other hand, if the crime drop creates the political space in which large-scale reforms can happen, it may be at once the best and most consequential trend in the long and troubled history of American criminal justice. The range of future possibilities is large.[24]

The pessimistic story sketched above is largely about a failure of self-governance. The sovereign people are only a plaything of their own moods; those moods are channeled by the most effectively organized interests to achieve their own purposes, and cannot, except by accident, address our actual problems in a reasonable way. For example, the dispiriting possibility is that the rhetoric that is effective in the only available means of communication favors increasing escalation of ever more punitive policies and renders any more moderate possibilities politically unavailable. I have described such a dynamic leading to many of the features of our system today. The interest-group nature of our liberalism[25] also plays a part: communities dependent upon prisons and prison-guard unions may favor the expansion of the prisons over the expansion of police forces, when the latter is more likely to prevent crime, rather than simply to incarcerate offenders. For example, the "Doris Tate Crime Victims' Bureau" strongly supported California's three-strikes-and-you're-out law:

> That organization, however, was a mouthpiece for prison guards: it received more than three-quarters of its funding from the state prison guards' union. The real interest at work was not concern for victims, but insiders' self interest in generating more jobs for themselves.[26]

Likewise, private prison companies have become increasingly powerful lobbying forces.[27]

The question then is whether our political institutions, designed to fragment power, can address our actual problems, whether they contain "spaces of freedom" such that deliberation and good judgment can sometimes prevail. The Supreme Court's ruling in *Citizens United*,[28] unleashing large amounts of money to support often ideologically driven policies, give little reason for optimism. That money flows largely into the coffers of advertising agencies that know how to both constitute and focus public moods through thirty-second sound bites so as to remove the real freedom that comes from "the discipline of the evidence." It is only the latter that can realize practical judgment, that can, in Kafka's language, render the people worthy of administering the law themselves (or in E. P. Thompson's language, "administering themselves"), not as something mysterious but something that should express their own common sense, disciplined and elevated by consideration of the issues.

Appellate courts can be spaces of freedom as well, though the Court's unleashing of corporate money in state judicial races[29] tends to drag those courts into the deterministic world of political pressure we have been examining in the legislatures, *especially* with regard to criminal law, the area in which populist contests to be ever more "tough on crime" tend to be fought. Appellate courts, and notably the Supreme Court, have qualities of publicity and reasoned decision making that Kafka's remote highest court, whose ways "you don't know and you don't want to know," lack.

Theodore Lowi wrote forty years ago that the Supreme Court functions as the creator of our public philosophy.[30] There are a number of changes within reach of appellate courts, mostly having to do with more robust interpretations of the Fourteenth Amendment (actually more consistent with its original intent) that would address the "underpolicing of violent neighborhoods, along with the consequent underenforcement of violent felonies in those neighborhoods" so that this "would be more than a policy failure," but rather "a constitutional violation, one that governments at all levels would be obliged to remedy." Likewise, claims of discrimination in the exercise of prosecutorial discretion against black defendants could receive a more serious scrutiny. These changes would require a serious, though not at all radical, change in equal protection law.[31] This law has been constricted systematically over the past forty years. Such changes will not happen unless the prevailing philosophy in the federal courts changes. Whether the prevailing philosophy will change is anyone's guess and has more to do with court composition and presidential elections than anything else.

Probably more difficult for the appellate courts would be a rethinking of the deceptive complexity of the law of criminal procedure, the way the actual "law in action" is hidden, as we saw, by the immense superstructure of procedural law. In our terms, the law in action is virtually unknowable, especially if we start from the ordinary public sources in the written law. Because all this complexity has to be considered by counsel in every case, trials tend to be complicated and focused away from the factual and moral truth of an event.[32] (The complexities of the law of evidence contribute to this for the few cases that actually get to trial.[33]) There is little likelihood of starting over here. That would bring what are now issues of criminal procedure to be decided in a binary way in pretrial practice to contextual consideration within trials, where the lack of voluntariness of a confession or admission might provide the jury a "political" reason to reject it or where police practices had rendered the confession unreliable. The problem with the scaling back of the exclusionary rule, of course, is our lack of political will in providing other means of enforcement, by way of serious disciplinary actions against police and prosecutors or civil liability that actually provides a deterrent to the individual and the organization.

The Jury Trial as a Solution to the Antinomies of Modern Law

I want to suggest here that the jury trial, which is of constitutional stature in the United States and deeply intertwined with our political self-understanding, presents a possibility unknown and hardly imagined for Kafka.[34] Our appellate courts, legislatures, and bureaucracies should, in effect, work in different ways to empower the jury. The experience of democratic self-governance in the colonial period and through the Revolution convinced the founding generation of the possibility of self-government, that Kafka's dream of a people who could possess the law could be a reality. Probably nowhere was that experience more concretely realized than in the American jury trial. The jury remained, even after the ratification of the written Constitution, a place where the primordial sovereignty of the people perdured, initially in its authority to decide questions of law and fact. Supreme Court Justice James Wilson expressed a dominant view when he said in 1790 that the jury "should pay much regard" to the court's opinion as what the law is, but in the end if, "a difference of sentiment takes place between the judges and jury, with regard to a point of law, . . . the jury must do their duty, and their whole duty; they must decide the law as well as the fact."[35] As Akhil Amar has pointed out, the unreviewable nature of jury acquittals, the prohibition on directed verdicts against the defendant in criminal cases, the absence of binding special interrogatories in criminal cases, and a number of other doctrines contain an echo of this kind of structured sovereignty that lasts to this day. And when political theorist Paul W. Kahn looked for an example of full sovereignty in the United States today, he found it in the jury:

> The democratic revolutions that displaced Europe's sacral monarchs had the quality of dispersing the claim to sovereign power. That power could now appear anywhere and thus everywhere. What mattered was the exercise of the decision and the community's perception of the sovereign will at that point of decision, where in the streets of Paris or on the common of Lexington. . . . The closest thing we have to the sacral-monarch's power to create the exception to law may not be the executive pardon but jury nullification, which is best seen as a localized expression of the popular sovereign willing the exception.[36]

Discussions of sovereignty, which have become quite common among political theorists today, tend to consider sovereignty as a matter of decision, more particularly of *will*, and to focus on the dramatic either-or situation where a sovereign power "wills the exception." The American self-understanding of democratic and particularly jury power is somewhat different.[37] The legitimacy of the jury stems from its superior ability to discern the morally appropriate decision in the individual case, "true law" as it was sometimes put. As it was put on the floor of the Massachusetts Constitutional Convention of 1853:

> Which is the best tribunal to try [a] case? This man who sits upon the bench, and who . . . has nothing in common with the people; who has hardly seen a common man in twenty years. . . . Is he the better man to try the case than they who have the same stake in community, with their wives, and children, and their fortunes, depending on the integrity of the verdicts they shall render.[38]

The American trial has the power to reveal the practical truth of a human event or situation. The relationship between the jury's judgment and the law of rules is enormously more complex than most discussions of sovereignty imagine. It can converge on a practical truth by an activation or realization of practical intelligence. This occurs through the creation of a set of almost unbearable tensions, most prominently, the tensions between each party's narrative theory of the case expressed in opening statements and the presentation of highly detailed evidence "in the language of perception" that occurs in direct examinations.[39] There are tensions as well between the role of judge and lawyer and of lawyer and witness. It proceeds through the construction and deconstruction of competing narratives, narratives in which are embedded the commonsense judgments of the community. Each direct examination is subject to cross-examination in which an alternative story (employing the witness's own commitments and beliefs) can be proposed, the facts recharacterized or reordered to suggest alternative conclusions, the witness's character revealed, or his credibility attacked through a dozen or so rhetorical commonplaces of witness impeachment. In short, the trial has an "anticonfluential"[40] nature: it multiplies perspectives so that the audience has a many-voiced view of the event, but no one unified view. Each perspective is always in contest. It is the crucible of democracy.

> The jury box is where people come into the court; the judge watches them and the jury watches back. . . . The jury attends in judgment, not only upon the accused, but also upon the justice and humanity of the law. . . . Justice is not a set of rules to be "administered" to a people. Verdicts are not "administered"; they are *found*. And the findings, as matters of "public importance," cannot yet be done by microchip. Men and women must consult their reasons and their consciences, their precedents and their sense of who we are and who we have been.[41]

This is the conception of the trial that Nazi legal theorists, like Kafka's court, thought inconvenient: "Developed by German legal scholars, it was explained by Heinrich Henkel, a professor of criminal law as follows: 'By freeing ourselves from the notion of parties [to a lawsuit], we free ourselves from the liberal notion of a trial as a conflict of aims, an unleashing of a struggle to find the truth, which by its very nature as a conflict between two parties makes finding the truth difficult. We thus become free to set against the liberal system of opposing forces a new order, in which the participants have unanimity of aim.'"[42] The American trial's giving the defendant an equal right to speak effectively in a public forum through his representative reflects a respect for his human dignity that we find nowhere in the vast hydraulics of power in *The Trial*. We now defeat the American trial's potential through our preferred methods of actual criminal enforcement, interrogation and plea bargaining. As we saw, plea bargaining allows the prosecutor to play cards that often amount to offers that cannot be refused. Interrogation's methods can yield confessions that render the trial almost hopeless.

The American jury trial offers a solution to the otherwise unsolvable conflict of the jurisprudence with which Kafka was acquainted. For us, it offers some hope that we are not in quite the iron cage in which he found himself. Central European legal debates, as Kafka knew well, tended to revolve around the contrast between legal positivism and formalism, on the one hand, and "Free Law," on the other. The debate took place, however, against the background of a judiciary that tended to be decidedly upper class and conservative. The judges whom Kafka parodies in *The Trial* are the triers of "fact and law," as we might say. They were also officials. The persistent criticism of positivism and formalism was that its separation of law from morality and its application in a mechanical manner could elevate a mindless and oppressive bureaucracy that had lost sight of the purposes of the law, "rule by nobody." (Kafka's officials seem to operate this way, except that nobody has any idea of what the rules actually are: even the secret law books are just pornographic novels.) The alternative was the "Free Law" approach, which suggested that the *judge* should ignore the literal meaning of the law and apply his own sense of right and wrong to the issues before him. As applied by the authoritarian judges in the Third Reich, "right and wrong" became heavily ideologized and so identified with the program of the Nazi Party in a way that could occur anywhere that ideologically committed officials decided all cases. The languages and practices of the American jury trial actualize a common sense that, in a sense, *prevents* individual jurors and the jury as a whole from acting arbitrarily, deciding the case as a matter of sovereign will without regard to what that common sense, absorbed in the trial's performances, requires.

Hannah Arendt's American Surprise

Hannah Arendt was surprised by her experience of the American jury in a way that illustrates the point I am making about the discontinuity of our institutions with those that Kafka knew and that formed his imagination. Of course, Arendt emphasizes through her writing the importance of the political dimension of "the human condition." In part, this was due to her conclusion that it was the absence of mature political institutions and practices in Europe that led to the "totalitarian catastrophe"[43] that engulfed Europe and that she barely escaped. Her mature view was that such institutions and practices could guard against the worst results of "the onslaught of modernity."[44] For Arendt, the human condition embraces fundamentally different modes of activity. When we engage in labor, we participate in the endless, and often exhausting, rhythms of life-sustaining productivity; when we "work," we create the stable world structures, physical and otherwise, that house and protect us from nature; when we engage in politics, we can enjoy public freedom and engage in action. In political forums, we engage in "the processes of persuasion, negotiation, and compromise, which are the processes of law and politics,"[45] and enjoy the "actual content of political life—the joy and the gratification that arise out of being in the company of our peers, out of acting together and appearing in public, out of inserting ourselves into the world by word and deed."[46] The existence of a political dimension to the human condition allows for an experience of meaningful life. It does not require the achievement of an Archimedean point from which to make judgments. Rather, it recognizes the irreducible plurality of perspectives in the public world, and frames its arguments to the multiple perspectives that exist in the world of commonsense moral judgment.

For much of her career, Arendt was, in effect, a traditional positivist and formalist. She distinguished quite sharply between the processes of law and those of politics. In the main, she placed law largely in the sphere of "work," that is, of creating and maintaining the "stable worldly structure" within which we live and sometimes act. She appreciated the ability of the American founders, alone among modern revolutionaries, to "found a new authority . . . to assure perpetuity, that is, to bestow upon the affairs of men that measure of stability without which they would be unable to build a world for their posterity."[47] She conceded that constitutional texts have to be interpreted, but still believed that they, in conjunction with accepted canons of interpretation, can provide *some* degree of stability: a "house" within which political processes can go forward. It is within this world that political action becomes possible and this stable structure can serve to protect life, liberty, and property from tyrannical government. "Foremost among the stabilizing factors, more enduring than customs, manners, and traditions are the legal systems that regulate our life in the world and our daily affairs with each other."[48] In the context of the criminal law, she emphasizes the limitations of what law should seek to achieve: "Lawfulness sets limitations to actions, but it does not inspire them; the greatness but also the perplexity of law in free societies is that they only tell what one should not, but never what one should do."[49] She notes too that the obsessive concern of the criminal trial with simple factual truth, regardless of the opinions of the participants, celebrates what she calls a nonpolitical value.[50] In decent societies, one can see "the grandeur of court procedure that . . . is concerned with meting out justice to an individual, and remains unconcerned about everything else—with the Zeitgeist or opinions that the defendant may share with others."[51] In short, the constitutional law's concern for institutional stability pays homage to human plurality, and the criminal law's concern for factual truth pays homage to "those things which men cannot change at will, which show that the political sphere, its greatness notwithstanding, is limited—that it does not encompass the whole of man's and the world's existence."[52]

Arendt's concern for stability and for the values of individual justice quite obviously spring from her experience of the legal world of the Third Reich. For Arendt, "[p]ositive laws . . . are primarily designed to function as stabilizing factors for the ever changing movements of men."[53] Under the Reich, in her wonderful phrase, "all laws have become laws of movement."[54] The burning of the Reichstag in 1933 provided the excuse for a declaration of a state of emergency in Germany, but "[w]hat was actually decreed was the loss of all personal rights during the Third Reich. The freedom of the individual, the inviolability of the home from unwarranted search, the privacy of the mails, freedom of speech and assembly, the right to form organizations, and even the right to own property were suspended 'until further notice.'"[55] And in both the ordinary criminal courts and then, to an extreme degree in the informal "People's Courts" that followed, the nature of the trial was fundamentally transformed into a pure instrument of natural necessity, understood ideologically.

Given this background, there can be little surprise about Arendt's concern for law as providing protection for civil rights and a relatively stable structure within which ordinary political processes could go forward. That is why it is so remarkable that her own American jury service convinced her that the jury trial in what trial lawyers call "triable cases"—cases that have some level of uncertainty about them—was in-

deed an appropriate occasion for an understanding of law discontinuous
with her earlier formalism:

> We have the last remnant of active citizen participation in the republic in the
> juries. I was a juror—with great delight and with real enthusiasm. Here again,
> all these questions are somehow *really* debatable. The jury was extremely re-
> sponsible, but also aware that there are *different viewpoints*, from the two
> sides of the court-trial, from which you could look at the issue. This seems to
> me quite clearly a matter of *common public interest*.[56]

Arendt argued that the jury trial provided an example of the kinds of
issues that "really *belong* in a public realm" and "of the very places where
a non-spurious public still exists."[57] It seems to me that what Arendt discovered in the American jury trial was a public forum that did not have
the cancerous ideological character[58] of the "post-positivist" German legal system, an American forum where it was decidedly not true that "all
the laws are laws of motion" whose "consciously structured hybrid of
languages and practices" provided the necessary stability. Legal positivism and formalism turn out not to be the only protections for human decency and human liberty, though they have a place in that enterprise.[59]
That was a judgment that the judges and thinkers of Central Europe did
not have the experience to make. It allows, as Arendt put it in her interpretation of the political dimension of Kafka's work, a law that is an expression of ordinary human judgments and values.

Actually Arendt was doubly surprised at her experience on the jury.
In *On Revolution*, which Justice William Douglas recognized to be a
"classic treatise," Arendt had provided an appreciative account of the
accomplishment of the founding generation in the United States against
the background of Western political thought. She argued that, alone
among modern revolutionaries, the Americans had, in the Constitution,
created a stable foundation for liberty and for the protection of rights.
What they lost, she then concluded, was a place where the political liberty they had known during the Revolution could be exercised directly.
Public participation in political deliberation was the "lost treasure" of
the founding generation. What Arendt discovered in her jury service was
that the treasure had not been lost, but rather continued to reside in the
jury trial.[60] She also implicitly realized that, in the structured world of
the trial, there was greater continuity between the world of law and that

of politics than she had imagined, and that this continuity did not have to have the cancerous nature it had in Central Europe.

And so a higher level of public participation in the administration of the criminal justice system does not necessarily translate into the excesses of "penal populism," best symbolized by "three strikes" laws in California and other states, and which has led some commentators to despair of a criminal justice system consistent with the spirit of American laws.[61] Understandably, these commentators tend to look favorably on European systems deferential to apolitical expert judgment.[62] It seems to me that such systems are likely to be politically unavailable in America and that "participatory institutions that expect citizens to share responsibility for the criminal law is [sic] a better solution for pluralist and state-skeptical countries like the United States."[63] We have already seen the ways in which the American criminal justice system increasingly conforms to the "organizational gothic" patterns of Weberian bureaucracy. We have likewise seen how important decisions about individual cases are increasingly made at a great distance from the individual case, approximating the Kafkaesque "highest court" and the bureaucratic "rule by nobody." Nobody, at least nobody who has taken the time fairly to familiarize himself with the details of the individual case, is responsible for issues of guilt and innocence and, in cases of guilt, for the appropriate sentence. The system increasingly resembles Packer's dystopian picture: "an assembly-line conveyor belt down which moves an endless stream of cases, never stopping, carrying the cases to workers who stand at fixed locations and who perform on each case as comes by the same small but essential operation that brings it one step closer to being a finished product."[64] As Arendt intuited in her jury service, the taut balance between the claim of the "law of rules" and norms that emerge from the jury's lifeworld, between the complex normative claims embedded in relatively unconstrained opening statements and the painful detail of witness examination, and between professional norms and lay participation create a highly constrained force field where a more individualized justice may emerge. And it is a justice for which we may take a democratic responsibility.

For this to occur, more cases have to get to trial, and trials themselves have to be far less bureaucratized. The law of evidence still operates to disfigure the evidentiary base on which the jury decides the case. Or rather, given the open texture of evidence law described above, the law of evidence provides the rationale for a trial judge to disfigure it. A jury that is responsible for the outcome should be permitted, to the extent feasible, to weigh all of the evidence that has any normative weight in the case. And juries should have the same sort of authority over sentencing in the range of cases that they have in capital cases. For this to occur, we have to convey to juries what it means to serve two years or ten years or life in one of our penitentiaries.

A More Democratic Criminal Justice System?

William Stuntz's "short answer" to improving the American criminal justice system is that it must become "more democratic."[65] The increased reliance on the jury is an important part of that, as we will see, but more broadly, it relies upon our legislatures and appellate courts actually being "spaces of freedom" where self-governance can actually occur.

> So the source of the criminal justice system's key problem is also the biggest obstacle to its solution. When and where criminal justice was an exercise in local self-government, the system worked reasonably well: it controlled crime without today's massive prison population or equally massive racial disparities in criminal punishment. The justice system stopped working when a particular kind of local democracy—the kind in which residents of high-crime neighborhoods shape the law enforcement that operates on their streets—ceased to govern the ways police officers, prosecutors, and trial judges do their jobs. A more distant and more detached democracy governs today's system.[66]

That democracy should, in his view, even permeate our bureaucracies, as it has begun to in the rise of "community policing" and even a nascent "community prosecution" movement, where there is a higher level of consultation with the local community with regard to prosecution policies. Stephanos Bibas, himself a former prosecutor, has offered a broad range of specific suggestions to increase the levels of transparency of prosecutorial decision making and to increase the level of public participation in charging and plea-bargaining decisions.[67] He urges that "[i]nstead of seeking perfect rules," the default solution of formalism, "we should give public participation a greater role in guiding and tempering official discretion"[68] and endorses the proposals of other writers:

Scholars have proposed various ways to involve the local community more thoroughly even in cases that are plea bargained. Kevin Washburn suggests using neighborhood grand juries for each zip code, so neighbors play a role in charging decisions. Jason Massone proposes lay plea panels to review the voluntariness and fairness of individual plea bargains. Josh Bowers suggests using lay panels at the charging stage. Laura Appleman, Richard Bierschbach, and I have endorsed plea juries—lay tribunals that would inject community notions of retribution, expression, and fairness into pleas and sentences. Jurors would be drawn from a cross-section of the community, to inject community values and check excessive harshness or leniency in plea bargaining.[69]

Similarly, sentencing in tried cases should not be the exclusive preserve of the judiciary, as they are now outside the death penalty context. Bibas recommends jury determinations on sentencing free of statutory minimum sentences to "restore checks and balances to our system, counterbalancing what had become unilateral prosecutorial power to plea bargain," and so to "restore a measure of sanity and common sense to offset overcriminalization."[70] These jury proceedings would be "free of technicalities and staged largely by the parties and their neighbors":

> The parties could blame, apologize and heal face to face, while their community sat in judgment. What we need are restorative juries at sentencing for at least the most serious crimes, blending the best of restorative justice procedures with the expression and retribution of traditional trials. Victims, wrongdoers, their families, and their friends ought to *see* justice done by doing justice themselves.[71]

That "distant and detached democracy," however, exercised in Congress and in state legislatures, continues to hold real power. As we saw, Stuntz concludes that hope, not optimism, is in order. After all, our legislatures contain the democratically elected representatives of the sovereign people, not a wholly mysterious and aloof source of a law administered by "the nobles." The question, in our terms, is whether our legislatures really can be self-governing outside the context of strict interest-group politics. The question is whether our legislatures can be "attentive" enough not simply to be a forum where opportunistic exploitation of shifting public moods, something that *does* resemble Kafka's dark source of law, takes place. Has our democracy become a vast organism where background interests keep any real change from occurring, or can our legislatures become spaces of freedom? To echo Stuntz's final verdict, it is helpful to recall a favorite saying of Heinrich Blucher, Arendt's husband, "Pessimists are cowards, and optimists are fools."

It is striking that the concrete suggestions that Stuntz and Bibas make for the improvement of the American system involve the removal of the Kafkaesque qualities that it has taken on. At the center of the former's prescriptions is an increase in the importance of the jury trial, in effect making the criminal justice system less bureaucratic, in our terms. The vast increase in jury trials would return plea bargaining to its appropriate role as "as means of settling easy cases" rather than "guilty pleas and the quick bargains that precede them" being "the system's primary means of judging criminal defendants' guilt or innocence. Given the quick-and-dirty character of the bargains, the judging is bound to be done badly."[72] Jury trials' attention to the details of the act being tried[73] would overcome the casualness about the facts of the case that characterized *The Trial* and plea bargaining's bureaucratic methods. Stuntz suggests as well returning to a contained criminal law, addressing a limited range of traditional, morally salient issues, where the jury is the judge not only of the "facts of the case" but also explicitly, in the way in which the crime is defined, of the "wrongfulness" of the act and the appropriateness of punishment for what the defendant has done. This would explicitly legitimize a traditional understanding of the way in which juries do their work, one in which their value judgments affect the very "fact-finding" process itself.[74] In particular, Stuntz recommends that federal and state law no longer cut across subject areas, so that federal law does not metastasize into every area, but rather addresses a limited range of issues for which it can be held accountable.[75] Part of rejuvenating the jury trial and the curtailing of the bureaucracy would involve ending the kind of marginalization of defense counsel parodied by Kafka. Although the case pressure on prosecutors has risen dramatically over the past thirty years, there is every reason to believe that the pressure on public defenders is more extreme still. "If the number of guilty pleas is to fall, as it must in a system that punishes less promiscuously than ours does, the number of lawyers doing the litigating—and the amount of public money spent on criminal litigation—must rise, and substantially."[76] Here optimists really are fools.

Formality and Publicity in the Bureaucracies

As we saw, Kafka's law proceeds through informal methods that are wholly secret. Our legal culture elevates formality and publicity in our understanding of due process and the right to a public trial, and then almost completely undermines those commitments in practice. We have already weighed the melancholy possibility that this eviscerating of our public commitments by the bureaucracy and the market is intrinsic to the maintenance of the "equilibrium" established by the real power sources in our vast social organism.

The hopeful, though not optimistic, possibility is that some of these commitments to publicity and formality (in addition to the commitments to democracy discussed above) may migrate into our police and prosecutorial bureaucracies. After all, in Kafka's world such ideals of formality, publicity, and democracy did not exist *anywhere*. In philosophical language, "Our task is less to create constantly new forms of life than to creatively renew actual forms by taking advantage of their internal multiplicity and their tensions and frictions with one another."[77] In particular, our bureaucracies should understand themselves as the servants of the sovereign people gathered on juries and modify their practices to improve the level of jury deliberations, not circumvent or undermine them.

For example, Richard Leo, Steven Drizen, and others have been working resolutely to increase the level of, first, publicity and, then, almost inevitably, formality in police interrogation by requiring as a matter of state law the taping of the entire interrogation.[78] Leo has argued persuasively that taping serves all the purposes of criminal procedure: fostering truth finding, serving as a check on state power, and protecting the legal rights of the defendant. (It seems unthinkable today, but reformers in the thirties proposed that interrogation should be supervised by an impartial magistrate.) Leo has proposed a series of additional formalities that would lessen the psychological pressure that occasions false confessions, but more broadly, expresses a lack of respect for the person being questioned. A return to our traditional doctrine, one that really could only be enforced if we taped interrogations, would prohibit threats and promises to the suspect. And we could require probable cause, as determined by an "impartial magistrate," as a precondition for interrogation at all, conceding, in effect, that detectives will inevitably want to

win the "game" of interrogation in the interests of the "competitive enterprise of ferreting out crime." More obvious, again only enforceable if
interrogations were taped, would be prohibitions on the pervasiveness
of deception in the interrogation process, especially lying about the existence of physical evidence. And juveniles and persons with intellectual
limitations need additional protection. Finally, cautionary instructions
might be devised to warn jurors that certain sorts of evidence are intrin-
sically unreliable.

Bibas likewise recommends a much higher level of publicity and citizen participation in the business of policing. Following Kahan and
Meares, he suggests that specific police tactics should be adopted "in
consultation with neighborhoods." These meetings may have broader
democratizing effects: "By building social networks of trust, police can
help neighbors help themselves."[79] Further, "citizen advocates, drawn
from a cross-section of the community, could rotate through police departments and prosecutors' offices for a few weeks at a time. They would
review enforcement priorities, indictments, pleas agreements, and sentence recommendations."[80]

Reforms in the criminal justice system will require the efforts of people of good will in many forums, in appellate courts, legislatures, prosecutors' offices, and police departments. "And the diverse pathologies require more than a single national law or Supreme Court decision, or even
a central planned reform agenda. They need diverse grass-roots pressures to reform criminal justice at the levels of counties, cities, neighborhoods, and even individual cases."[81] Opportunities, big and small,
to break through what appear to be organic necessities will continually
present themselves. Whether the deterministic story is true or not, we
must act as if it were not. Even with the best efforts of persons of good
will, failure is often likely, even with the decided advantages that our traditions of publicity, formality, and citizen participation offer. After all,
as Kafka's law practice allowed him to appreciate deeply, "something
has gone wrong with creation"

Seventy years ago, John Dewey and Reinhold Niebhur argued about
the possibilities for true reform that liberal democracy offered in what
the latter emphasized was a sinful world. Niebuhr doubted the likelihood
that education could ever overcome the claims of self-interest in public
institutions. Dewey responded that we had little choice but to rely on education and the "method of intelligence" even if it was, to some extent,
an illusion. Niebuhr insisted in turn that "the problem of sin cannot be

eliminated," but agreed with Dewey that "some wrongs can be righted, some distortions of self-interest can be corrected, and new structures of justice can be created." And he agreed with Dewey on the "wisdom of the American democratic system which maintains a separation of government powers and has criticism built into the system."[82] Kafka, whose vision has been called "Augustinian" in his appreciation for the darkness that inheres in institutions, allows us to see more clearly the features of our law that express pure domination and thereby to grasp what is to be done. There is some reason for hope, if not for optimism. "Reforming a system so broken seems hopeless, but we must keep hope alive."[83]

Notes

Preface

1. This extremely compressed account is taken from Ernst Pawel, *The Nightmare of Reason: A Life of Franz Kafka* (New York: Farrar, Straus, Girouz, 1984), and Max Brod, *Franz Kafka: A Biography*, trans. G. Humphreys Roberts and Richard Winston (New York: Da Capo Press, 1995; German edition originally published in 1937).

Introduction

1. The account is taken from Richard A. Leo, *Police Interrogation and American Justice* (Cambridge: Harvard University Press, 2008), 204–7.

2. People who have never been interrogated probably have little imagination for how taxing lengthy questioning can be.

3. The term "detective" tends to summon up a picture of a slightly built, cerebral gentleman given to deductive reasoning and close observation. I can say from personal experience that such a picture is, shall we say, incomplete.

4. Id., 205–6 (references omitted).

5. If the extant studies are representative, "they indicate that a false confessor whose case goes to trial stands a 73 to 81 percent chance of being convicted, even though there is no reliable evidence corroborating his confession." Id., 250. A dramatic example is provided in a case litigated and finally won by Northwestern's Center on Wrongful Convictions. The defendant, who gave a confession shown to be false by DNA evidence, was convicted *three times* by Lake County, Illinois, juries, as the prosecution devised increasingly implausible scenarios to explain the evidence. It took a decision of the Illinois Appellate Court to end the case. *People v. Rivera*, 962 N.E.2d 53 (2011). The case certainly provides strong evidence for Justice Brennan's observation that "no other class of evidence is so

profoundly prejudicial." *Colorado v. Connelly*, 479 U.S. 157, 182 (1986) (dissenting opinion).

6. Leo, *Police Interrogation and American Justice*, 206–7, citing Steven Drizin and Richard Leo, "The Problem of False Confessions in the post-DNA World," *North Carolina Law Review* 82 (2004), 891–1007 (emphasis added).

7. Leo, *Police Interrogation and American Justice*, 249.

Chapter One

1. Breon Mitchell, "The Life of Franz Kafka," in Franz Kafka, *The Trial*, trans. and with a preface by Breon Mitchell (New York: Schocken Books, 1998), 267, 268. The agency combined features of our Social Security Administration and the Occupational Safety and Health Administration. Kafka was quite effective in his professional roles, a counterweight to understanding him as an otherworldly prisoner in the bureaucracy: "[F]ar from being a nameless cog in a giant machine run amok, he was from the very beginning in decision-making positions and contributed his share toward significant reduction of crippling and fatal accidents in some of Bohemia's major industries." Ernst Pawel, *The Nightmare of Reason: A Life of Franz Kafka* (New York: Farrar, Straus, Girouz, 1984), 189.

2. Kafka, *The Trial*, 6. All additional page references to *The Trial* will be inserted directly into the text.

3. Robert P. Burns, *A Theory of the Trial* (Princeton: Princeton University Press, 1999), 183.

4. I have argued that this parallels our own trials as we conduct them. The truth that emerges at trial cannot, without remainder, be translated into any different language. Id., 235–38. See Michael Pardo, "Commentary: Upsides of the American Trial's 'Anticonfluential' Nature: Notes on Richard K. Sherwin, David Foster Wallace, and James O. Incadenza," in *Imagining Legality: Where Law Meets Popular Culture*, ed. Austin Sarat (Tuscaloosa: University of Alabama Press, 2011), 133–51.

5. James Rolleston, "Introduction: On Interpreting *The Trial*," in *Twentieth Century Interpretations of "The Trial": A Collection of Critical Essays*, ed. James Rolleston (New York: Prentice Hall, 1976), 4.

6. See David Luban, *Legal Modernism* (Ann Arbor: University of Michigan Press, 1997), 201 ("We narrate stories in order to make manifest whatever unsayable meaning resides in them"). The trial as we have it is more than storytelling, however. It is a "consciously structured hybrid" of languages and practices, only some of which are narrative.

7. I have provided an account of *The Trial* in this chapter and a description of major issues surrounding its meaning in the next chapter that presuppose no prior familiarity with the work. It has been said that Kafka's undeniable place as

a great twentieth-century novelist lies with *The Trial*. It is also the most immediately relevant of his longer works to questions surrounding legal procedure. This is not to say that *The Castle*, among his three longer works, and "In the Penal Colony" or "The Judgment," among his shorter, are irrelevant. In order to keep this book balanced between explication, on the one hand, and interpretation and application, on the other, I have chosen to focus on *The Trial*.

8. Mirgan R. Damaska, *The Faces of Justice and State Authority: A Comparative Approach to the Legal Process* (New Haven: Yale University Press, 1986), 51–53.

9. James Rolleston, *Kafka's Narrative Theater* (University Park: Pennsylvania State University Press, 1974), 86–87. In the second chapter, K. literally "reenacts" the interrogation for Fraulein Bursner, his neighbor and erotic interest, referring to the participants as a "cast of characters," though he initially forgets to include himself as a character. He begins the description by saying, "Now the action really begins" (31).

10. Another theme of the book is K.'s lack of an inner life that could resist the anonymous and relentless pressure exerted through the various officials who surround him. In the controversies surrounding the vulnerability of German countries to totalitarian regimes, some commentators stressed the lack of well-grounded moral convictions among modern populations, while others stressed the lack of developed "external" democratic political institutions with deep cultural and historical anchors. For the first, see Alan Donagan, *The Theory of Morality* (Chicago: University of Chicago Press, 1979). For the second, Elisabeth Young-Bruel, *Hannah Arendt: For Love of the World* (New Haven: Yale University Press, 1982). On Kafka as a religious thinker for whom the ethical realm, the realm that recognizes the claim of the other as other is primary, see Beth Hawkins, *Reluctant Theologians: Kafka, Celan, Jabes* (New York: Fordham University Press, 2003). On the link between "thoughtlessness" and immorality, see Hannah Arendt, *The Life of the Mind: One/Thinking* (New York: Harcourt Brace Jovanovich, 1977), 179–93.

11. Heinz Politzer suggests that the grim poignancy of the scene may stem from the knowledge that Kafka and his friends had that they might soon be conscripted by Franz and sent to the kind of death that Josef K. will soon endure. "Franz Kafka's Language," in *Franz Kafka's "The Trial,"* ed. Harold Bloom (New York: Chelsea House, 1987), 35.

12. Again, here begins Josef K.'s inability to exercise spontaneity, to act against the inevitable flow of events.

13. Again, the suggestion is that what is "in the mind" is itself powerful, and is inexorably intertwined with public institutions, a suggestion that is picked up by the book's great final parable, "Before the Law."

14. See the short piece "The Problem of Our Laws," discussed in chapter 2, below. In Arthur Koestler, *Darkness at Noon* (New York: Scribners, 2006), a his-

torically important novel describing the Stalin show trials, the protagonist is persuaded that his own ideological commitments logically entail his own execution, which should be passively accepted in the interests of the revolution.

15. So K.'s "fool fear" is exploited to keep him in line. In the parable "Before the Law," which forms the penultimate chapter of *The Trial* and which I discuss below, the protagonist, with whom K. naturally identifies, chooses not to confront a guard who orders him not to enter the door, though the door, we learn, was meant only for him.

16. Hannah Arendt, "Franz Kafka: A Revaluation," in Hannah Arendt, *Essays in Understanding, 1930–1954* (New York: Harcourt Brace & Company, 1994), 69–80.

17. Young-Bruel, *Hannah Arendt*, 76.

18. There are wonderful interrogation scenes, again both grim and funny, throughout Kafka's works, no doubt the product of his own experience in an "inquisitorial" legal system. They manifest the deep unfairness of a forum in which the person who controls the procedure and determines the questions to be asked is intent on establishing his own predetermination of guilt and the impossibility of the victim of this kind of questioning showing the other side of the issue. See *Amerika: The Missing Person*, trans. Mark Harman (New York: Schocken Books, 2008), 3–35, 162–71. Malcolm Waner argues that this latter scene, in its procedural unfairness, could be an illuminating case study in industrial relations. "Kafka, Weber, and Organizational Theory," *Human Relations* 60, no. 7 (2007). As a practicing lawyer, I have seen this happen, and, as a dispirited defense lawyer (now a judge!) once told me about the ability of a deeply unfair judge to twist the proceedings, "You have to have been there to understand." For a description of the unfair browbeating of effectively unrepresented capital defendants by English judges, see John H. Langbein, *The Origins of the Adversary Criminal Trial* (Oxford: Oxford University Press, 2003), 271–72. Simone Weil describes the evil of this abuse of power: "[T]hose who most often have occasion to feel that evil is being done to them are those who are least trained in the art of speech. Nothing, for example, is more frightful than to see some poor wretch in the police court stammering before a magistrate who keeps up an elegant flow of witticisms." Simone Weil, "Human Personality," quoted in James Boyd White, *Living Speech: Resisting the Empire of Force* (Princeton: Princeton University Press, 2006), 224–25. For the American experience, see Leo, *Police Interrogation and American Justice*, discussed in chapter 3, below.

19. Ziolkowski suggests that exchange parodies a feature of Austro-Hungarian procedure, where the prosecutor becomes involved only after the largely secret investigation of the examining magistrate is over. Theodore Ziolkowski, *The Mirror of Justice: Literary Reflections of Legal Crises* (Princeton: Princeton University Press, 1997), 226.

20. "Wooden, arm-slinging Rabensteiner, block Kullich with his deep-set eyes, and Kaminer, with his annoying smile, produced by a chronic muscular twitch" (18). In the next chapter, K. calls them into his office at the bank just to observe them, just as the inspector had done to him (21). K. claims that he would have been able to handle the appearance of the guards if they had appeared at his bank, where he was fully in his public role, not in his vulnerable personal isolation (23). (We will see later that isolating the suspect is a key step in the dominant form of American interrogation.) K. later complains that they had been obviously brought along to spread the news of his arrest and undermine his position at the bank (48). And so another leitmotif is sounded in this prologue: the different spheres of life, here business and personal life, cannot be kept distinct. In a foreshadowing of totalitarian regimes, the law compresses all such distinctions for its own purposes and invades every sphere of life.

21. In the humanities and in certain understandings of the law school "Socratic method," this pattern of questions is thought to yield a kind of enlightenment: something important becomes manifest, though it cannot be reduced to a set of assertions. This is true, I think, for Kafka's reader, though not often for his protagonists.

22. *Omnis homo mendax est* (Every man is a liar), St. Augustine tells us. Or in famous contemporary terms, "the odor of mendacity" is almost everywhere.

23. In the next chapter, K. meets his building caretaker's son standing in front of their building and addresses him with a note of forgiveness "as if the fellow had done something truly wrong, but he was willing to forgive him," though he had, in fact, done nothing wrong. So K. himself exploits the human inclination to assume one's own guilt. K. apologizes to the typist whose room the inspector used, claiming that "in a sense it was my fault, [although] it was done by strangers and against my will" (28). There follows this bizarre exchange with the typist that in some ways parallels that with the inspector:

> "[T]here was a commission of inquiry here," K. added, since the young woman was staring at him with a questioning look. "Because of you?" the young woman asked. "Yes," K. replied. "No," the young woman cried with a laugh. "Oh yes," said K. "Do you think I am guiltless, then?" "Well, guiltless . . . ," said the young woman, "I don't want to make a hasty judgment. . . . [A]nd I don't really know you." (29)

24. Frau Grubach, K.'s landlady, contrasts his arrest to that of a thief, "[T]his arrest: it seems like something scholarly. I'm sorry if that sounds stupid, but it seems likes something scholarly that I don't understand, but that I don't need to understand either" (23).

25. Later in the novel, Titorelli, the artist, and a priest give faint glimmers of hope (which come to nothing) of breaking out of the process.

26. Again, as biological beings, death is our universal fate. To anticipate, the novel describes a bureaucracy that is identifying both with the inevitable demands of nature and also, as we will see, the prerogatives of the God of Nature.

27. *Losung,* "solution," has the same root as our "dissolution."

28. Sundays were chosen, K. is told, so as not to disrupt his "professional life." Official business is thus intruding into a traditional "day of rest." On the merging of everything into the law, see the discussion in chapter 2, below. Of course Sunday morning is also the traditional time of Christian religious observance. On the merging of law and religion, see chapter 2, below.

29. In another dreamlike episode, on the way to court, K. spots all three of the bank clerks who were present at the initial interrogation (37). In "The Public Prosecutor," described below, we are told that the law decides which of its proceedings will be public and which will be secret.

30. Another leitmotif is sounded: bureaucracies may act like nightmares, beyond control by anyone's conscious mind.

31. Jury trials were known in Austrian practice, but were abolished in the late nineteenth century.

32. Yet another theme is set: the law is relatively indifferent to factual matters and is more interested in the entirety of K.'s character, as it is seen from its own (unknowable) perspective.

33. The washerwoman informs K. later that he was not disadvantaged by the hubbub that may have provided a distraction from a speech that led to his being "judged quite unfavorably later" (55).

34. She also informs K. later that these encounters are the price she and her husband, an usher at the court, have to pay in order for him to keep his job (56). This world of power expresses itself, in different ways, sexually. It's another aspect of the corruption that surrounds the process.

35. Burns, *A Theory of the Trial,* 168 n. 61.

36. It turns out that the assembly hall is actually the apartment of a court usher and his wife, who have to move their furniture out when there is court. She tells K. of an episode in which, after she and her husband had gone to sleep, the magistrate, who had been studiously writing reports until late at night, appeared at her bedside to make mildly suggestive remarks (60).

37. Hannah Arendt, "Truth and Politics," in Hannah Arendt, *Between Past and Future: Eight Exercises in Political Thought* (New York: Penguin Books, 1977), 259–64.

38. See Kafka's short essay, "The Problem of Our Laws," discussed in chapter 2, below. The unknowability of the law is one of the major themes in *The Trial.*

39. On the value of publicity of a legal order, see John Rawls, *A Theory of Justice* (Cambridge: Harvard University Press, 1971) 54–60.

40. The interpenetration, so to speak, of the law with human sexuality is another theme of the novel. At a fundamental level Kafka is toying with the Nietz-

schean idea that the world of power simply is life, vitality. At another level, he suggests that political power will "use" sexuality to keep the ruled within its grip. When K. lingers in the law's offices, the "severe" young woman tells him he has to leave because he will interfere with the "intercourse" within the law's offices. The German word (*Verkehr*), like the English, can mean either sexual intercourse or simply "business" or "traffic."

41. See Robert M. Cover, *Justice Accused: Antislavery and the Judicial Process* (New Haven: Yale University Press, 1984), for the rhetorical subterfuges used by American judges who considered slavery immoral, but still enforced fugitive slaves laws. See also Steven Lubet, *Fugitive Justice: Runaways, Rescuers, and Slavery on Trial* (Cambridge: Harvard University Press, 2010), for an account of the tensions at the trial level in enforcing those laws. On bureaucracy as "rule by nobody," that is, by no responsible individual, see chapter 2, below.

42. Charles Taylor argues that one of the distinctive features of the modernism that Kafka represents and of the modern temper is a reverence, often religious, for ordinary life. *Sources of the Self: The Making of the Modern Identity* (Cambridge: Harvard University Press, 1992).

43. The flogger caustically dismisses that claim, claiming that the guard, who eats the breakfast of *everyone* he arrests, is much too fat to be a flogger. The values and aspirations of the officials have become distorted by the incentives for rising in the system. See *Eichmann in Jerusalem: Notes on the Banality of Evil* (New York: Viking Press, 1962). Alfred Weber, Max Weber's brother and, ironically, Kafka's examining professor for his doctorate in law, "describes the tragic cost of the bureaucrat's obsession with security and social prestige in terms of spiritual paralysis":

> One seeks with every possible means to bind [the bureaucrats] to their positions and to the apparatus, so that they are incorporated into it. One offers them security and a comfortable existence instead of the restlessly uncertain struggle in the stream of life: in return, one demands a lifelong attachment to the apparatus, demands "obedience." One offers them the possibility of advancing from position to position within the apparatus, the prospects of a "career" and of future power; as compensation one demands the strength of all their labor. One offers them "prestige" and social status, nice titles for the state and the community; in return, not only is the strength of their labor demanded but also their humanity, their "souls."

Richard Heinemann, "Kafka's Oath of Service: 'Der Bau' and the Dialectic of the Bureaucratic Mind," *Proceedings of the Modern Language Association* 111, no. 2 (1996), 256–70, 258, quoting Alfred Weber, "Der Beamte," in *Die neue Rundschau* 4 (1910), 1321–39, 1327. Weber's essay was "almost certainly known to Kafka." Heinemann, "Kafka's Oath of Service," 269 n. 5.

44. Several critics have noted that the action in *The Trial* does not actually progress, as a drama typically does. Each scene is a kind of reenactment without

resolution of exactly the same enigmatic situation, as in a dream, or in eternity, until, of course, K.'s death, which itself can't be said to *resolve* the conflicts previously enacted.

45. K. later reflects, "I recruit women helpers, he thought, almost amazed: first Fraulein Burnstner, then the court usher's wife, and now this little nurse, who seems to have an inexplicable desire for me." Once again, near the end of the novel, a priest advises K. that he is too ready to accept help, especially from women, who really can't help.

46. The lawyer later explains to K. that Leni is so "forward" because she finds "most defendants attractive. She's drawn to all of them, loves all of them, and of course appears to be loved; she occasionally amuses me with stories about it, when I let her" (184). Huld explains that all defendants, innocent or guilty, are, in fact, more attractive because "of the proceedings being brought against them, which somehow adheres to them" (185).

47. This sounds shocking to our sensibilities. It turns out that, through the early nineteenth century, criminal defendants in England were forbidden to have copies of the indictments, though their contents were often orally translated from the Latin to them at their arraignments. John H. Langbein, *The Origins of the Adversary Criminal Trial* (Oxford: Oxford University Press, 2005) 27 n. 88, 51 n. 198.

48. Defense counsel are not permitted to accompany witnesses before our grand juries. Attorneys sit outside the grand jury rooms and try to "surmise" what has gone on within based on what their clients tell them. Sometimes they can offer some advice based on their guesses as to the significance of what has happened within.

49. For a contemporary fictional depiction of this kind of judicial culture, based on the author's own experiences as a prosecutor of judicial corruption in Chicago, see Scott Turow, *Personal Injuries* (New York: Farrar, Straus, & Giroux, 1999).

50. Hubert L. Dreyfus, *Being-in-the-World: A Commentary on Heidegger's "Being and Time"* (Cambridge: MIT Press, 1990).

51. In my own legal education, a recurring professorial suggestion was that any progressive change in the law was futile because the dominant party could simply insist on "contracting around" the change (insisting on the waiver of the right by the weaker party). The implicit message was that the market served as this sort of unchangeable organism. Practicing lawyers in Chicago have sometimes referred to the "rule of cool." One should never appear too enthusiastic for a result that seems too far from the way things usually go. That only undermines one's credibility and demonstrates lack of appreciation of the powerful background commitments of the system.

52. In *Amerika*, the protagonist's uncle, an immigrant from Austria-Hungary and a successful businessman in New York, embodies the economic rationality,

without much qualification by fellow feeling even within the family. This rationality protects him from "irrational" forces within and without. He has achieved what philosophers sometimes call negative freedom, freedom from external, in this case personal, constraints. Josef K.'s tragedy is in part that he cannot completely become *Homo economicus*, but remains in part *Homo religiosus*. The question that Kafka, of course, leaves unanswered, at least explicitly, is whether it is desirable to live the life of *Homo economicus*, even if it were possible (for some).

53. K. walks out on three potential clients who have been waiting hours for him with this off-putting suggestion:

> Pardon me, gentlemen, but unfortunately I have no time to receive you now. I do beg your pardon, but I have an urgent business errand to attend to and have to leave immediately. You see how long I've been tied up. Would you be so kind as to come again tomorrow, or some other time? Or could we possibly handle the matter by phone? Or could you tell me briefly [K. had already put his winter coat on!] now what it is you wanted . . .

K. concludes that his conduct was causing his career "irreparable damage" (139).

54. Not only does he use a pseudonym, but he has a propensity to lie (135). Kafka uses the same assertion and retraction style for the dialogue between K. and his client about Titorelli. K. suggests that Titorelli visit him at the bank, but his client points out that would probably be a bad idea, causing K. to question his own judgment concerning his trial.

55. The Titorelli scene is also a meditation on the meaning of art in the modern world. Titorelli tells K. that he has painted scenes from "myths," perhaps scriptural, that represent a kind of ultimate truth, though no one has actual experience of such "truth." Here art, like religion, expresses Hegel's "absolute point of view" in a graphic medium. Unfortunately, this function of art cannot help a defendant actually survive and may actually get in the way of survival. Walter H. Sokel, "The Three Endings of Joseph. K. and the Role of Art in *The Trial*," in *Franz Kafka's "The Trial*,*"* 84. But "art," in the flattering and false pictures of judges that he paints, also serves the interests of the power structure. Consider Leni Riefenstahl's brilliant film *The Triumph of the Will*, which glorified the nascent Nazi regime, or D. W. Griffith's *The Birth of a Nation*, which painted an effective and sympathetic picture of the Ku Klux Klan. And, in another form of decline, through the kitschy and repetitious landscapes Titorell pressures K. to buy, art can sell out to the demands of success in the mass marketplace.

56. Titorelli laments, in a sentiment that may be a wistful reflection on Kafka's own experience, that all of his contacts with the "gentlemen of the court" have caused him to "lose a good deal of artistic energy" (151).

57. At one level, there is some allusion here to the beautiful promises of salvation contained in the ancient scriptures. These legends may not be cited in court,

are not real precedent (154). Yet there seems to be something wrong with K.'s "realist" conclusion that "it's useless to talk about them then." At a more ominous level, these "beautiful" myths allow the law to claim an absolute justice, such that its actual determinations of guilt (and never innocence) are true absolutely. See chapter 4, below.

58. Hawkins argues that Kafka is closer to Augustine than to the heart of the Jewish tradition in that he views sin as an existential condition that precedes individual action. Hawkins, *Reluctant Theologians*, 25.

59. Sokel, "The Three Endings of Joseph. K.," 86.

60. Id., 83.

61. Id.

62. Id., 84–85.

63. Id., 85–86.

64. The German root, *Winkel*, connotes "angle." A "shyster" is not straight with people, and plays the angles. The merchant tells K. that court usage distinguishes among "great lawyers," "petty lawyers," and shysters, but the great lawyers are also inaccessible (179). Huld claims to be one of them, but Block dismisses that claim. Only the shysters promise immediate results (180).

65. Arendt emphasizes the ways in which totalitarian regimes operate in secrecy to isolate people and so to prevent any common or political action. See chapter 2, below.

66. K. is surprised that Block both acts in such a servile manner toward Huld and still has the gumption to lie to Huld about his having other lawyers.

67. It turns out that Block had been locked in the maid's room all day, pouring over documents given him by the lawyer, not so that he would understand them, but only to impress upon Block the "difficulty" of Huld's task.

68. Huld concedes that Block may have something to be anxious about, for, as we have seen, "in some cases the final judgment comes unexpectedly from some chance person at some random moment" (197).

69. K. is trapped in part because he knew a little Italian and had some knowledge of art history, which "had become known at the bank and blown far out of proportion because for a time, and solely for business reasons as it happened, K. had belonged to the Society for the Preservation of Municipal Works of Art." When the Italian client arrives and begins to speak in his native language, K. realizes that he cannot follow the conversation that occurs between the client and the bank's president. And so K.'s career-driven pretenses place him in the relentless tide moving him to perdition (199–202).

70. The priest dismisses K.'s description of his planned rendezvous with the Italian as an "irrelevancy." There is, it seems, a deeper necessity operating here through what appear to be contingencies. It goes without saying that deception is systematically deployed against the defendant.

71. On the standard ploy in American criminal interrogation always to assume the guilt of the suspect, see chapter 3.

72. It seems implied that such texts have been available to commentators for some time and have spawned the contradictory interpretations that the priest describes. In other writings, Kafka describes the law as utterly unknowable. See chapter 2, below.

73. The parable was separately published before being integrated into *The Trial*. Kafka said initially that he did not himself understand the parable when he wrote it, but that the meaning of the parable came to him somewhat later. Similarly, the stand-alone story "The Stoker" became the first scene in *Amerika*. It has often been observed that the "chapters" in Kafka's novel are really a sequence of parables, which repeat the same dynamic in different contexts.

74. Harold Bloom, "Introduction," in *Franz Kafka's "The Trial,"* 20.

75. "Enter through the narrow gate, for the gate is wide and the path broad that leads to destruction and there are many who enter through it." Matthew 7:13.

76. "[T]he hermeneutic debate between K. and the prison chaplain itself suggests that indeterminacy is one central characteristic of sacredness, which this parable places at the heart of the Law's power—an example of the sacred's 'inexhaustible morphology.'" Martha Merrill Umphrey, Austin Sarat, and Lawrence Douglas, "The Sacred in Law: An Introduction," in *Law and the Sacred*, ed. Austin Sarat, Lawrence Douglas, and Martha Merrill Umphrey (Stanford: Stanford University Press, 2007).

77. The Augustian-Lutheran view that there exists a yawning gulf between the City of God and the City of Man can often counsel an acceptance of the public status quo.

78. On the varied ways in which false necessity is deployed as an anodyne against change, see chapter 4, below.

79. Arendt argued that modern totalitarianism eliminates the distance between men in a way that surpassed even traditional tyrannies:

> By pressing men against each other, total terror destroys the space between them; compared to the condition within its iron band, even the desert of tyranny, insofar as it is still some sort of space, appears like a guarantee of freedom. Totalitarian government does not just curtail liberties or abolish essential freedoms; nor does it, at least to our limited knowledge, succeed in eradicating the love for freedom from the hearts of man. It destroys the one essential prerequisite of all freedom which is simply the capacity for motion which cannot exist without space.

Hannah Arendt, *The Origins of Totalitarianism* (New York: Harcourt Brace Jovanovich, 1973), 466.

Chapter Two

1. J. P. Stern, "The Law of the Trial," in *On Kafka: Semi-Centenary Perspectives*, ed. Franz Kuna (New York: Harper & Row, 1976), 22–41. Of course, the importance of a "political reading" does not exclude and, in fact, deepens other readings as well.

2. Id., 24.

3. Sokel, "The Three Endings of Joseph K.," 88.

4. Arendt, "Franz Kafka: A Revaluation."

5. Waner, "Kafka, Weber, and Organizational Theory."

6. Stern, "The Law of the Trial," 38. See chapter 1, note 10, above. In the words of the poet, "the center cannot hold," while "the best lack all conviction, and the worst are filled with passionate intensity." W. B. Yeats, "The Second Coming." The upper-middle-class defendants whom we meet in the offices of the law are bowed over. "As a class they have evolved their own social rules, their own superstitions. They comfort and torment themselves with the formula that waiting is not a waste of time, whereas any form of 'independent action' most certainly is." Martin Walser, "On Kafka's Novels," in *Franz Kafka's "The Trial,"* 115, 121.

7. Walser, "On Kafka's Novels," 127.

8. Id., 119.

9. Id., 121.

10. Stuart Hampshire, *Justice Is Conflict* (Princeton: Princeton University Press, 2000).

11. Id., 123.

12. Id.

13. Id., 124–25.

14. Theodore Ziolkowski, *The Mirror of Justice: Literary Reflection of Legal Crisis* (Princeton: Princeton University Press, 1997), 239 (emphasis added).

15. David I. Grossvogel, "The Trial: Structure as Mystery," in *Franz Kafka's "The Trial,"* 107. As Arendt intimates, the novel is filled with exaggeration and parodies of the actual procedures of Austrian justice. For example, the entire process of criminal investigation and evidence gathering by the Austrian examining magistrate was secret until he decided to file his charge, when more formal procedures took hold. Kafka exaggerates this structure, by eliminating *all* legitimate public and formal processes, assimilating all process to the "pre-trial" stage. Ziolkowski, *Mirror of Justice*, 226. I will only note here what I will explore at much greater length below: that in more than 95 percent of American criminal cases, there is only pretrial procedure and no formal trial at all.

16. Ziolkowski, *Mirror of Justice*, 215, 217.

17. Id., 215.

18. We will see that forms of abusive police interrogation, combined with the high credibility given by judges and juries to confessions, can have precisely this same effect today.

19. Stern, "The Law of the Trial," 30. Stern writes that the question, "'Why do you think we would summon anybody unless they have committed some crime?' is not a quotation from *The Trial*, but the remark of a Gestapo official to a Gentile husband who wants to know what his Jewish wife has done that she should be deported to her death." Id., 29. I recall a state prosecutor asking me about a client, "Do you think we have nothing better to do that to prosecute the innocent?" Because he was an American prosecutor, I like to think that he said it with an ironic self-aware smile.

20. Ziolkowski, *Mirror of Justice*, 239.

21. Arendt, "Franz Kafka: A Revaluation," 80.

22. Id., 4.

23. Hawkins, *Reluctant Theologians*, xxix.

24. Arendt, "Franz Kafka: A Revaluation," 70–71.

25. Id., 71.

26. Id., 70.

27. A. E. Dyson, "Trial by Enigma," in *Franz Kafka's "The Trial,"* 61.

28. Id., 69.

29. Robin West, "Authority, Autonomy, and Choice: The Role of Consent in the Moral and Political Visions of Franz Kafka and Richard Posner," *Harvard Law Review* 99 (1985), 384, 387.

30. Id., 390.

31. Sokel, "The Three Endings of Joseph K.," 93.

32. Heinemann, "Kafka's Oath of Service."

33. As Heschel put it, awe can lead to faith and wisdom, and without awe, "the universe becomes a marketplace," as it has for the Uncle Jacob in *Amerika*. Hawkins, *Reluctant Theologians*, 29. But, sadly, those same "religious" sensibilities can lead to K.'s end in *The Trial*. By contrast, Job's sufferings, however absurd, are fruitful in that they "sustain a dialogue with a transcendent party" (id., 12) who does not accuse Job of wrongdoing. It is "the satan" who is "the accuser," the meaning of the Hebrew word. Gustavo Gutierrez, *On Job: God-Talk and the Suffering of the Innocent*, trans. Matthew J. O'Connell (Maryknoll: Orbis Books, 1987).

34. Sokel, "The Three Endings of Joseph K.," 265.

35. *Sources of the Self: The Making of the Modern Identity*, 506. Other modernist authors include T. S. Eliot, Rainer Maria Rilke, and James Joyce. Only Eliot in this group could be described as conventionally religious.

36. Iris Murdoch writes that the heart of the Christian message is, "Be ye perfect!" (Her Platonism may have something to do with her choice of this particular injunction.) *The Sovereignty of Good* (London: Routledge, 2001).

37. Wayne C. Booth, "Deconstruction as a Religious Revival," in *Christianity and Culture in the Crossfire*, ed. David A. Hoekema and Bobby Fong. On Kafka's "gnosticism," a vision of a sharp discontinuity between the ideal and the fallen world, see Bloom, "Introduction," in *Franz Kafka's "The Trial,"* 1.

38. It will turn out that K. errs in both the guilt he feels and the guilt he fails to feel, a function of the confusion of the religious and legal realms that is at the heart of the novel, and which Kafka sees in his own legal order.

39. Booth, "Deconstruction as a Religious Revival," 144.

40. Id. Booth points out that traditional religious perspectives, such as those T. S. Eliot embraced, accept that God may intervene to heal this brokenness and that our efforts must in some way be in harmony with his will. It is very hard to find any hope for this in Kafka. His conversation with his friend Brod is often quoted: to Kafka's remark, "We are nihilist thoughts that came into God's head," Brod "explained to Kafka the gnostic notion that the Demiurge had made his work both sinful and evil. 'No,' Kafka replies, 'I believe we are not such a radical relapse of God's, only one of His bad moods. He had a bad day.' Playing straight man, the faithful Brod asked if there was hope outside our cosmos, Kafka smiled, and charmingly said: 'Plenty of hope—for God—no end of hope— only not for us.'" Bloom, "Introduction," in *Franz Kafka's "The Trial,"* 1. Booth also describes an aspect of Derrida's religious sensibility that bears an analogy to Kafka's, the conviction that "we live in a world of perpetual elusiveness; every statement about it can be shown, as earlier negative theologians insisted, to be disappointingly inadequate; we never get to the essence," id., 147, a conviction reflected in Kafka's choice of the parable form. Kafka writes cryptically, "A veering round. Peering, timid, hopeful, the answer prowls round the question, desperately looking into its impenetrable face . . ." "That he tells us, 'We have *not yet* eaten of the Tree of Life, provides hope as it emphasizes the fact that the task that may provide the means for redemption is, nevertheless, an unfinished task." Hawkins, *Reluctant Theologians*, xxiii, 28.

41. Dyson, "Trial by Enigma" 57, 72.

42. Id. This perspective is consistent with the perspective of one of Kafka's great inspirations, Dostoyevsky. See *Sources of the Self*, 451. To accept the guilt assigned by the state is, however, quite a different thing.

43. Erich Heller, "Man Guilty," in *Twentieth Century Interpretations of "The Trial,"* 94, 97.

44. Bloom, "Introduction," in *Franz Kafka's "The Trial,"* 20.

45. Politzer, "Franz Kafka's Language," 33, 39.

46. Id.

47. R. G. Collins, "Kafka's Special Methods of Thinking," in *Franz Kafka's "The Trial,"* 41, 56.

48. Dyson, "Trial by Enigma," 63. One of my best teachers mentioned casually one day that only the very greatest philosophers "don't leave much out."

49. Id., 63, 66.

50. Hawkins, *Reluctant Theologians*, 58.

51. Id., 58, 57 (quoting Kafka's Notebooks, 39).

52. Grossvogel, "*The Trial*: Structure as Mystery," 95, 104.

53. Id.

54. Politzer, "Franz Kafka's Language," 36.

55. Bernard J. F. Longergan, *Insight: A Study of Human Understanding* (New York: Philosophical Library, 1957), 385–87.

56. Camus, who emphasizes the religious and existential aspects of the book, recognizes its relevance, as well, to legal and political matters. Albert Camus, *The Myth of Sisyphus and Other Essays*, trans. Justin O'Brien (New York: Vintage Books, 1955) , 127 n. 1.

57. Joyce Carol Oates, "Kafka as Storyteller," in *Franz Kafka: The Complete Stories and Parables* (New York: Quality Paperbacks, 1983), quoted in West, "Authority, Autonomy, and Choice." Oates's "feelingly" recalls Taylor's notion of "subjective resonance."

58. Politzer, "Franz Kafka's Language," 52.

59. Id. I argued in *A Theory of the Trial* that this is true for the meaning that emerges from adversary presentation in the American trial: that meaning cannot be simply restated in any other language than the "consciously structured hybrid of languages" in the trial itself. One critic finds a source for Kafka's commitment to a multiplicity of conflicting perspectives to his legal training, where a range of plausible interpretations of legal texts was often possible and there was "error . . . in . . . immediately passing judgment on anything." Collins, "Kafka's Special Methods of Thinking," 41, 46. At a higher level of reflexivity, the grim ending of the novel serves as an internal critique of art's mythologizing tendencies.

60. Franz Kafka, *Parables and Paradoxes* (New York: Schocken Books, 1958), 155.

61. Id.

62. Id.

63. Id., 155, 157.

64. Id., 157.

65. Id.

66. Id., 159.

67. Id.

68. Thomas Green, *Verdict according to Conscience: Perspectives on the English Criminal Trial Jury, 1200–1800* (Chicago: University of Chicago Press, 1985).

69. Ingeborg Henel, "The Legend of the Doorkeeper and Its Significance for Kafka's Trial," in *Twentieth Century Interpretations of "The Trial,"* 40, 44.

70. Germany abolished the jury in 1924, as Austria had some decades before.

71. Arendt, "Franz Kafka: A Reevaluation," 70.

72. Id., 71.

73. Id., 73.

74. Id, 75.

75. Sheldon Wolin, *Politics and Vision* (London: G. Allen and Unwin, 1961) , 354, quoted in Waner, "Kafka, Weber, and Organizational Theory," 1019, 1028.

76. Id., 1033.

77. Id., 1032.

78. Id., 1027. This focus recurs in many of Kafka's other works as well. We find it in *The Metamorphosis* "in Gregor Samsa's office, where the 'head clerk' and 'the boss' exert their wills in the social space of the workplace. The latter 'sits on top of his desk and from a great height addresses his employees, who must step up very close because of the boss's deafness. . . . In 'The Stoker (the first chapter of what was later published as *Amerika*) he befriends this fellow, the unnamed one, who is abused by his boss. He witnesses 'the sufferings of the underdog at the hand of the powerful' and tries to speak up for him. As the talk continues, he reveals the hustle and bustle of the capitalist marketplace, the 'Tayloristic' working conditions in a prototype of a 'call-centre,' as well as a striker's demonstration and so on. . . . In chapter 5, where Karl becomes a lift boy, there is a very strong almost Dickensian empathy with the workers in the Hotel Occidental, vis-à-vis the harsh work discipline there; when he encounters a lift boy asleep on his feet, he retorts that a 'ten or twelve hour day is just a bit much for a boy like that.' The protagonist himself is later unjustly 'sacked.' K. vividly depicts Karl's rebuff in this 'materialistic Eden.' The 'dismissal' sequence reads like an industrial relations case study." Id., 1025–26.

79. Id., 1029.

80. Stern, "The Law of the Trial," 41.

81. The woman tells K. that he has to leave the offices because his presence would interfere with the "intercourse" that is going on there. The German word, again, has the same double meaning as does the English word.

82. Sokel, "The Three Endings of Josef K.," 75.

83. Franz Kafka, *Dearest Father: Stories and Other Writings*, trans. Ernst Kaiser and Eithne Wilkins (New York: Schocken Books, 1954), 330–36.

84. Id., 332.

85. Franz Kafka, *Hochzeitvorbereitungen auf dem Lande und andere Prosa aus dem Nachlass* (Frankfort: Schocken, 1953), 369.

86. Id.

87. Kafka, *Dearest Father*, 332.

88. Id., 333.

89. Id., 335–36.

90. Arendt, "Truth and Politics," 227–64.

91. Stern, "The Law of the Trial," 26.

92. Id., 26–27.

93. Ziolkowski, *The Mirror of Justice*, 244.

94. Stern, "The Law of the Trial," 28.

95. There is a family resemblance between this religious dialectic in Kafka's parable and that in Dostoyevsky's parable "The Grand Inquisitor" in *The Brothers Karamazov*. In both cases, religion, as we have it, is too often a device that "saves" the believer from the burden of freedom. In Kafka's parable, the gatekeeper discourages the man from the country from taking the leap of faith necessary to walk through the open door to the radiance beyond.

96. Arendt, "Franz Kafka: A Revaluation," 70.

97. Id., 70–71.

98. Id., 71.

99. Id., 70.

100. Id., 72.

101. Id., 80.

102. West, "Authority, Autonomy, and Choice."

103. Sokel, "The Three Endings of Josef K.," 91.

104. Heinemann, "Kafka's Oath of Service," 258.

105. Arendt, "Franz Kafka: A Revaluation," 70.

106. Id., 74.

107. Id.

108. Id., 71.

109. Id., 91.

Chapter Three

1. Ziolkowski, *Mirror of Justice*, 239.

2. Id.

3. Robert P. Burns, *The Death of the American Trial* (Chicago: University of Chicago Press, 2009).

4. *Southern Union Co. v. United States*, 132 S. Ct. 2344, 2371 (Breyer, J., dissenting), citations omitted and emphasis added.

5. *Police Interrogation and American Justice.*

6. Jonathan Simon, *Governing through Crime: How the War on Crime Transformed American Democracy and Created a Culture of Fear* (Oxford: Oxford University Press, 2007), 106. Simon argues that this preference for rage over planning has led us to prefer prisons over policing in our crime-control policy. Id.

7. Hannah Arendt, *On Revolution* (New York: Penguin Books, 1965). Winnifred Sullivan insightfully analyzes the striking fact, to which we will return, that America has both the highest rate of church membership, is a place where "religion proudly and independently flourishes," and the highest imprisonment rate

in the developed world. Winnifred Sullivan, *Prison Religion: Faith-Based Reform and the Constitution* (Princeton: Princeton University Press, 2009), 2.

8. David Garland, *The Culture of Control: Crime and Social Order in Contemporary Society* (Chicago: University of Chicago Press, 2001), 3. Garland adds, "Not even the most inventive reading of Foucault, Marx, Durkheim, and Elias on punishment could have predicted these recent developments—and certainly no such predictions ever appeared." Id. "Neo-conservatism introduced into political culture a strikingly *anti-modern* concern for the themes of tradition, order, hierarchy, and authority." These themes were articulated by both the religious right and secular neoconservative intellectuals. They were opposed to the culture of the sixties, which was blamed for most of our woes. The path forward was through the reassertion of "family values," "individual responsibility," and a "generalized return to a more orderly, more disciplined, and a more tightly controlled society." Id., 99.

9. William J. Stuntz, *The Collapse of American Criminal Justice* (Cambridge: Harvard University Press, 2011), 46–50.

10. Garland, *The Culture of Control*, 178.

11. Stuntz, *Collapse of American Criminal Justice*, 47.

12. Id., 48–49.

13. Garland uses the provocative term "toxic waste" prisons. This sort of prison has the politically appealing characteristic that they can really not fail, since they have given up any aspirations to rehabilitation, and that the prison walls provide the only resource that is important.

14. Garland, *Culture of Control*, 194.

15. Karl Polanyi, *The Great Transformation* (Boston: Beacon Press, 1944).

16. See the more extended discussion in chapter 4, below.

17. Simon, *Governing through Crime*, 62.

18. Id., 160.

19. Id., 100.

20. Garland, *Culture of Control*, 25.

21. Garland argues that it coexists with a more pragmatic, adaptive strand that holds more promise.

22. Id., 138.

23. Stuntz, *Collapse of American Criminal Justice*, 249.

24. William E. Connolly, "The Ethos of Sovereignty," in *Law and the Sacred*, 148. Connolly puts it more succinctly: "In American democracy, sovereignty circulates uncertainly among a Supreme Court now sanctioned *positionally* (after an early period of struggle and self-assertion) to decide contested issues authoritatively, a populace marked by an uneven distribution of power, and orientations to the sacred into which the Court and much of the populace are inducted." Id., 151.

25. Stuntz identifies six mechanisms through which popular anger led to "ex-

tremism and excess." *Collapse of American Criminal Justice*, 253. Garland argues that we have concluded that "certain offenders once they offend, are no longer 'members of the public' and cease to be deserving of the kinds of consideration we typically afford to each other." In his view, this imaginative divide between "us" and "them" has made "many complacent about the emergence of a more repressive state power," "characterized by a more unvarnished authoritarianism" than in earlier regimes. *Culture of Control*, 181.

26. See *Miles v. Dorsey*, 61 F.3d 1459 (10th Cir. 1995) (plea held voluntary despite prosecutors' threats to charge defendant's parents); *United States v. Pollard*, 959 F.2d 1011 (D.C. Cir. 1992) (plea held voluntary despite prosecutors threat to charge defendant's wife), quoted in Stuntz, *Collapse of American Criminal Justice*, 373 n. 61.

27. For a partial inventory drawn from actual cases, see Monroe H. Freedman, "The Use of Unethical and Unconstitutional Practices and Policies by Prosecutors' Offices," *Washburn Law Journal* 52 (2012), 1–21.

28. Daniel S. Medwed, *Prosecution Complex: America's Race to Convict and Its Impact on the Innocent* (New York: New York University Press, 2012), 2.

29. *Imbler v. Patchtman*, 424 U.S. 429 (1976).

30. Garland, *Culture of Control*, 133. It is not long ago that our methods were not too distant from those that Foucault famously described. The "third degree," which amounted to physical torture was, into the thirties, our dominant "system of administering punishment and dispensing justice." Ernest Hopkins described it in the thirties as a kind of "pre-trial secret inquisition." "[O]ur police are getting not so much evidence as verdicts. The third degree is our predominating type of trial for crime. It tries more men, convicts more men, acquits more men, in felony cases, than the regular courts ever see. The former police lieutenant W. R. Kidd would echo Hopkins nine years later. . . . The policeman has no legal authority to act as judge, but we know from practical experience that far more cases are disposed of in this manner than ever reach the court." Quoted in Leo, *Police Interrogation and American Justice*, 57. In *Brown v. Mississippi*, 297 U.S. 278 (1936), the Supreme Court ruled that convictions resting on confessions extracted by torture violated the due process clause of the Fourteenth Amendment. The case involved confessions extracted by brutal whipping that the Court described as reading "more like pages torn from some medieval account, than a record made within the confines of a modern civilization which aspires to an enlightened constitutional government."

31. Id., 135.

32. Austin Sarat, "Capital Punishment as a Fact of Legal, Political, and Cultural Life: An Introduction," in *The Killing State: Capital Punishment in Law, Politics, and Culture* (Oxford: Oxford University Press, 1999), 15.

33. Peter Fitzpatrick, "'Always More to Do': Capital Punishment and the (De)Composition of Law," in *The Killing State*, 118.

34. Simon, *Governing through Crime*, 23 (summarizing Garland's argument).

35. This is partially for historical reasons. The demanding generalizations were largely established in the early years of the Warren court and have been slowly eroded through the efforts of the conservative courts that have sat since Richard Nixon's appointees in the late sixties.

36. Anthony G. Amsterdam, "Perspectives on the Fourth Amendment," *Minnesota Law Review* 58 (1974) 349, 353–54. The Fourth Amendment provides "[t]he right of the people to be secure in their persons, houses, papers, and effects, against unreasonable search and seizures, shall not be violated, and no Warrants shall issue, but upon probable cause, supported by Oath or affirmation, and particularly describing the placed to be searched, and the person or things to be seized." Interpreting the amendment today is so challenging because it was written against the background of institutions and threats to liberty profoundly different from those that prevail today. Thomas Y. Davies, "Recovering the Original Fourth Amendment," *Michigan Law Review* 58 (1999), 547. Stuntz criticizes the "proceduralism" of the Bill of Rights and its lack of important substantive limitations, for example, explicit limits on what range of behavior can be criminalized. *Collapse of American Criminal Justice*, 74–85. But see *Griswold v. Connecticut*, 381 U.S. 479 (1965), and *Lawrence v. Texas*, 539 U.S. 558 (2003).

37. *Duncan v. Louisiana*, 391 U.S. 145 (1968).

38. *Weeks v. United States*, 232 U.S. 383 (1914).

39. *Mapp v. Ohio*, 367 U.S. 643 (1961).

40. *Katz v. United States*, 389 U.S. 347 (1967). Justice Harlan's concurring opinion became the major source for post-*Katz* jurisprudence. The concurrence required both a subjective expectation of privacy and a general normative judgment that the expectation was deserving of protection. It became clear that the second criterion was more significant, because the first could be reduced simply by the general knowledge of government intrusion.

41. Id.

42. *Oliver v. United States*, 466 U.S. 170 (1984).

43. *United States v. White*, 401 U.S. 745 (1971).

44. As constitutional protection was withdrawn, it became a matter of legislative judgment as to the protection offered personal records and information about telephone calls and other communications.

45. *California v. Ciraolo*, 476 U.S. 207 (1986); *Florida v. Riley*, 488 U.S. 445 (1989).

46. *Minnesota v. Carter*, 525 U.S. 83 (1998). Doctrinally, such a person would not have "standing" to raise the constitutional claim, or as Justice Rehnquist, much preferred, that he "personally had an expectation of privacy in the place searched." Thus a passenger in someone else's car may not urge suppression of (his) drugs found in the glove compartment, because of the standing doctrine. *Rakas v. Illinois*, 439 U.S. 128 (1978).

47. *Kylo v. United States*, 533 U.S. 27 (2001).

48. Scott E. Sundby, "Everyman's Fourth Amendment: Privacy or Mutual Trust between Government and Citizen," *Columbia Law Review* 94 (1994), 1751, 1789–90, quoted in Joshua Dressler and George C. Thomas III, *Criminal Procedure: Principles, Policies and Perspectives*, 4th ed. (St. Paul: West Publishing, 2010), 137.

49. "Misleadingly" because a reading of the actual case law must occasion the conclusion that "a man of reasonable caution" is, in fact, not very cautious.

50. *Brinegar v. United States*, 338 U.S. 160 (1949) (quoting *Carrol v. United States*, 267 U.S. 132 (1925)).

51. Is the reader beginning to be more and more confused about the applicable law? So there's another variable: the question of a need for warrant added to the underlying question of whether there exists probable cause.

52. *Illinois v. Gates*, 464 U.S. 213 (1983).

53. On police lying, see Morgan Cloud, "The Dirty Little Secret," *Emory Law Journal* 43 (1994), 1311. The circular relationship between police practices and legal doctrine, even at the Supreme Court level, is part of what Connolly means when he says that sovereignty "circulates" among the Court, the police, and other actors.

54. Another mystifying feature that pervades this law is that most of it is established in criminal litigation where crimes have almost certainly occurred: where a search yields no such evidence, the case will probably not be litigated. Thus officers in the field can be fairly confident that any credibility determination will be resolved in their favor, a conviction that cannot but encourage them to "push the envelope." This style of reasoning is a pallid echo of an even more ominous claim made in the South: that truly awful trials were excusable because they were better than lynching. Michael J. Klarman, "The Racial Origins of Modern Criminal Procedure," *Michigan Law Review* 99 (2000), 48, 56–57.

55. *Leon v. United States*, 468 U.S. 897 (1984). There is an indeterminate exception where there is evidence of abuse, such a low level of detail in the supporting affidavit, for example, that it appears to have been obvious that the warrant was an immunizing sham or that is was supported by an intentional lie. Those criteria will seldom (and unpredictably) be met.

56. If it is a requirement: again there is a dispute as to whether the Fourth Amendment ever requires a warrant, so long as there is probable cause. See Akhil Reed Amar, "Fourth Amendment Principles," *Harvard Law Review* 107 (1994), 757.

57. An arrest in a public place does not require a warrant. *Payton v. New York*, 445 U.S. 573 (1980).

58. *Maryland v. Buie*, 494 U.S. 325 (1990).

59. In the cynical slang, "DWB," "driving while black" provides the "probable cause."

60. *When v. United States*, 517 U.S. 806 (1996).

61. *Arizona v. Gant*, 556 U.S. 332 (2009). This last limitation was long in coming: even the conservative justices came to see that there needs to be *some* limit on the gap between the rule and its justification in protecting the officer's safety.

62. *New York v. Belton*, 453 U.S. 454 (1981).

63. Compare *Michigan Department of State Police v. Sitz*, 496 U.S. 444 (1980) (stops to prevent drunken driving permissible) with *City of Indianapolis v. Edmond*, 531 U.S. 32 (2000) (stops to prevent drug trafficking not permissible).

64. *South Dakota v. Opperman*, 428 U.S. 364 (1976).

65. *United States v. Mendenhall*, 446 U.S. 544 (1991).

66. For empirical evidence that this is not the case, see Janice Nadler, "No Need to Shout: Bus Sweeps and the Psychology of Coercion, *Supreme Court Review* 2002, 153. Here is another Kafkaesque twist. The Court assumes a freedom to walk away from a policeman. The Court has ruled that the fact that a young man in a high-crime neighborhood *ran* away from a policeman provided grounds for his detention and search. Apparently, you can walk away, just not too fast!

67. *Schneckhoff v. Bustamente*, 412 U.S. 218 (1973).

68. *Arizona v. Hicks*, 480 U.S. 321 (1987).

69. *Minnesota v. Dickerson*, 508 U.S. 366 (1993).

70. 392 U.S. 1 (1968). The case is fascinating and important for many reasons that go beyond my purposes here.

71. In *Floyd v. City of New York*, ____ F. Supp. ____, 2013 WL 4046209 (S.D.N.Y., August 12, 2013), the district court, after a trial, found that New York's policies violated the Fourth Amendment. The decision came down as this went to press, and the city has vowed to appeal.

72. In *Florence v. Board of Chosen Freeholders of the County of Burlington*, 132 S. Ct. 1510 (2012), the Court again deferred to law enforcement in allowing a full strip search of anyone placed in jail custody, even if there is no reason to believe he possesses drugs or weapons. In that case, the individual was arrested and jailed on an incorrect warrant for driving without a license.

73. Simon, *Governing through Crime*, 112.

74. Leo, *Police Interrogation and American Justice*, 124.

75. Id., 280. The effect has been to allow "chiefly recidivists and white collar defendants" to avoid questioning. Stuntz, *Collapse of American Criminal Justice*, 224.

76. Leo, *Police Interrogation and American Justice*, 291.

77. 446 U.S. 291 (1980).

78. *North Carolina v. Butler*, 441 U.S. 369 (1979).

79. *Oregon v. Estad*, 470 U.S. 298 (1985).

80. Stuntz, *Collapse of American Criminal Justice*, 210. See Gary Fields and John R. Emshwiller, "As Criminal Laws Proliferate, More Are Ensnared," *Wall*

Street Journal (July 24, 2011) (describing convictions for digging for arrowheads on federal land, unknowingly driving a snowmobile in a blizzard onto federal land, violating a *federal* criminal statute prohibiting the otherwise legal and unthreatening ownership of guns while under a *state* restraining order that didn't mention the guns, for importing lobsters into the United States in violation of a *Honduran* law prohibiting undersized lobsters).

81. Fields and Emshwiller, "As Criminal Laws Proliferate."

82. *United States v. Behrman*, 258 U.S. 280 (1922), discussed in Stuntz, *Collapse of American Criminal Justice*, 176.

83. Id. For an argument that this is an essential element of law in a liberal society, see H. L. A. Hart, *Punishment and Responsibility: Essays in the Philosophy of Law* (New York: Oxford University Press, 1968).

84. "He who murdereth a man drunk, sober shall be hanged" is the picturesque way my teacher Norval Morris liked to put it (with his charming Australian accent).

85. Stuntz, *Collapse of American Criminal Justice*, 262.

86. This latter was too much for the Supreme Court in *Skilling v. United States*, 130 S. Ct. 2896 (2010), which chose to rewrite the statute more narrowly. The decision, though in some ways welcome, has been criticized for *still* not bringing clarity to such a vague statute.

87. All the examples are from Stuntz, *Collapse of American Criminal Justice*, 262–64.

88. Simon, *Governing through Crime*, 109.

89. Id., 192.

90. Id., 263. Multiple-count trials can be particularly unfair in that they can prevent the jury from focusing on a manageable number of issues of fact.

91. Douglas Husak, *Overcriminalization: The Limits of the Criminal Law* (Oxford: Oxford University Press, 2008), 12.

92. Id., 27, 31.

93. National Research Council, National Academy of Sciences, *Strengthening Forensic Science in the United States: A Path Forward* (2009).

94. Robert P. Burns, "The Withering Away of Evidence Law," *Georgia Law Review* 47 (2013), 665; "A Short Meditation on Some Remaining Issues in Evidence Law," *Seton Hall Law Review* 38 (2008), 1435; "Notes on the Future of Evidence Law," *Temple Law Review* 74 (2001), 69.

95. See Federal Rule of Evidence (FRE) 104(b) and 901(a).

96. See FRE 104(a). This rule's "admissibility of evidence" applies most significantly to the hearsay exceptions.

97. I recall such a boast from a truly terrible trial judge.

98. This is embedded in FRE 403.

99. Brandon L. Garrett, *Convicting the Innocent: Where Criminal Prosecutions Go Wrong* (Cambridge: Harvard University Press, 2012).

100. Including, by their own admission, the last three presidents of the United States, though one of them claimed not to have inhaled.

101. Husak, *Overcriminalization*, 25.

102. Id., 24.

103. Id., quoting Stuntz.

104. Eric Luna, "Overextending the Criminal Law," in *Go Directly to Jail: The Criminalization of Almost Everything*, ed. Gene Healy (Washington, DC: Cato Institute, 2004), 1; "The Overcriminalization Phenomenon," *American University Law Review* 54 (2005), 703, 706, quoted in Husak, *Overcriminalization*, 35.

105. Simon, *Governing through Crime*, 141; see Michelle Alexander, *The New Jim Crow: Mass Incarceration in the Age of Colorblindness* (New York: The New Press, 2012).

106. On the other hand, Simon points out that the categorical nature of our criminal law now makes it less likely that a middle-class white person may avoid conviction and prison by virtue of an individualized judicial determination.

107. Kaaryn S. Gustafson, *Cheating Welfare: Public Assistance and the Criminalization of Poverty* (New York: New York University Press, 2011).

108. Stuntz, *Collapse of American Criminal Justice*, 159.

109. Id., 171.

110. David J. Langum, *Crossing over the Line: Legislating Morality and the Mann Act* (Chicago: University of Chicago Press, 1994), 1–3, 182–85, explained on 171, and 358 nn. 37 and 38. Johnson was not actually prosecuted for his relationship with his future wife, but was later prosecuted for sleeping with a white prostitute. Id.

111. Stuntz contrasts this with the criminal liquor laws under Prohibition, which criminalized neither possession nor serving liquor in one's own home. *Collapse of American Criminal Justice*, 267. All three of our authors, to different degrees, offer explanations that blend strategic behavior by public officials with public moods that have a darker, more Kafkaesque quality.

112. Id., 268.

113. Garland, *Culture of Control*, 132. See Michelle Alexander, *The New Jim Crow: Mass Incarceration in the Age of Colorblindness* (New York: New Press, 2010).

114. The trials that occur in the remaining 5 percent of cases (1) have certain bureaucratic characteristics, too many in my view, such as the judge's control of the evidence the jury sees through its evidentiary rulings, and (2) can be distorted by the bureaucracies on which it relies, the police and prosecutors, through the various forms of misconduct.

115. Stuntz, *Collapse of American Criminal Justice*, 250.

116. Id., 251.

117. Alasdair MacIntyre, *After Virtue: A Study in Moral Theory*, 3rd ed. (Notre Dame: University of Notre Dame, 2007), 25.

118. Roberto Mangabeira Unger, *Law in Modern Society: Toward a Criticism of Social Theory* (New York: The Free Press, 1977).

119. Id.

120. Simon, *Governing through Crime*, 165.

121. *Coleman v. Thompson*, 111 S. Ct. 2546 (1991).

122. Albert W. Dzur, *Punishment, Participatory Democracy, and the Jury* (Oxford: Oxford University Press, 2012) 100 (quoting Thoreau).

123. G. K. Chesterton, *Tremendous Trifles* (London: Methuen, 1920), 65, 67–68. Of course, we have taken the next step and largely supplanted the judge with the prosecutor.

124. George Fisher, *Plea Bargaining's Triumph: A History of Plea Bargaining in America* (Stanford: Stanford University Press, 2004), 175.

125. Id., 176.

126. Dzur, *Punishment, Participatory Democracy, and the Jury*. "There is also a new and all-pervasive managerialism that affects every aspect of criminal justice . . . performance indicators and management measures." *Culture of Control*, 18.

127. See Burns, *A Theory of the Trial*, for an account of how this kind of judgment is actualized by the practices of the trial. See *The Death of the American Trial*, for an account of the significance of the loss of the jury trial.

128. Legal historian William Nelson describes a case in which jurors were shocked to learn that a kind of compromise verdict they reached believing that the defendant would receive a year or two in prison actually resulted in a very, very long sentence. Afterward the stunned jurors said they would never have reached that result if they had been aware of the consequences. ____ *William and Mary Law Review* ____ (2014, forthcoming).

129. Brian Forst, *Errors of Justice: Nature, Sources, and Remedies* (Cambridge: Cambridge University Press), 17.

130. Id., 87.

131. Daniel S. Medwed, *Prosecution Complex: America's Race to Convict and Its Impact on the Innocent* (New York: New York University Press, 2012), 77.

132. Id.

133. Barbara O'Brien, "A Recipe for Bias: An Empirical Look at the Interplay between Institutional Incentives and Bounded Rationality in Prosecutorial Decision-Making," *Missouri Law Review* 74 (2009), 999; see Monroe H. Freedman, "The Use of Unethical and Unconstitutional Practices and Policies by Prosecutors' Offices," *Washburn Law Journal* 52 (2012), 1.

134. I have often been impressed at the willingness of "marginal" people to tell the truth at no benefit, and often extreme disadvantage, to themselves. It serves as a counterbalance to the sociopathic willingness of others to lie, prom-

inently the "jailhouse snitches" upon whom prosecutors often rely. Freedman, "The Use of Unethical Practices," and Policies 16–17.

135. Stuntz, *Collapse of American Criminal Justice*, 203. Stuntz uses the case to demonstrate the very limited power of procedural solutions to injustice in the American criminal justice system.

136. Michael McConville and Chester L. Mirsky, "Understanding Defense of the Poor in State Courts," *Studies in Law, Politics, and Society* 10 (1990), 217.

137. Dzur, *Punishment, Participatory Democracy, and the Jury*, 163.

138. Id.

139. Simon, *Governing through Crime*, 35.

140. Id., 40.

141. Harry Kalven Jr. and Hans Zeisel, *The American Jury* (Chicago: University of Chicago Press, 1966), 270, 293, 305, 319, 338 (providing examples that suggest leniency uncountenanced by the law of rules: the defendant was seriously injured at the time of the crime, the victim is reluctant to prosecute, the prosecution for this kind of crime is rare, the defendant's action would not be a crime over the border of a nearby state, the defendant was unrepresented, he was suffering great personal tragedies while events were unfolding, or he used a toy rather than a real gun in a robbery).

142. Stuntz, *Collapse of American Criminal Justice*.

143. The account is condensed from the essay by Bryan Smith, "Kevin Fox: They Promised to Stop the Grilling—If He'd Just Say It Has Been an Accident," in *True Stories of False Confessions*, ed. Rob Warden and Steven A. Drizin (Evanston: Northwestern University Press, 2009), 107–29. A few of the facts are from the account in the US Court of Appeals for the Seventh Circuit, affirming in part, a civil rights judgment against the detectives involved and Will County.

144. Id., 113–14.

145. Id., 120.

146. Id., 110.

147. Burns, *Death of the American Trial*, 98–101.

148. Leo, *Police Interrogation and American Justice*, 186.

149. Id., 31.

150. Id., 33.

151. Arendt observed that simple factual truth such as the existence of the camps was far more offensive to and feared by the regime than were challenges to its ideology. Arendt, "Truth and Politics," 236.

152. *Leviathan*, chap. 11, quoted in Arendt, "Truth and Politics," 230.

153. Frank Zimring, "The Executioner's Dissonant Song," in *The Killing State*, 144.

154. MacIntyre, *After Virtue*, 23–24.

155. 360 U.S. 315 (1959).

156. See, e.g., *Bram v. United States*, 168 U.S. 532 (1897).

157. Leo, *Police Interrogation and American Justice*, 5–6.

158. Id. 11.

159. Id., 322.

160. Id, 190.

161. Id., 166, quoting Mike Hepworth and Bryan S. Turner, *Confession: Studies in Deviance and Religion* (London: Routledge & Kegan Paul, 1982), 148.

162. For many more, see *True Stories of False Confessions*.

163. The account is in *Police Interrogation and American Justice*, 177–81.

164. Id., 178, quoting Lowery's testimony.

165. Id.

166. Id. 181.

167. The account is at id., 181–86.

168. Id., 182, quoting Godschalk's statement.

169. Id., 185, quoting the detective's testimony.

170. Id., 186.

171. The account is at id., 255–60.

172. Id., 258.

173. Id., 257.

174. Id., 190.

175. Friedman, "The Use of Unethical and Unconstitutional Practices and Policies."

176. Stuntz, *Collapse of American Criminal Justice*, 57–58.

177. Detectives are taught to assume guilt and prevent the suspect from even expressing his claims of innocence.

178. Daniel Givleber, "Meaningless Acquittals, Meaningful Convictions," *Rutgers Law Review* 49 (1997), 1317 As we will see below, in many ways the fight is hardly fair.

179. Edward Connors et al., *Convicted by Juries, Exonerated by Science: Case Studies in the Use of DNA Evidence to Establish Innocence after Trial*, in *National Institute of Justice Report* (1996).

180. After the profound embarrassment of one after another exoneration in death penalty cases, Illinois finally created a limited form of deposition practice in capital cases. It never went into practice because Governor Ryan first commuted the sentences of all prisoners on death row (finding some factually innocent) and the legislature then abolished the death penalty completely.

181. It is unethical for prosecutors to counsel witnesses not to speak with defense counsel. ABA Model Rules of Professional Conduct 3.4(f). No one other than the participants knows what is actually said in these conversations between prosecutors and witnesses.

182. If the surprise is important enough, defense counsel can beg for a short continuance, which it is almost completely within the court's discretion to deny.

183. Bennett L. Gershman, "Litigating *Brady v. Maryland*: Games Prosecutors Play," *Case Western Reserve Law Review* 57 (2007), 531.

184. American Law Institute, *Restatement Third: The Law Governing Lawyers*, sec. 116.

185. National Research Council, National Academy of Sciences, *Strengthening Forensic Science in the United States: A Path Forward* (2009). "Professor Jane Moriarty attributes unreliable forensic evidence to a slew of factors: 'fraud and negligence in the laboratory; the failure to use blind testing procedures; the lack of meaningful standards to judge the validity of a given theory; inadequate or nonexistent proficiency testing; and inadequate or nonexistent data base from which to draw comparisons.' A common theme in the forensic science disciplines is that they blossomed within the corridors of government crime laboratories rather than those of universities. As a consequence, they have not faced the rigorous validation tests applied to the 'hard' sciences. . . . Creatures of the crime lab, not the academy, forensic scientists operated in offices lacking a scientific culture—environments that may value the ends of the process (ideally, a match) far more than the means." Medwed, *Prosecution Complex*, 94.

186. *State v. Krone*, 897 P.2d 621 (Ariz. 1995).

187. This "science" is one of the forms of proof most often discredited.

188. George C. Thomas III, *The Supreme Court on Trial: How the American System of Justice Sacrifices Innocent Defendants* (Ann Arbor: University of Michigan Press, 2006), 7. The inclination to jump at the first hypothesis and ignore all the other evidence is the reason why the London police always got it wrong. The ability to maintain alternative hypotheses and evaluate the evidence for each of them is the reason Sherlock Holmes always got it right. See Umberto Eco and Thomas A. Sebeok, eds., *The Sign of Three: Dupin, Holmes, Peirce* (Bloomington: Indiana University Press, 1988).

189. Medwed, *Prosecution Complex*, 55. "Thirty-one of the thirty-nine convictions obtained in the Tulia, Texas scandal—in which a rogue white undercover narcotics officer fabricated evidence against black men and women—came from guilty pleas. After the officer was wholly discredited, all those convictions were overturned on the basis of actual innocence." Id., 54. One estimate is that about 7 percent of exonerations involve guilty pleas: *guilty pleas*, not just false confessions.

190. Simon, *Governing through Crime*, 196. One housing authority sought automatically to evict a woman who was attacked in her own apartment by her former husband or boyfriend. Id., 197.

191. Anthony G. Amsterdam, "Selling a Quick Fix for Boot Hill: The Myth of Justice Delayed in Death Cases," in *The Killing State*, 153. Amsterdam describes the Court itself being incorrect in the prediction of the way it is likely to rule on legal matters related to the issues raised in stays.

192. Simon, *Governing through Crime*, 43.

193. Id.

194. Fisher, *Plea Bargaining's Triumph*, 48.

195. Simon, *Governing through Crime*, 112–13. In *Republican Party of Minnesota v. White*, 536 U.S. 765 (2002), the US Supreme Court struck down state rules of judicial conduct that limited the partisan nature of campaigning for judgeships. Many of the most partisan statements tend to be promises to be relentlessly "tough on crime."

196. Medwed, *Prosecution Complex*, 79.

197. All the examples are from id., 1. Prosecutors have opposed the request in about half the cases where DNA evidence testing has been sought. Then there are the cases of straightforward prosecutorial misconduct: James Giles served ten years in prison because prosecutors didn't hand over evidence that a different man by the same name was the perpetrator. David Wong spent seventeen years in prison based on the false testimony of a jailhouse snitch who received a recommendation for parole. Bruce Godschalk spent fifteen years in prison for a sexual assault he did not commit, the last seven of which were spent trying to pry physical evidence out of the prosecutor's office for DNA testing.

198. Id., 109–10.

199. Id., 142.

200. Leo, *Police Interrogation and American Justice*, 9, quoting Saul Kassn. This is true despite the evidence, noted above, that the initial surmises as to who is the guilty party are wrong in a significant minority of cases.

201. Id., 23. And so it is often the case where a full confession cannot be obtained, detectives will try to keep the suspect talking, so that he will almost inevitably make a mistake. The latter can then be portrayed as a lie designed to obscure guilt.

202. Id., 37.

203. Id., 165. "Police accountability systems do not generally provide incentives for the police to improve the quality of arrest brought forward for prosecution." Forst, *Errors of Justice*, 102.

204. Garland, *Culture of Control*, 179. This occurs at a time when the victims of crime are increasingly personalized. Id.

205. Id., 172 (emphasis added).

206. Leo, *Police Interrogation and American Justice*, 21.

207. Id., 58. This is somewhat less startling than the response given by detectives to the investigators who created the Wickersham report on American criminal process: "[F]irst, there wasn't any third degree; and second, they couldn't do their work without it."

208. Id., 85. The polygraph is only one of a number of "scientific" methods of distinguishing guilt from innocence, all of which are even less reliable than the polygraph. Id., 89–106.

209. Id., 135.

210. Id., 227.

211. Austin Sarat, "Capital Punishment as a Fact of Legal, Political, and Cultural Life: An Introduction," in *The Killing State*, 5.

212. Ingo Muller, *Hitler's Justice*, trans. Deborah Lucas Schneider (Cambridge: Harvard University Press, 1991), 76.

213. Id., 79.

214. Garland, *Culture of Control*, 135–36 (emphasis added).

215. Id., 165.

216. Id., 188.

217. Id., 191.

218. *Ewing v. California*, 538 U.S. 11 (2003), upheld the result in the latter case.

219. Medwed, *Prosecution Complex*, 164 (first emphasis added).

220. Sullivan, *Prison Religion*, 2.

221. It is ironic given that these forms of Protestantism tend to find their roots in the antinomian forms of the radical Reformation most skeptical of state authority.

222. Id., 221.

223. Martha Merrill Umphrey, Austin Sarat, and Lawrence Douglas, "The Sacred in Law: An Introduction," 13.

224. Connolly, "The Ethos of Sovereignty," 137.

225. Garland, *Culture of Control*, 185.

226. Id., 99.

227. Id., 100.

228. Franklin E. Zimring, *The City That Became Safe: New York's Lessons for Urban Crime and Its Control* (Oxford: Oxford University Press, 2012), 181.

229. Id.

230. Leo, *Police Interrogation and American Justice*, 217.

231. Stuntz, *Collapse of American Criminal Justice*, 255.

Chapter Four

1. Stephanos Bibas, *The Machinery of Criminal Justice* (Oxford: Oxford University Press, 2012), 164, 132, 155.

2. Gordon Wood, *The Creation of the American Republic* (Chapel Hill: University of North Caroline Press, 1969).

3. Polanyi, *The Great Transformation*, 257–58.

4. See *Bracy v. Gramley*, 520 U.S. 899 (1997).

5. *Mathews v. Eldridge*, 424 U.S. 319 (1976).

6. *Milliken v. Bradley*, 418 U.S, 717 (1974).

7. Loïc Wacquant, *Punishing the Poor: The Neoliberal Government of Social Insecurity* (Durham: Duke University Press, 2009), 312.

8. Id., 307.

9. Id.

10. Id., 308. Wacquant obviously considers "authoritarian moralism" intrinsic to the neoliberal state. Other theorists see the relationship as looser, a "temporary fix on the chronic instability and functional failings of neoliberalism." Id., 311, characterizing the views of David Harvey in his *Brief History of Neoliberalism* (New York: Oxford University Press, 2007). The latter view offers greater hope for changes in the criminal justice system in the absence of larger economic transformations.

11. Wacquant, *Punishing the Poor*, 313.

12. Stuntz, *Collapse of American Criminal Justice*, 275.

13. The murder rate remained much higher than it had been in 1950 (up 386 percent in Boston, up 135 percent in New York, up 567 percent in Detroit).

14. Albert W. Alshuler and Andres G. Deiss, "A Brief History of the Criminal Jury in the United States," *University of Chicago Law Review* 61 (1994), 867, 921. Bibas writes the entire history of the criminal justice system as a downward spiral created by the tensions between "insiders," officials within the system, and "outsiders," the general public, often manipulated by politicians. *The Machinery of Criminal Justice*, 29–53.

15. If one were to substitute "elites" for "nobles," in Kafka's parable, "Problem of Our Laws," we come fairly close to Fisher's account of the triumph of plea bargaining.

16. I tried to argue in *A Theory of the Trial* that these convictions were not illusory and that, in some form, they fairly describe the disappearing contemporary trial. They are discontinuous with the assumptions of ordinary political discussions and with standard social scientific perspectives. Marianne Constable, *Just Silences: The Limits and Possibilities of Modern Law* (Princeton: Princeton University Press, 2007); *The Law of the Other: The Mixed Jury and Changing Conceptions of Citizenship, Law, and Knowledge* (Chicago: University of Chicago Press, 1991).

17. Judith N. Shklar, "The Liberalism of Fear," in *Liberalism and the Moral Life*, ed. Nancy L. Rosenblum (Cambridge: Harvard University Press, 1989), 28–29, quoted in Dzur, *Punishment, Participatory Democracy and the Jury*, 14.

18. Id.

19. Steven C. Rockefeller, *John Dewey: Religious Faith and Democratic Humanism* (New York: Columbia University Press, 1991), 436.

20. Stuntz, *Collapse of American Criminal Justice, 281*.

21. Id., 309.

22. Bibas, *The Machinery of Criminal Justice*, 131.

23. Stuntz, *Collapse of American Criminal Justice*, 276.

24. Id., 280–81.

25. Theodore J. Lowi, *The End of Liberalism: The Second Republic of the United States*, 2nd ed. (New York: W. W. Norton & Company, 1979).

26. Bibas, *The Machinery of Criminal Justice*, 93.

27. *Gaming the System: How the Political Strategies of Private Prison Companies Promote Ineffective Incarceration Polices* (Washington, DC: Justice Policy Institute: June 2011).

28. 558 U.S. 310 (2010).

29. *Republican Party of Minnesota v. White*, 536 U.S. 765 (2002).

30. Lowi, *The End of Liberalism*.

31. Stuntz, *Collapse of American Criminal Justice*, 291.

32. William T. Pizzi, *Trials without Truth: Why Our System of Criminal Trials Has Become an Expensive Failure and What We Need to Do to Rebuild It* (New York: New York University Press, 2000). I agree more with Professor Pizzi's descriptions than on his prescription for reform.

33. Burns, "The Withering Away of Evidence Law: Notes on Theory and Practice." Justice Scalia's affection for originalism has created an increasingly complex law surrounding the confrontation clause, one that applies to all federal and state criminal trials and now runs parallel and can be discontinuous with the federal or state hearsay law that also applies. Here again the pattern is robust initial assertion (*Crawford v. Washington*, 541 U.S. 36 (2004)), followed by hard-to-discern qualifications. Some of the important derivative cases were decided by a deeply divided court.

34. It is also hardly imagined among all the great social theory that emerged from Central Europe in the late nineteenth and early twentieth century. The alternatives for them were largely bureaucratic government of the left and bureaucratic government of the right. Arendt, *On Revolution*.

35. Abramson, *We, the Jury*, 76. See, generally, *The Death of the American Trial*, 49–68.

36. Paul W. Kahn, *Political Theology: Four New Chapters on the Concept of Sovereignty* (New York: Columbia University Press, 2011), 40.

37. Arendt, *On Revolution*.

38. Abramson, *We, the Jury*, 84.

39. Burns, *A Theory of the Trial*, 176–82.

40. Michael Pardo, "Commentary: Upsides of the American Trial's 'Anti-confluential' Nature: Notes on Richard K. Sherwin, David Foster Wallace, and James O. Incadenza," in *Imagining Legality: Where Law Meets Popular Culture*, ed. Austin Sarat (Tuscaloosa: University of Alabama Press, 2011), 133–51.

41. E. P. Thompson, *Writing by Candlelight* (London: Merlin Press, 1980),

107–9. For the importance of judgments of political identity at trial, see *A Theory of the Trial*, 172–76.

42. Muller, *Hitler's Justice*, 64.

43. Melvin Hill, ed., *Hannah Arendt: The Recovery of the Public World* (New York: St. Martin's Press, 1979), 314.

44. Arendt, *On Revolution*, 196.

45. Id., 86–87.

46. Arendt, "Truth and Politics," 263.

47. Arendt, *On Revolution*, 182.

48. Hannah Arendt, "Civil Disobedience," in Hannah Arendt, *Crises of the Republic* (New York: Harcourt, Brace, Jovanovich, 1972), 79.

49. Arendt, *The Origins of Totalitarianism*, 467.

50. Arendt, "Truth and Politics," 263.

51. Arendt, "Civil Disobedience," 199.

52. Arendt, "Truth and Politics," 263–34.

53. Arendt, *Origins of Totalitarianism*, 463.

54. Id., 463.

55. Muller, *Hitler's Justice*, 47.

56. Hill, ed., *Hannah Arendt*, 317 (interview with Richard Bernstein).

57. Id., 318.

58. Even Roberto Unger, often thought to be an extreme legal realist, warns that the consequences that flowed from the Weimar courts' dispensing with the constraints of formalism stand as a warning to any desire to cut through formal law: "The German case may also serve to point out the enormous danger to freedom involved in the decline of the legal order and the high risks critical intelligence runs when it attacks the idea of positive law in behalf of an ideal of a self-governing community. Many of the trends of Weimar were repeated on a brutal scale under the Nazis. The withdrawal and weakening of the legal order was followed by the expansion of terror. The ideology of corporativist union became a pretext for unchecked bureaucratic dictatorship." Robert Mangabeira Unger, *Law in Modern Society: Toward a Criticism of Social Theory* (New York: The Free Press, 1976), 220.

59. For the ways in which the American trial both honors and relativizes the claims of formalism, see Burns, *A Theory of the Trial*. The richness of the "consciously structured hybrid of practices" embedded in the trial and its normative significance for both theory and practice remains underappreciated.

60. Justice Brennan's concurrence in *Teamsters Local No. 391 v. Terry*, 494 U.S. 558 (1990), in the context of the civil jury, similarly argues that the Seventh Amendment embodies an acceptance of a form of republicanism discontinuous with our current institutions and intuitions.

61. For a balanced assessment of the inevitable effects of broader political culture on the criminal justice system, see Nicola Lacey, *The Prisoner's Dilemma:*

Political Economy and Punishment in Contemporary Democracies (Cambridge: Cambridge University Press, 2008).

62. James Q. Whitman, *Harsh Justice: Criminal Punishment and the Widening Divide between America and Europe* (New York: Oxford University Press, 2003).

63. Dzur, *Punishment, Participatory Democracy, and the Jury*, 163. I follow closely Professor Dzur's argument for the promise of increased democratization of the criminal justice system, one that parallels in a somewhat different idiom William Stuntz's prescriptions for the system described below.

64. Herbert Packer, *The Limits of the Criminal Sanction* (Stanford: Stanford University Press, 1968), 159.

65. Stuntz, *Collapse of American Criminal Justice*, 287.

66. Id., 308–9.

67. Bibas, *The Machinery of Criminal Justice*, 144–53.

68. Id., 148.

69. Id.

70. Id., 149.

71. Id., 157.

72. Id., 302.

73. Burns, *Theory of the Trial*, 125–54.

74. Kalven and Zeisel, *The American Jury*, 111–14. It is more likely that the relatively few differences between judges and juries that Kalven and Zeisel found were based on "evidence problems" rather than any explicit inclination of the jury to nullify the law of rules. Id.

75. Stuntz, *Collapse of American Criminal Justice*, 305.

76. Id., 299. He seems to think that if the number of defense counsel increases, there will be substantial pressure to increase the number of prosecutors as well. Bibas's conclusion about the likelihood of adequate funding of public defender services is similar: "I will not hold my breath awaiting that needed reform." *The Machinery of Criminal Justice*, 155.

77. David Kolb, *The Critique of Pure Modernity, Hegel, Heidegger and After* (Chicago and London: The University of Chicago Press, 1986), 259.

78. Steven Drizin and Richard A. Leo, "The Problem of False Confessions in the Post-D," *North Carolina Law Review* 82 (2004), 891–1007; Steven Drizin and Marissa Reich, "Heeding the Lessons of History: The Need for Mandatory Recording of Police Interrogations to Accurately Assess the Reliability and Voluntariness of Confessions," *Drake Law Review* 52 (2004), 619–46. Given the gamesmanship that surrounds police investigation, there is little doubt that detectives would set about trying to circumvent these protections, probably by questioning a suspect in noncustodial surroundings, obtaining admissions, and only then turning on the tapes.

79. Bibas, *Machinery of Criminal Justice*, 147.

80. Id., 148.

81. Id., 131.

82. Rockefeller, *John Dewey: Religious Faith and Democratic Humanism*, 460–66.

83. Bibas, *The Machinery of Criminal Justice*, 164.

Index